Frommer's®

Portable

Charleston

5th Edition

by Darwin Porter & Danforth Prince

WILEY

Wiley Publishing, Inc.

Published by:

WILEY PUBLISHING, INC.

111 River St.
Hoboken, NJ 07030-5774

ISBN 978-0-470-88731-8 (paper); ISBN 978-1-118-07199-1 (ebk);
ISBN 978-1-118-07200-4 (ebk); ISBN 978-1-118-07201-1 (ebk)

Editor: Andrea Kahn
Production Editor: Jana M. Stefanciosa
Cartographer: Andrew Dolan
Photo Editor: Richard Fox
Production by Wiley Indianapolis Composition Services

Front cover photo: A pond at Magnolia Plantation Gardens. © H. Mark
Weidman Photography / Alamy Images

For information on our other products and services or to obtain technical
support, please contact our Customer Care Department within the U.S. at
877/762-2974, outside the U.S. at 317/572-3993 or fax 317/572-4002.

Wiley also publishes its books in a variety of electronic formats. Some
content that appears in print may not be available in electronic formats.

Manufactured in the United States of America

5   4   3   2   1

CONTENTS

LIST OF MAPS

ABOUT THE AUTHORS

As a team of veteran travel writers, **Darwin Porter** and **Danforth Prince** have written dozens of previous titles for Frommer's, including many of their guides to Europe as well as the Caribbean, Bermuda, and the Bahamas. They are also the authors of *Frommer's The Carolinas and Georgia* and *Portable Savannah*. Porter, a noted celebrity biographer, is a native of North Carolina and has lived in both Georgia and South Carolina. He is joined by Danforth Prince, formerly of the Paris bureau of *The New York Times* and today the president of Blood Moon Productions.

HOW TO CONTACT US

In researching this book, we discovered many wonderful places—hotels, restaurants, shops, and more. We're sure you'll find others. Please tell us about them, so we can share the information with your fellow travelers in upcoming editions. If you were disappointed with a recommendation, we'd love to know that, too. Please write to:

Frommer's Portable Charleston, 5th Edition
Wiley Publishing, Inc. • 111 River St. • Hoboken, NJ 07030-5774

AN ADDITIONAL NOTE

Please be advised that travel information is subject to change at any time—and this is especially true of prices. We therefore suggest that you write or call ahead for confirmation when making your travel plans. The authors, editors, and publisher cannot be held responsible for the experiences of readers while traveling. Your safety is important to us, however, so we encourage you to stay alert and be aware of your surroundings. Keep a close eye on cameras, purses, and wallets, all favorite targets of thieves and pickpockets.

FROMMER'S STAR RATINGS, ICONS & ABBREVIATIONS

Every hotel, restaurant, and attraction listing in this guide has been ranked for quality, value, service, amenities, and special features using a **star-rating system.** In country, state, and regional guides, we also rate towns and regions to help you narrow down your choices and budget your time accordingly. Hotels and restaurants are rated on a scale of zero (recommended) to three stars (exceptional). Attractions, shopping, nightlife, towns, and regions are rated according to the following scale: zero stars (recommended), one star (highly recommended), two stars (very highly recommended), and three stars (must-see).

In addition to the star-rating system, we also use **seven feature icons** that point you to the great deals, in-the-know advice, and unique experiences that separate travelers from tourists. Throughout the book, look for:

(Finds)　　Special finds—those places only insiders know about

(Fun Facts)　　Fun facts—details that make travelers more informed and their trips more fun

(Kids)　　Best bets for kids and advice for the whole family

(Moments)　　Special moments—those experiences that memories are made of

(Overrated)　　Places or experiences not worth your time or money

(Tips)　　Insider tips—great ways to save time and money

(Value)　　Great values—where to get the best deals

The following **abbreviations** are used for credit cards:

AE	American Express	**DISC**	Discover	**V**	Visa
DC	Diners Club	**MC**	MasterCard		

TRAVEL RESOURCES AT FROMMERS.COM

Frommer's travel resources don't end with this guide. Frommer's website, **www.frommers.com,** has travel information on more than 4,000 destinations. We update features regularly, giving you access to the most current trip-planning information and the best airfare, lodging, and car-rental bargains. You can also listen to podcasts, connect with other Frommers.com members through our active-reader forums, share your travel photos, read blogs from guidebook editors and fellow travelers, and much more.

The Best of Charleston

Charleston's rich history has made this city the backdrop of countless Gothic romances, the last major one being *Scarlett,* the faintly praised sequel to *Gone With the Wind.* Although a relatively small state—40th in size among the 50 states—South Carolina has had an enormous impact on the nation at numerous points throughout history, none more significant than the firing on Fort Sumter in Charleston Harbor that launched the Civil War.

Charlestonians manage to maintain a way of life that in many respects has little to do with wealth. Many local families still live in homes built by their planter ancestors. The simplest encounter with locals seems to be invested with a social air, as though the visitor were a valued guest. Yet there are those who detect a certain snobbishness in Charleston—and truth be told, you'd have to stay here a hundred years to be considered an insider.

A minimum stay of 3 days is necessary if you wish to discover Charleston by day and by night. Try to include a trip over the Cooper River Bridge to a string of islands that include Pawleys Island, Isle of Palms, Sullivan's Island, and Edisto Island.

To fortify you before you go, here's some background on one of America's most colorful, historic, and romantic port cities.

1 FROMMER'S FAVORITE CHARLESTON EXPERIENCES

- **Playing Scarlett & Rhett at Boone Hall:** Imagine you're one of the romantic figures in *Gone With the Wind* while paying a visit to this 738-acre Mount Pleasant estate, a cotton plantation settled by Maj. John Boone in 1681. Its gorgeous Avenue of Oaks was used for background shots in *Gone With the Wind* and the miniseries *North and South.* See chapter 6.
- **Going Back to Colonial Days:** At Charles Towne Landing, gain insight into how colonists lived 300 years ago when they established the first English settlement in South Carolina. Even the

animals the settlers encountered, from bears to bison, still roam about. Enjoy some 80 acres of gardens while walking along the marsh or biking past lagoons that reflect blossoming camellias and azaleas. See chapter 6.

- **Taking in the View from the Battery:** The Battery, as locals call White Point Gardens, offers the best perspective of the Historic District. The gardens lie at the end of the peninsula, opening onto Cooper River and the harbor, where Fort Sumter sits. For the best walk, head along the sea wall on East Battery Street and Murray Boulevard. Later you can relax in the landscaped park beneath wonderful live oaks. See chapter 6.

- **Tasting She-Crab Soup:** She-crab soup is to the local Charlestonian what clam chowder is to a New Englander. This rich delicacy has many permutations, but in most kitchens it is concocted from butter, milk, heavy cream, sherry, salt, cayenne pepper, crabmeat, and the secret ingredient: crab roe. See chapter 5.

- **Shopping Along King Street:** In 1854, painter Charles Fraser wrote of King Street and its "dazzling display of goods emulating a Turkish bazaar." The street's decline began with the Civil War and continued through subsequent natural disasters and 20th-century suburban sprawl. Today, King Street has bounced back and ranks as one of the most attractive shopping promenades in the South. See chapter 7.

- **Exploring Fort Sumter:** Few events have had such a far-reaching impact on American history as the first shot of the Civil War, fired here on April 12, 1861. As you tour this fortress, its gun emplacements and artifacts on shining display, you can almost hear the bombardment as Yankee ships fired on the fort, whose Confederate troops valiantly resisted until the final day of surrender 4 years after that fateful shot. See chapter 6.

- **Spending the Night in a B&B:** Few places in the South recapture that antebellum feeling the way that a restored Charleston B&B can. The Old English theme always prevails, with muslin curtains, draped rice beds, exposed beams, and crystal chandeliers. Listen for the clank of an iron gate in front of a columned house as the scent of jasmine fills the air. See chapter 4.

- **Strolling Through the City as a Garden:** The entire district of Charleston seems to be one lush garden—not just the public plantings, such as the oleanders that line the Battery, but also the nooks and crannies of private courtyards, planted with everything from wisteria to Confederate jasmine, tea olives to ginger lilies. Pink-blossomed crape myrtles line the streets, and camellias and magnolias sweeten the air.

- **Hiring a Horse & Carriage:** Nothing captures the languid life of the Low Country better than a horse-drawn-carriage ride through the semitropical landscape. Most times of year, the heavenly scent of tea olive, jasmine, or wisteria blossoms pervades the streets. You'll feel like you're back in the antebellum South as you slowly clip-clop past sun-dappled verandas and open-air markets selling fruit, vegetables, and straw baskets. See "Organized Tours" in chapter 6.

2 BEST HOTEL BETS

See chapter 4, "Where to Stay," for complete reviews of all of these accommodations.

- **Best Classical Hotel:** Visiting dignitaries and celebs bunk at the **Charleston Place Hotel,** 205 Meeting St. (© **888/635-2350** or 843/722-4900; www.charlestonplace.com), which rises like a post-modern French château out of the Historic District. Acres of Italian marble, plush bedrooms, and a deluxe restaurant await you. See p. 47.
- **Best & Most Prestigious Inn:** One of the signers of the Declaration of Independence built the **John Rutledge House Inn,** 116 Broad St. (© **800/476-9741** or 843/723-7999; www.johnrutledge houseinn.com), which has been restored to its former Federalist grandeur. All of the typical modern comforts have been added to the gracious, antique-filled bedrooms. See p. 48.
- **Best B&B:** One of the most outstanding bed-and-breakfasts in the Southeast, **Palmer Home View,** 5 East Battery (© **843/853-1574;** www.palmerhomebb.net), was constructed in 1848 by John Ravenel, who designed the forerunner of the submarine. Since 1977, it's been rated one of the most beautifully decorated B&Bs in the area, with its bedrooms opening onto views of Charleston Harbor. See p. 57.
- **Best Small Luxury Hotel:** For those who like their inns on the small scale but as luxurious as any first-class competitor, there's the **Planters Inn,** 112 N. Market St. (© **800/845-7082** or 843/722-2345; www.plantersinn.com). This beautiful little hotel next to the Old City Market was opulently renovated in 1994, transforming it into an enclave of Colonial charm. One of Charleston's best restaurants and bars is on-site. See p. 48.
- **Best Survivor of the Gilded Age:** The landmark **Wentworth Mansion,** 149 Wentworth St. (© **888/466-1886** or 843/853-1886; www.wentworthmansion.com), is an 1886 Second Empire building

filled with the kind of architectural details with which America's robber barons decorated their lavish estates: hand-carved marble fireplaces, Tiffany stained-glass windows, and elaborate wood and plasterwork. Built by a rich cotton merchant, the mansion has been successfully converted into one of South Carolina's grandest hotel addresses. See p. 50.

- **Best Boutique Hotel:** The facade of the **French Quarter Inn at Market Square,** 166 Church St. (© **866/812-1900** or 843/722-1900; www.fqicharleston.com), evokes an 18th-century town house in Paris. Although it has been modernized, the hotel blends in beautifully with the surrounding neighborhood. You'll stay in dignified comfort, enjoying nostalgic reminders of the architecture of yesterday, such as high ceilings, monumental staircases, and wrought-iron fixtures. See p. 53.

- **Best Harbor View:** No inn in Charleston is more aptly named than **HarbourView Inn,** 2 Vendue Range (© **888/853-8439** or 843/853-8439; www.harbourviewcharleston.com), set in the heart of Charleston, across from Waterfront Park. From its windows, you can look out at one of the best city seascapes in South Carolina, a historic setting where the first round in the Civil War was fired. The sea-grass rugs and rattan chairs are of the sort Charleston sea captains used to bring back from their voyages. See p. 54.

- **Best Historic Hotel:** Constructed in grandeur and steeped in the history of Charleston, the **Mills House Hotel,** 115 Meeting St. (© **800/874-9600** or 843/577-2400; www.millshouse.com), has welcomed everyone from Robert E. Lee to Elizabeth Taylor. Many of the original furnishings remain from 1853, when it was built for the then-astronomical price of $200,000. Although it's been heavily altered over the years, it still maintains much of its antebellum charm. See p. 57.

- **Best Modern Hotel:** For the best of contemporary living, head to the **Inn at Middleton Place,** 4290 Ashley River Rd. (© **800/543-4774** or 843/556-0500; www.theinnatmiddletonplace.com), a modern luxury hotel secluded among tall pines and live oaks on the grounds of the historic 18th-century Middleton Plantation, one of the area's major sightseeing attractions. It was the creation of Charles Duell, one of the descendants of Middleton's original owners, who wanted to offer an alternative to "ersatz Colonial." See p. 55.

3 BEST DINING BETS

See chapter 5, "Where to Dine," for complete reviews of all of these restaurants.

- **Best Low Country Cuisine:** Hip and stylish, **Anson,** 12 Anson St. (② **843/577-0551;** http://ansonrestaurant.com), is filled with Low Country charm. The way this place handles the foodstuffs of coastal South Carolina is reason enough to visit. Time-tested recipes are given imaginative twists, as exemplified by the lobster, corn, and black-bean quesadillas or the cashew-crusted grouper in champagne sauce. See p. 68.

- **Best Historic Restaurant:** Of course, George Washington no longer stops at **McCrady's,** 2 Unity Alley (② **843/577-0025;** www.mccradysrestaurant.com), on his visits to Charleston, but this citadel of upmarket American/French cuisine is still going strong. Set in a historic tavern of exposed beams and wide-plank floors, it was recently heralded by *Esquire* as one of the best restaurants in the U.S. Even the most basic dish is magical—take potato soup, for example. Here it's creamy and enlivened with chive oil, truffles, and leek foam. See p. 70.

- **Best for Sunday Brunch:** Sunday brunch at the historic Mills House Hotel's **Barbados Room Restaurant,** 115 Meeting St. (② **843/577-2400;** www.millshouse.com/amenities/dining.html), is a Charleston tradition. In an antebellum setting, you can enjoy some of the best Low Country brunch specialties in the city. Shrimp and grits are traditional, but who can resist the jumbo crab cakes? See p. 70.

- **Best for Seafood:** Most restaurants in Charleston serve seafood, but for authentic Low Country fish dishes, head to **Hank's,** 10 Hayne St. (② **843/723-3474;** www.hanksseafoodrestaurant.com), a converted turn-of-the-20th-century warehouse overlooking Old City Market. The she-crab soup, that invariable Charleston appetizer, is prepared to perfection here. See p. 73.

- **Best for Steak:** Since the '90s, **High Cotton,** 199 E. Bay St. (② **843/724-3815;** www.mavericksouthernkitchens.com), has been winning over a clientele devoted to its steaks. Made from the finest cut of meats, the steaks here are tender, juicy, and succulent. To go the full Southern route, ask for a steak with bourbon sauce. See p. 69.

- **Best for Oysters:** Long known for its oysters, **A. W. Shuck's,** 70 State St. (② **843/723-1151;** www.a-w-shucks.com), settles the demands of city dwellers who really know their bivalves. Oysters, perhaps the best in the South, are prepared here in various delightful ways, including, of course, chilled and served on the half shell. See p. 76.

- **Best for Down-home Favorites:** When you get a hankering for the likes of Carolina quail, peanut-butter pie, and jambalaya, head to **Poogan's Porch,** 72 Queen St. (© **843/557-2337;** www. poogansporch.com). The restaurant is housed in a restored 1891 building where locals come for a good "tuck-in." See p. 79.

- **Best Gullah Cuisine:** Gullah cooking, for some, evokes Creole flavors, and the most authentic is at the aptly named **Gullah Cuisine,** 1717 U.S. 17, Mount Pleasant (© **843/881-9076**), across the bridge from the center of Charleston. Here you'll be served some of the best okra gumbo or andouille sausage in the area. See p. 82.

- **Best Restaurant in South Carolina:** In the town of Summerville, outside Charleston, some of the most discerning palates in the South have ruled that the elegant **Dining Room at Woodlands,** 125 Parsons Rd. (© **843/875-2600;** www.woodlandsinn.com), is the finest in the state. Readers of *Condé Nast Traveler,* in fact, have rated it one of the top restaurants in North America for several years in a row. Low Country cuisine is prepared here to near perfection. See p. 82.

- **Best for Romantic Dining:** In the carriage house of Wentworth Mansion, **Circa 1886 Restaurant,** 149 Wentworth St. (© **843/ 853-7828;** http://circa1886.com), is Charleston's most elegant setting for a romantic dinner. That it also serves some of the city's best Low Country and French cuisine comes as an added bonus. To get in the right mood, take in the water views from the restaurant's cupola. See p. 65.

- **Best for Kids:** A short walk from the Old City Market, **Bocci's,** 158 Church St. (© **843/720-2121;** www.boccis.com), has one of the best family dining rooms in Charleston, known for its good-value Italian cuisine. Kids love to dig into the full-flavored pasta dishes; there's even a special children's menu. See p. 71.

Charleston in Depth

In the closing pages of *Gone With the Wind,* Rhett tells Scarlett that he's going back home to Charleston, where he can find "the calm dignity life can have when it's lived by gentle folks, the genial grace of days that are gone. When I lived those days, I didn't realize the slow charm of them." In spite of all the changes and upheavals over the years, Rhett's endorsement of Charleston still holds true.

If the Old South lives throughout South Carolina's Low Country (the coastal region that stretches from Charleston to Savannah), it positively thrives in Charleston. All our romantic notions of antebellum days—stately homes, courtly manners, gracious hospitality, and, above all, gentle dignity—are facts of everyday life in this old city, in spite of a few scoundrels here and there, including an impressive roster of pirates, patriots, and presidents.

Located on the peninsula between the Cooper and Ashley rivers in southeastern South Carolina, Charleston is the oldest and second-largest city in the state. Notwithstanding a history dotted with earthquakes, hurricanes, fires, and Yankee bombardments, Charleston remains one of the best-preserved cities in America's Old South. It boasts 73 buildings that predate the Revolutionary War, 136 from the late 18th century, and more than 600 built before the 1840s. With its cobblestone streets and horse-drawn carriages, Charleston is a place of idyllic images and sensory pleasures. The Old City Market is bustling with craftspeople jammed under the covered breezeways. Sweetgrass basket weavers hum spirituals; horse-drawn carriages clop down the street; and thousands of tourists eat, drink, and shop their way through town. The scents of jasmine and wisteria fill the air; the aroma of she-crab soup (a local favorite) wafts from sidewalk cafes; and antebellum architecture graces the historic cityscape. "No wonder they are so full of themselves," said an envious visitor from Columbia, which may be the state capital but lacks Charleston style.

In its annual reader survey, *Condé Nast Traveler* magazine named Charleston the number-two city to visit in America. Visitors are drawn here from all over the world. Each spring the city hosts the **Spoleto Festival U.S.A.,** one of the most prestigious performing-arts events in the country.

Does this city have a modern side? Yes, but it's well hidden. Chic shops abound, and there are a few supermodern hotels, but Charleston has no skyscrapers. You don't come to Charleston for anything cutting edge—you come to glimpse an earlier, almost-forgotten era.

1 CHARLESTON TODAY

Many historic buildings still remain intact in Charleston, and this is something of a miracle considering that tornadoes, hurricanes, and several wars (including the Civil War) have swept across this low-lying city. In 1886, Charleston was almost destroyed by an earthquake that measured 7.5 on the Richter scale. In 1989, Hurricane Hugo devastated the city, destroying three-quarters of the homes in the Historic District and causing more than $2.8 billion in damage. And let's not leave out urban renewal in the 20th century, which leveled many landmark structures.

Today, as the city with the most history and antebellum glamour, Charleston is one of the main tourist attractions in the Southeast. It contains some of the most luxurious hotels in the Deep South, and is also known for the quality of its restaurants.

But hardly lost in its Scarlett-and-Rhett past, Charleston has definitely moved into the 21st century. It is the second-largest container seaport on the East Coast, and is also the primary medical center for the eastern part of South Carolina, with several major hospitals, including the sixth oldest continuously operating school of medicine in the United States.

Many locals are employed in the information-technology industry, at companies such as Modulant, Google, and CSS. The U.S. Navy's Space and Naval Warfare Systems Center became the largest employer in the metropolitan area in 2004, trailed by the Medical University of South Carolina.

In demographics, the population of Charleston is 65% white and 32% African American, with only a few percent identified as Latino/Hispanic or of Asian descent.

In 1995, Marjabelle Young Stewart, the country's leading etiquette expert, named Charleston "the best mannered city in the United States." It still remains at the top of that list. A former mayor said, "When it comes to hospitality, we take second place to no one. C'mon down and see us, y'all hear?"

2 LOOKING BACK AT CHARLESTON

COLONIAL DAYS

It is estimated that some 18,000 Native Americans were living in what is now the state of South Carolina when the first European invaders arrived in the 16th century. The Spanish, sailing from what is now the Dominican Republic and entering South Carolina waters through St. Helena Sound (btw. Beaufort and Edisto Island), landed ashore on August 18, 1520. The next year, two more Spanish galleons arrived at Winyah Bay (north of Charleston), the site of present-day Georgetown. Indian settlers ran out to greet them—a big mistake. The choicest specimens were taken back to the Dominican Republic as slaves.

The first Spanish settlement in South Carolina was founded by Lucas Vásquez de Ayllón of Toledo, a Spanish don, who sailed into South Carolina waters in 1526 with an estimated 500 settlers. The resulting community, San Miguel de Guadalpe, predated the English settlement at Jamestown, Virginia, by exactly 81 years. Unfortunately, attacks by hostile Indians,

DATELINE

- **1520** The Spanish arrive from the Caribbean.
- **1562** French Huguenots first settle in the Charleston area.
- **1670** First permanent settlement by the English; plantation economy launched.
- **1740s** Mass importation of slaves to work the plantations.
- **1776** Charleston becomes a major battleground of the American Revolution.
- **1780** British troops under Cornwallis occupy Charleston.
- **1793** Eli Whitney's cotton gin revolutionizes local economy.
- **1860** South Carolina secedes from the Union.
- **1861** Firing on Fort Sumter in Charleston Harbor marks the beginning of the Civil War.
- **1863** Charleston bombarded by Union ships.
- **1865** Sherman invades South Carolina as the South loses the war.
- **1870s** Reconstruction era marks long decline of Charleston's once-golden economy.
- **1918** Some 70,000 men from South Carolina join U.S. military during World War I.

widespread disease, and a particularly bad winter forced the settlers to abandon their colony. Only 150 men and women survived to be evacuated.

In 1562, fleeing religious persecution from the French Catholics, Huguenot settlers sailed into Port Royal Sound (btw. Hilton Head and the town of Beaufort). Under their leader, Jean Ribaut, they came ashore at Parris Island, today the site of a U.S. Marine Corps station.

Their little settlement was to last only 4 years. In 1566, the conquistador Pedro Menéndez de Avilés attacked the colony and routed the Huguenots. Under his command, Fort San Felipe was constructed.

By 1586, with Sir Francis Drake and his British warriors raiding St. Augustine in Florida, the Spanish settlers withdrew.

The British began settling the area in the 1670s. In London, King Charles II awarded the territory of "Carolina," stretching from Virginia to Spanish Florida, to eight so-called "Lord Proprietors."

THE RULE OF THE LORD PROPRIETORS

From the British-held colony of Barbados in the southern West Indies, the lord proprietors recruited sugar-cane and tobacco planters. The first shipload came in 1670, arriving at Albemarle Point on the Ashley River.

- **1941** Military training centers established in South Carolina, as 173,642 people join in World War II effort.
- **1960** Civil rights demonstrations launched.
- **1961** Desegregation extended to public transportation.
- **1975** James Edwards becomes first Republican governor in a century.
- **1980s** Massive return of blacks from Northern cities to their homeland in South Carolina.
- **1989** Category 5 Hurricane Hugo causes mass destruction to the barrier islands around Charleston.
- **2002** Strom Thurmond, Dixiecrat poster boy and U.S. senator from South Carolina for 47 years, resigns at the age of 100.
- **2003** The so-called "Granddaddy of South Carolina"— Strom Thurmond—dies, as scandal erupts.
- **2005** New Copper River Bridge links Charleston to Mount Pleasant.
- **2007** Population explosion makes Charleston "Second City" of South Carolina.
- **2010** South Carolina elects its first woman governor, a Tea Party–backed Republican lawmaker to succeed scandal-stained Gov. Mark Sanford. Nikki Haley will become the nation's second Indian-American governor.

Throughout the 1670s, these planters crossed the river to found Charles Towne, which in time became Charleston.

In the 18th century, the plantations launched by these settlers from Barbados spread throughout the Sea Islands and the Low Country. Settlers were constantly harassed by American Indians, especially the Cherokees, Westoes, and Yemassees, and they also endured attacks from pirates, notably Blackbeard. Even the Spanish raided ships sailing north from Florida. In spite of all the hardships, Charles Towne became the richest colony in America, a prize highly valued by the throne in London.

The importation of slaves to work the land continued at such a rapid rate that nearly 25,000 slaves (figures vary) were said to be living in and around Charleston in the 1740s—outnumbering the white population three to one. Most of the slaves were shipped over from Sierra Leone and Senegal.

Slaves were used for the most monumental of tasks, such as clearing swamps and constructing dikes. Rice, which was in great demand at this time, became the crop of choice for American colonists. Rice production increased annually, and plantation owners grew rich with British pounds. Indeed, the merchants, shippers, and plantation owners in and around Charleston were the richest people in 18th-century America, when direct trade with England was six times in Charleston what it was in the other colonies. Ships arriving from London brought fashionable goods and exotic spices to the port of Charles Towne. While slaves toiled in the rice fields, Charleston's landed gentry celebrated with balls, races, concerts, and festivities.

THE REVOLUTIONARY WAR

Change was in the air in the latter part of the 18th century. Word of the Battle of Bunker Hill in Massachusetts reached the colony of South Carolina. Less than a month later, on July 12, 1775, local rebels seized Fort Charlotte in McCormick County. This was the first English military installation to be captured in the oncoming Revolutionary War.

In the minds of many, South Carolina is more strongly associated with the Civil War than the Revolutionary War. But the state was actually a major battleground of the American Revolution. A total of 137 battles were fought on South Carolina soil.

So severe was hatred against Tory Loyalists that they were rounded up, tarred, feathered, and then paraded through the streets of Charleston.

The Revolutionary War hero of South Carolina was Francis Marion, a descendant of the Huguenots. Born in a settlement near Georgetown in 1732, he was brought up in the South Carolina Up

Country, the swamps and thickets that comprise the northwestern corner of the state. What Marion learned about guerilla warfare fighting the Cherokees in the Up Country, he used to his state's advantage against the British, who in time nicknamed him the "Swamp Fox." He made periodic raids on British installations, and then disappeared with his men into the swamps, where he could not be routed.

With the help of log fortifications (such as Fort Moultrie, which can be visited today), the rebels delayed the advance of British troops into Charleston until 1780. Lord Cornwallis, who had established himself as the ruler of Charleston, planned to join forces with Up Country colonials still loyal to the crown and advance against the forces of George Washington in Virginia.

But when Up Country colonials learned that English forces had massacred rebels of the Continental Army as they were surrendering at Lancaster, the Up Country colonials became so incensed that they at long last joined the Low Country rebellion.

Up Country rebels defeated the Cornwallis forces at the Battle of Kings Mountain in October 1780, marking a turning point in the war. After that, the British surrender at Yorktown in 1781 became inevitable.

ANTEBELLUM DAYS

A major blow to the prestige of Charleston came in 1786, when the capital of South Carolina was moved from that city to the more centrally located Columbia, a newly created city in the sort of border territory between the Low Country and its traditional rival, the Up Country. In 1788, South Carolina would ratify the U.S. Constitution, becoming the eighth state to join the newly emerging Union.

Charleston was profoundly affected by the invention of Eli Whitney's cotton gin in 1793. In time, rice barons turned to growing cotton, and Sea Island cotton became highly valued for its long, silky fibers. By the mid-1830s, South Carolina's annual cotton crop was nearing 70 million pounds, accounting for more than half of America's exports to Europe. Cotton would remain king in and around South Carolina right up to the advent of the Civil War.

Charleston's bankers and shippers constructed canals to export slaves outward from their arrival point at the city's port, and to bring cotton from the interior of South Carolina quickly to the harbor in Charleston, where ships were waiting to take it abroad.

"The Best Friend of Charleston," as the new South Carolina Canal & Railroad Company was called, opened up newer and faster markets, as rail lines in the 1840s were extended as far as the Up Country.

Overproduction by cotton plantations in Georgia and Alabama eventually brought havoc to local South Carolina cotton planters.

Impressions

To describe our growing up in the lowcountry of South Carolina, I would have to take you to the marsh on a spring day, flush the great blue heron from its silent occupation, scatter marsh hens as we sink to our knees in the mud, open you an oyster with a pocket-knife and feed it to you from the shell and say, "There. That taste. That's the taste of my childhood." I would say, "Breathe deeply," and you would breathe and remember that smell for the rest of your life, the bold, fecund aroma of the tidal marsh, exquisite and sensual, the smell of the South in heat, a smell like new milk, semen, and spilled wine, all perfumed with seawater.
— Novelist Pat Conroy, *The Prince of Tides*

Nonetheless, politics in the antebellum South were still dominated by South Carolina, with Charleston wielding the greatest influence.

The emerging spokesperson for South Carolina's interests was the towering John C. Calhoun, who was married to a Low Country plantation heiress. Resigning as the vice president to Andrew Jackson in 1832, he devoted all his considerable intellect and power to preserving both the cotton industry and slavery. Elected to the U.S. Senate, he fought against federal export taxes on cotton.

Threats to secede were issued by South Carolina from 1832 until the actual outbreak of the Civil War. Charleston financiers and Low Country planters, more than any other force in the South, took the dangerous steps to divide the nation, especially in the wake of the election of Abraham Lincoln, who swept into the presidency without a single electoral vote south of the Mason-Dixon line.

THE CIVIL WAR

That dreadful day, one of the most important in the history of America, came on April 12, 1861, as South Carolina troops began their bombardment of Fort Sumter under Union control. The Union troops held out for 34 hours of shelling before surrendering their citadel. By May 11, President Abraham Lincoln in Washington had declared war against the Confederate States of America.

Although the port of Charleston came under heavy bombardment by Union forces, especially in 1863, South Carolina was hardly a major battleground during the Civil War—certainly not in the way it was during the American Revolution. The state's major battle—not among the great Civil War conflicts—was the Battle of Rivers Bridge in February 1865, just 2 months before Robert E. Lee surrendered at Appomattox.

The port of Charleston did play a major role in blockade running during the war, however. Amazingly, only 7 months after the firing on Fort Sumter, Union forces occupied Hilton Head, Beaufort, and St. Helena Island on the doorstep of Charleston and remained in control there throughout the war.

Even by 1863, Union forces had begun land redistribution, awarding parcels of Sea Island and various hunks of plantations to freed slaves. Some 40,000 freedmen took over nearly half a million acres of plantation lands. It was to be only a temporary grant, however. By 1866, President Andrew Johnson had given most of the land back to the former white landowners, the landed gentry.

At the end of the war, victors from the North occupied Charleston, filling the city with "carpetbaggers," the name derisively given to carpetbag-carrying Yankees who flooded the South during Reconstruction, hoping to make a quick buck. The golden age of antebellum life was over, and South Carolina remains to this day one of the poorest states in America.

MODERN TIMES

Charleston remained under Union forces until 1877. The abolition of slavery and the end of the plantation era brought economic stagnation that would not be relieved until the coming of World War II.

It wasn't that king cotton wasn't being produced. It was, and in greater bulk than it had been during its antebellum heyday. It was *too* plentiful, as it would turn out. Planters grew more and more cotton, causing the price to fall lower and lower.

Rice and cotton met bitter ends: A fierce hurricane in 1911 destroyed rice production, and the pesky boll weevil finished off the Sea Island cotton industry around 1922.

One positive result of the ongoing poverty of post–Civil War Charleston was that few could afford to revamp their homes in the latest Victorian style. "Too poor to paint; too proud to whitewash," went the rallying cry. The result is a city whose collection of antebellum architecture is unsurpassed.

Many communities in South Carolina became cotton-mill towns, with low wages granted to the all-white mill workers. Smallpox became the curse of the mill towns. Charleston and South Carolina sank deeper and deeper into depression long before the actual Depression was set in motion by the Wall Street crash of 1929.

On the eve of America's entry into World War I, South Carolina had barely a dozen public schools. Locals, especially mill owners, opposed sending the children to schools, wanting them to work in factories instead. Farmers kept their children on the family spread, toiling in the sun.

> **Fun Facts**   **A Nationwide Craze**
>
> In the 1920s, the musical *Running Wild* introduced the Charleston, which quickly became a nationwide craze. Silent movies, such as *Our Dancing Daughters* with Joan Crawford, were particularly fond of depicting the dance. Even the stuffy Duke of Windsor took Charleston lessons.

At the outbreak of World War I, some 70,000 men from South Carolina, many of them from Charleston, joined the military; during World War II, more than double that number of men (and women) signed up for military duty.

But few suffered more than the state's black populace, who had little chance of making a living in the South. During the first 4 decades of the 20th century, black Southerners began a vast migration to Washington, New York, Cleveland, Detroit, and Chicago, among other cities. On the eve of the Japanese attack on Pearl Harbor, more white people than black were living in Charleston and South Carolina at large. This had not been true since the dawn of the 18th century.

Much of the history of modern South Carolina has been marred by ugly racial conflicts. Civil rights demonstrations began in 1960, followed by desegregation in 1961. Often the front lines in the battle for racial fairness stretched bitterly across schoolyards, college campuses, and public-transportation facilities. By 1970, the first blacks elected to the legislature since the dawn of the 20th century were voted into office.

Feeling betrayed by their long-cherished Democratic Party, right-wing conservatives in 1975 elected James Edwards, the first Republican governor in more than a century.

South Carolina legislators disgraced themselves and their state in the 1980s and early 1990s. In the 1989 sting operation "Operation Lost Trust," 17 members of the state legislature—among others—were arrested for selling their votes for money.

The death of the oldest living senator, Strom Thurmond, in 2003 was followed immediately by headlines. Although Thurmond had stood for "segregation today, segregation tomorrow, segregation forever," it was revealed that he was the father of a child born out of wedlock and conceived in an illicit affair with a black woman.

The latest trends show a reversal of the great emigration pattern in the early decades of the 20th century that saw some 6.5 million blacks uproot themselves and head north. Urban decay and increasing violence in many Northern cities have led to a reverse emigration pattern. At the post-millennium, figures showed a return by thousands of blacks to the South and burgeoning growth in their population figures.

In 2005, at long last, the Arthur Ravenel, Jr., Bridge (or the New Copper River Bridge) linked downtown Charleston with the suburb of Mount Pleasant. With a main span of 1,546 feet, it is the longest cable-stayed bridge in the Western Hemisphere. The bridge is designed to endure wind gusts in excess of 300 mph and earthquakes of up to 7.4 on the Richter scale. It also includes a shared bicycle-pedestrian path called Wonders' Way.

The latest population estimate put Charleston at an estimated 125,560 citizens. This made it the second most populous city in South Carolina, rivaled only by the state capital, Columbia.

In the November 2010 elections, Nikki Haley, the Republican nominee, was elected governor of South Carolina. She became the second Indian American governor ever elected, after Louisiana's Bobby Jindal. She also became the first female governor ever elected in South Carolina, and, surprisingly, has even been suggested as a long-shot presidential candidate for 2012.

3 ART & ARCHITECTURE

The epitome of Southern graciousness, the plantation culture of Charleston and its surrounding Low Country spans 2 centuries that saw everything from a glorious antebellum past (for the landed gentry, not the slaves) to depression, decay, and the passing of a way of life.

The most remarkable buildings were constructed between 1686 and 1878 (yes, 13 years after the Civil War, during Reconstruction) along the South Carolina coastal plain centered at Charleston.

Many of these once-elegant structures still stand today to enchant us, although they are in varying states of preservation, some no more than ruins. Only the camera has captured some of these stately Low Country manses for posterity. From churches to gardens, chapels to memorable homes, plantation houses to graceful frame structures, Charleston has it all.

THE ARCHITECTURE OF CHARLESTON

All you need to do is walk down Broad Street in the center of Charleston to see three dozen ornately decorated and historic structures, on the block between East Bay and Church streets. Much of what has been saved was thanks to an ordinance passed in 1931 that preserved whole sectors of town—and not just individual buildings. Although some other American cities now have this, Charleston was the first city in the world to adopt such a preservation law.

To many visitors today, the so-called historic core lies **south of Broad Street.** This sector is certainly one of the great districts of architecture in the Deep South. But the landed gentry in the heyday of the plantation era also built many superb homes and mansions in other sections of the city, such as **Harleston Village** and **Radcliffeborough.** Harleston Village lies west of the Historic District. Directly north of Harleston is the neighborhood of Radcliffeborough, beginning north of Calhoun Street. Some of the grandest Victorian manses stand around **Colonial Lake.** These neighborhoods deserve at least an hour of your time: Lacy iron gates, 19th-century ornaments, towering old trees, and private gardens make it a worthwhile stroll, even if you're not particularly interested in architecture.

The Georgian Palladian style reigned supreme in historic Charleston, lasting over the centuries, and surely there are more columns in Charleston today than in a small Greek city in classical days. One of the finest Georgian mansions in America stands at **64 S. Battery St.,** built in 1772 by William Gibbes, a successful ship owner and planter. He modeled it after English designs but was also inspired by Palladio. The house is not pure Georgian, however, as Adamesque features, such as wrought-iron railings, were added later.

The columned single house prevailed for 250 years—there are perhaps some 3,000 such houses standing in Charleston today. Its most defining feature is its single-room width; it's also set at right angles to the street. One of the most evocative examples of a Charleston single house is the **Col. Robert Brewton House,** at 71 Church St. The domestic structure of the single house is one of Charleston's greatest contributions to city architecture in America.

Almost from the day the first settlement of Charles Towne was launched, locals showed a surprising, almost feverish, interest in the shape of their domestic dwellings. Some were more lavish than others, of course, but even less expensive dwellings were adorned with wrought-iron balconies or two-columned porches. Today, some of the city's grander manses, churches, and banks still evoke the entrance to Greek temples.

Although much of the great architecture is gone, what remains is impressive: 73 buildings from the colonial period, approximately 136 from the late 18th century, and more than 600 built during the antebellum heyday before the coming of the Civil War.

Colonial to Adamesque

In Charleston's early days, from roughly 1690 to 1740, there was the colonial style, with such defining features as clapboard wooden siding, low foundations, and steeply pitched roofs. The **John Lining House,** at 106 Broad St., is the most evocative building of that period. Coexisting for a certain time with colonial architecture was Georgian, a style that flourished between 1700 and 1800. Its defining features are box chimneys, hipped roofs, flattened columns, and raised basements. Nowhere is this style better exemplified than in the **Miles Brewton House,** at 27 King St.

As colonial and Georgian faded, another style of architecture appeared, peaking in popularity during a 3-decade span beginning in 1790. Although it was called Federalist architecture in the North, most Charlestonians referred to the structures of this era as "Adamesque" or from the "Adam period," a reference to what those brothers from Scotland, James and Robert Adam, were creating in the British Isles. The heyday of the Adam influence was in the mid-1700s. The best example of Federalist/Adamesque architecture in Charleston is the **Nathaniel Russell House,** at 51 Meeting St., which is open to the public (see chapter 6).

Constructed around the same time as the Nathaniel Russell House, the **James Moultrie House,** at 20 Montagu St., is an Adamesque treasure of delicate proportions. Although it was built by a planter, Daniel Cobia, it became more famous as the address of the Moultrie family in 1834. Dr. Moultrie, related to the Revolutionary War hero Gen. William Moultrie, was one of South Carolina's early physicians, founding its first medical school.

A magnificent Adamesque mansion, the **Gaillard-Bennett House,** was constructed at 60 Montagu St. around 1802. The restored house was originally built by a rice planter, Theodore Gaillard. It is famous for its fluted columns with so-called "Tower-of-the-Winds" capitals, along with an elliptically shaped window in its portico gable and a modillion cornice, with other Palladian architectural motifs. In 1870,

Impressions

Outwardly discreet, the landscape masks extremes of beauty and terror. Hidden in the loveliest places are narratives of horror: Some of the region's most beautiful gardens were created by forced labor. Its peaceful cypress swamps, now refuges for alligators, egrets, and herons, were likewise built by slaves as freshwater impoundments for the cultivation of rice, which Africans were brought here to grow.

—John Beardsley, *Art and Landscape in Charleston and the Low Country*

5 years after the end of the Civil War, Robert E. Lee was a guest of the Bennett family, who then owned the manse, and he spoke to admiring well-wishers from the second-floor balcony.

Another stellar example of the Adamesque style is the **Jonathan Lucas House,** at 286 Calhoun St., built around 1808. Several generations of rice barons lived here, establishing rice milling as a big industry in the southeastern United States.

Greek Revival vs. Gothic Revival

The Regency style came and went quickly in Charleston, filling in a transitional period between Adamesque and the Greek Revival style. The most evocative example of Regency is the **Edmondston-Alston House,** at 21 E. Battery St., erected by Charles Edmondston in 1825. The purity of the original style was later altered by Charles Alston, a rice planter who added Greek Revival details. From its precincts, General P. G. T. Beauregard watched the attack on Fort Sumter in 1861, and Robert E. Lee once took refuge here when a fire threatened the Mills House Hotel where he was lodged. This historic home is open to the public (see chapter 6).

The Greek Revival period, which flourished roughly from 1820 to 1875 (a full 10 years after the Civil War), had an enormous impact on the cityscape of Charleston. Its defining features are, of course, heavy columns and capitals (often Doric), along with a hipped or gabled roof and a wide band of trim. One of the most solid examples of this form of bold architecture is the **Beth Elohim Reform Temple,** at 90 Hasell St., the oldest synagogue in continuous use in the United States, first organized in 1749.

However, the most spectacular example of the Greek Revival style is at **172 Tradd St.,** built in 1836 by Alexander Hext Chisolm, who made his fortune in rice. The lavish capitals are copies of those designed in Athens in 335 B.C. The architect is thought to be Charles F. Reichardt of New York.

At the turn of the 19th century, Gabriel Manigault, a French Huguenot, was the biggest name in the architecture of Charleston. Manigault's father, also known as Gabriel Manigault, was in his day not only the richest man in Charleston but also one of the wealthiest in the country. Unfortunately the architect's greatest buildings have been torn down, and those that remain have been only loosely attributed to him. One such structure is today's **City Hall,** at the corner of Broad Street at its junction with Meeting Street. Constructed in 1801, City Hall is a stellar example of the Adamesque-Palladian style of architecture. It was originally a bank building before becoming City Hall in 1818.

(Fun Facts   The Gullah Tongue Makes It to Broadway

In the 1920s, while he was living in Charleston, DuBose Heyward wrote *Porgy*, which in time became a Broadway play. Later, it became even more famous as a folk opera, written by George Gershwin and retitled *Porgy and Bess*. (Living for a time in Charleston, Gershwin incorporated sounds and rhythms of the Gullah language he'd heard in black churches around the Low Country.) Heyward was inspired by the city's rich heritage, even though the glorious mansions of old had fallen into disrepair and Charlestonians were going through hard times—"too poor to paint, too proud to whitewash." Heyward used not only the byways of Charleston for his setting but also the Gullah language for his dialogues.

One of the few buildings that can be directly traced to the architectural drawing board of Manigault is the **Joseph Manigault House,** at 350 Meeting St., which the architect designed for his brother Joseph in 1803. Many critics hail it as one of the most impressive Adamesque homes in the United States. It is one of the few historic homes in Charleston open to the public (see chapter 6).

Another national landmark attributed to Manigault is at **18 Bull St.,** an Adamesque manse constructed at the turn of the 19th century by William Blacklock, a wine merchant. At its lowest point, this mansion became a cheap boardinghouse that barely escaped bulldozers in 1958.

Robert Mills, who designed the Washington Monument, filled in when Manigault resettled in Philadelphia. But Mills was never as well received, although he left the monumental **First Baptist Church** (1819–22) on lower Church Street and the five-columned **Fireproof Building** (1822–26) at Chambers and Meeting streets.

When an 1838 fire destroyed a large part of antebellum Charleston, many districts were reconstructed in the Greek Revival style. Doric columns were particularly fashionable, along with rectangular shapes inspired by Greek temples, such as those found in Sicily.

A monumental "pillar" of Greek Revival is the columned **Centenary Methodist Church,** at 60 Wentworth St., an 1842 structure by Edward Brickell White. This is one of the grandest examples of a Greek Doric temple in America.

Then along came Andrew Jackson Downing, the mid-19th-century arbiter of American architectural taste, who ridiculed Charleston's obsession with Greek Revival. The way was paved for the emergence of E. B. White, who brought in the Gothic Revival design, which prevailed from 1850 to 1885 and is characterized by pointed arches and buttressed stone tracery. The best example of Gothic Revival is the **French Protestant (Huguenot) Church,** at 136 Church St.

Also dominating the 1850s, the decade before the Civil War, were the architects F. D. Lee and Edward C. Jones. Together and separately, they began to change the cityscape of Charleston, creating, for example, the Moorish-style fish market, their most exotic invention—alas, now gone. They pioneered the use of cast iron, which became a dominant feature in city architecture and can still be seen at its most abundant on the western side of Meeting Street, stretching from Hasell to Market streets.

Among the most talented of all Charleston architects, Jones designed the **Trinity Methodist Church,** on Meeting Street, in 1850. This impressive edifice has a pedimented Palladian portico of Corinthian columns. But in just 3 years Jones shifted his style to Italianate, which remained popular until the dawn of the 20th century. The Italianate style is defined by verandas, low-pitched roofs, and balustrades; an evocative example is the **Col. John Ashe House,** at 26 S. Battery St., which was designed by Jones.

In 1853, Jones designed his first commercial building in the Italianate Renaissance Revival style, at **1 Broad St.** Reminiscent of a corner building in London, it once housed a bank. At one time this building was owned by George A. Trenholm, a cotton broker and blockade runner, one of several 19th-century power brokers in Charleston who were said to have inspired Margaret Mitchell's character of Rhett Butler in *Gone With the Wind.*

Still one of the city's most magnificent landmarks, the columned building at **200 E. Bay St.** is the most stellar example of the Italian Renaissance Revival style. This U.S. Custom House was built over a period of 26 years, from 1853 to 1879, and was the creation of Ammi Burnham Young, a Boston architect who'd designed a similar building in his home city. Young was largely instrumental in launching the tradition of designing federal buildings, such as post offices, in a classical style. The Roman Corinthian portico of this splendid temple is much photographed by visitors.

About 20 years before Charleston got sucked up in the Civil War, all purism in architectural style vanished. Most architects and builders were more interested in a dramatic facade. This period saw the bastardization of much of Charleston's architectural landscape. Architects reached out internationally for inspiration—perhaps to the

Moors, to Persia, to the Norman style of church, or even Gothic Venice, if they were fanciful.

The best example of this adulterated though architecturally beautiful style is at **67 Rutledge Ave.,** the home that Col. James H. Taylor ordered built around 1851 "in the style of a Persian villa," with Moorish arches as ornamentation. This was a famous address in its heyday, entertaining the likes of such distinguished guests as the 19th-century politician, tastemaker, and orator Daniel Webster.

And then came the Civil War, when all building ceased except for fortifications. Much great architecture was destroyed during Union bombardments, especially in 1863.

After the Civil War

The Victorian style arrived in Charleston after the Civil War and prevailed from 1870 until the coming of World War I. This style was not as predominant here as it was in other American cities because many Charlestonians, wiped out economically from the effects of the war, did not have money to build. Nonetheless, you'll see some fine Victorian manses in Charleston today, notably the **Sottile House,** with its wide verandas opening onto Green Street on the College of Charleston campus.

When Victorian architects did design buildings in Charleston, they often created "fantasies," as exemplified by the manse that stands at **40 Montagu St.** Built by food merchant Bernard Wohlers in 1891, the house was restored in 1963. Its unique style combines Charles Eastlake with Queen Anne motifs. This startling house seems underappreciated in a city that prizes its colonial and antebellum homes more than Victorian grandeur.

Not all Charlestonians during the latter Victorian Age were building in the Victorian style. The architect and state senator Albert W. Todd, for example, constructed one of Charleston's most magnificent private residences, at **40 Rutledge Ave.,** in the Colonial Revival style at the turn of the 20th century. With its verandas and splendid columned portico, this house is worth a detour.

One of the most celebrated blocks in the city is **Rainbow Row,** 79–107 E. Bay St. It got its name in the 1930s, when the entire block was rejuvenated and painted in colors used by the colonials. The architecture is mainly of the so-called British style, in that there was a store on the ground floor with the living accommodations on the floors above. Rainbow Row is the longest such Georgian block of buildings in the United States, and it inspired DuBose Heyward's "Catfish Row" in *Porgy and Bess*.

Although it's an arguable point, a Florida professor, Sigmund Heinz, once stated: "For all practical purposes, the Civil War brought

THE ART OF CHARLESTON

As might be expected, Charleston is far more distinguished by its architecture than by its art. But it's had some high points over the years, and today boasts a creative core of artists whose works are displayed at the Spoleto Festival U.S.A. and in museums in the city—and often showcased in traveling exhibitions around the state.

In the colonial period, the art decorating the antebellum homes of Charleston—most often landscapes or portraits of dogs and horses—was imported from London and brought over by British ships sailing into Charleston Harbor. When families grew rich from rice and indigo, portrait painters, many of them itinerant, did idealized portraits of the founding father of a dynasty and his wife (always made out to be far more beautiful than she was), or else the whole brood gathered for an idealized family portrait.

Out of this lackluster mess, one artist rose to distinguish himself.

Charleston's Renaissance Man

Born in South Carolina in 1782 of Scottish descent, Charles Fraser became the best-known artist in Charleston for his miniature portraits, many of which you can see in the **Gibbes Museum of Art** (see chapter 6). Although he was also a distinguished landscape painter, today he is mainly known for his miniatures.

When the Marquis de Lafayette came to Charleston in 1825, he sat for a portrait by Fraser. In turn the artist gave the marquis one of his miniatures as a gift. Lafayette later wrote that the portrait was a "very high specimen of the state of arts in America."

Fraser received his artistic training at the age of 13 when he studied with Thomas Coram. He was educated at the Classical Academy, which in time became the College of Charleston. For 11 years he was a lawyer, before giving up his practice in 1818 to devote himself to art full-time.

As a miniaturist, he became quickly known in Charleston, and he captured the essence of many of the city's most distinguished citizens.

Impressions

Come quickly, have found heaven.

—Artist Alfred Hutty, in a wire to his wife
upon discovering Charleston

His color was relatively flat, but his compositions were filled with linear detail, and he was known for his delicate, lyrically stylized art.

Fraser had many other talents, not only as an attorney. He distinguished himself as a civil leader, and he was also a designer, having provided the plans for the steeple on **St. John's Lutheran Church** at 10 Archdale St. In 1854, he wrote a valuable history of the city, *Reminiscences of Charleston.* Charlestonians hailed Fraser as "a faithful citizen, a pillar, and an ornament."

The Charleston Renaissance

The long, dreary years of the Reconstruction era, when much of Charleston was mired in poverty, did not encourage the growth of great art. In the early 20th century, however, the "Charleston Renaissance" was born. This cultural movement spanned the decades between 1915 and 1940 on the eve of the U.S. entry into World War II. Fostered by artists, musicians, architects, and poets, the Renaissance rescued Charleston from the physical devastations of the Civil War and later from the deep mire of the Depression.

Laura Bragg, the director of the Charleston Museum from 1920 to 1931, presided over a salon at her home at 38 Chambers St. In time, this parlor grew as famous in the South as the salon of Gertrude Stein and Alice B. Toklas became in Paris. Much of the Southern literary world, including the novelist and playwright Carson McCullers from Georgia, dropped by.

Elizabeth O'Neill Verner (1883–1979) has emerged as the towering figure of the Charleston Renaissance artists. As she once put it, "I had two hobbies, art and love of Charleston. I combined them into one profession." Charleston-born and -bred, she studied art in Philadelphia from 1901 to 1903 before returning to Charleston. When she found herself unexpectedly widowed, she turned to art to earn a living to support herself and her two small children.

Verner specialized in beautiful etchings and drawings of Charleston scenes, as exemplified by her *Avenue at the Oaks.* As she aged, she switched to pastels. She chose such subjects as churches, beautiful homes, columns, porticos, and wrought-iron gates. But her forte was in depicting scenes of the vendors in the city market, none more evocative than her pastel on silk entitled *Seated Flower Seller Smoking Pipe.* Verner was instrumental in reviving an interest in art in Charleston during the 1920s and 1930s.

Another major artist of the period was **Alice Ravenel Huger Smith** (1876–1958), a Charleston native who was intrigued by the Low Country landscape, with its acres of marshes, cypress swamps, palmettos, rice fields, egrets, herons, and lonely beaches. Her sketches were filled with imagery. After 1924, she worked mainly in watercolor, which she found best for depicting the hazy mist of the Low Country. One of her most evocative works is the 1919 *Mossy Tree.* Her interest in Japanese-style prints led to the creation of the Charleston Etchers' Club.

Another native of South Carolina, **Anna Heyward Taylor** (1879–1956), found her inspiration in Charleston, which she considered a city of "color and charm." Her paintings, now in private collections and major galleries, are steeped in the misty aura of the Low Country. Our favorite among her works is the 1930 rendition of *Fenwick Hall,* in which she captured the rot, despair, and decay of this dilapidated plantation before its renovation.

Another notable artist, Michigan-born **Alfred Hutty** (1877–1954), began a lifelong love affair with Charleston when he was sent here to establish an art school for the Carolina Art Association. His greatest fame came as an etcher, although he was an accomplished painter as well. His *White Azaleas–Magnolia Gardens* (1925) captures the luxuriant vegetation of the Low Country as seen in the Ashley River plantations. Today his works are displayed in such institutions as the British Museum in London and the Metropolitan Museum in New York.

4 CHARLESTON IN POPULAR CULTURE: BOOKS, FILM & MUSIC

BOOKS

Many writers have tried to capture the legend and lore of Charleston. *Mary's World,* by Richard N. Cote, is notable in that it was based on more than 2,500 pages of unpublished letters, diaries, and journals written by a Southern aristocrat named Mary Pringle. This is a moving chronicle of the life her family led in antebellum Charleston, during the Civil War, and in the Reconstruction era.

For a quick overview of the city, *A Short History of Charleston,* by Robert Rosen, starts with the founding of Charles Towne and continues through Hurricane Hugo's destruction in 1989. It's all here—from the rice plantations in the Low Country to Charleston's roles in the Revolutionary War and again in the Civil War.

Charleston! Charleston! History of a Southern City, by Walter J. Fraser, tells the story of Charleston from 1670 to the present day—and what a saga it is. From the bars to the bedrooms of the bordellos, this is an insider guide to the city. You go into prisons and schools, churches and orphanages, meeting black and white, rich and poor. From economic booms to devastating busts, this book takes you on a roller coaster ride of local history.

The best and most helpful practical guide—virtually a street-by-street survey—is *Complete Charleston: A Guide to the Architecture, History, and Gardens of Charleston,* by Margaret H. Moore, with photographs by Truman Moore. Sold all over town, the book divides Charleston into 11 neighborhoods and takes you on a tour of each, a voyage of discovery of the city's world-class architecture and lush secret gardens.

Art and Landscape in Charleston and the Low Country, by John Beardsley, was published as part of the 21st season of the Spoleto Festival U.S.A. The color photographs of Charleston and the Low Country alone are reason enough to purchase this guide. Its chief focus is on contemporary art in the Low Country, landscape history, and garden design with many architectural perspectives.

For a fictional depiction, the 1991 bestseller *Scarlett,* by Alexandra Ripley, is set partially in Charleston. As the sequel to *Gone With the Wind,* it depicts Scarlett returning to Charleston to try to get her husband, Rhett Butler, back.

FILM

Directed by Nick Cassavetes, *The Notebook* (2004) used backdrop scenes set in Charleston. Shots included Mount Pleasant, the Battery, and the College of Charleston. Told in flashback, the film depicts James Garner reading to an old nursing home patient (Gena Rowlands), telling the star-crossed love story of a boy and a girl.

Based on Charles Frazier's best-selling novel of the same name, *Cold Mountain* (2003) features Charleston in some of its background scenes. Nicole Kidman and Jude Law were the stars in this drama directed by Anthony Minghella. In the waning days of the Civil War, a wounded Confederate deserter makes his way home to return to his true love.

Several portions of *The Patriot* (2000) were filmed on the College of Charleston campus. Hollywood's most controversial actor, Mel Gibson, and the late Heath Ledger star in this film shot entirely in South Carolina. An old-fashioned period drama, it tells the tale of a man swept up into the conflict of the Revolutionary War against his wishes.

Various television shows have also based themselves in Charleston. The miniseries *North and South* (1985), starring Patrick Swayze, was filmed in and around town. Two friends—one from the North, the other from the South—struggle to maintain their friendship as events move toward the outbreak of the Civil War.

More recently, the Lifetime series *Army Wives,* which premiered in 2007, was filmed in Charleston at the old Navy base. The drama centers on the lives of a group of military spouses living on a U.S. Army base.

The first musical society in North America, St. Cecilia Society, was founded in 1766 in Charleston. In the centuries to follow, Charleston and the state of South Carolina would produce a number of musicians who would attain world renown.

Born in Charleston, **Frederick (Freddie) William Green,** a self-taught musician on banjo and guitar, was discovered in New York in the 1920s. He played in the Count Basie Orchestra and went on to record with Benny Goodman, Lionel Hampton, Lester Young, and the legendary Billie Holiday.

John Birks (Dizzy) Gillespie, an African-American jazz trumpeter, bandleader, singer, and composer, and a South Carolina native, was once a major entertainer in the nightclubs of Charleston. He became a major figure in the development of bebop and modern jazz, and he was also a key player in founding Afro-Cuban jazz. Many music critics hail Dizzy as the greatest jazz trumpeter of all time.

James Brown, born in South Carolina, was one of the key players in the rock-'n'-roll era. He was often seen in Charleston, and in time he became one of the most influential figures in 20th-century music, a prime player in the evolution of gospel and rhythm and blues as it evolved into soul and funk. Today, the late musician is called the "Godfather of Soul."

Another Charleston native, **James Jamerson,** became a legendary Motown bassist. Critics claimed he single-handedly revolutionized bass playing.

Born and raised in Charleston, **Darius Rucker** formed **Hootie & the Blowfish,** the best-known rock band to hail from South Carolina, in 1986. The band became a mainstream pop music sensation in the mid-1990s. In 2002, Rucker recorded a solo R&B album, and his debut country album in 2008 was a big hit.

5 LOW COUNTRY COOKING

Charleston is the capital of the Low Country, an area that comprises some half a million acres of wetlands, and the site of former rice plantations. Although threatened by overdevelopment, these rivers, swamps, ponds, creeks, lakes, and bird-filled salt marshes have traditionally provided the foodstuffs for "sandlappers," as residents of the region are sometimes called.

For many generations, folks have literally lived off these marshy waters. The tables they set reflected their surroundings, where the economy was based for at least 2 centuries on the cultivation of rice.

The early settlers learned to thrive on crab, oysters, mullet, eel, shrimp, sturgeon, and shad, among other sea creatures.

In its high-rolling king-cotton days, Charleston developed a reputation for lavish productions of hearty fare from land and sea, served up in hospitable communal style—from turtle suppers (now merely a memory of a vanished era) and catfish stews to outdoor barbecues, oyster roasts, and venison feasts. One particularly over-the-top 19th-century Charleston dinner of record boasted some two dozen meat and poultry dishes. It was launched with green-turtle soup and salmon in an anchovy sauce, followed by saddle of venison, capons with truffles, roasted pheasant, wild turkey, grouse, legs of mutton in caper sauce, green-turtle steak in a Madeira sauce, and, of course, platters of fried oysters from the marsh. Eight different desserts, ranging from pyramids of crystallized fruit to omelet soufflés, followed.

The English colonists didn't just search the sea for foodstuffs. The early Spanish settlers had planted pomegranates, figs, and peaches, and these transplanted species thrived in South Carolina. The settlers also found forests filled with animals, including deer, bears, and birds of all kinds. Today, however, the bison, wolves, and panthers known to them are all gone.

The English and the French Huguenots brought their own tastes and recipes, but Low Country fare was also greatly influenced and seasoned by the black hands of Africa laboring in the open hearths and brick ovens of the plantations and town houses. These African slaves spiced up traditional recipes brought over from England and Scotland by tossing hot peppers into the pot to wake up their masters' taste buds. They brought over such African foodstuffs as peanuts and okra, which became staples in Southern cuisine. They also introduced Hoppin' John, a bean-and-rice pilaf traditionally served on New Year's Day, and made good use of field peas, up until then a crop planted mainly to enrich the soil. Sure, Low Country cooking has obvious ties to the Creole fare found in southern Louisiana. But Africans influenced the Low Country cuisine of South Carolina more than Louisiana blacks did the Cajun cuisine that eventually developed in that state.

Sephardic Jews from Iberia (Spain and Portugal) brought the tomato to Charleston long before it became a common foodstuff elsewhere in America. Italian-style pastas, along with such Mediterranean techniques as sun-drying tomatoes, were first introduced to America in Charleston. Charlestonians even made a port-scented tomato ketchup. Ketchup back then was an exotic condiment, its fame yet to spread to every hamburger joint in America.

As the area's sea captains began to fan out across the world during Charleston's antebellum heyday, they brought back spices and exotic foodstuffs, including fine wines and olive oils. From Cuba came the rich fruits of the West Indies. Charleston gardens were growing sorrel, hyssop, salsify, and scorzonera well before the rest of the country took to these garden plants.

Some of the foodstuffs were unique to the Low Country, including Sieva beans (pronounced *siv*-vy). This delectable flageolet remains the tiniest and tastiest of all butter beans (baby limas).

SOUP KETTLES & THE SHE-CRAB

The quintessential Low Country soup is the celebrated **she-crab soup.** In recipe books, the first mention of this soup was in *Two Hundred Years of Charleston Cooking.* Published in 1930, the cookbook attributed its she-crab recipe to "Mrs. Rhett's able butler." His name was William Deas, and he was hailed—at least locally—as one of "the greatest cooks in the world."

The soup is best in midwinter, when she-crabs are full of roe, as the roe is essential for the flavor of this soup—hence, no he-crabs will do.

Of course, Low Country cooks use more than she-crab to make soups, turning out variations of **shrimp soup** (cream and sherry), **gumbo, fish chowder, oyster soup,** and such old Southern dishes as **calf's head soup.** There's even a version of **turnip soup** made with a "scrag of mutton."

As in Cuba, **black-bean soup** remains a local favorite, often prepared with chopped smoked sausage. **Beaufort stew** is a meal unto itself, made with shrimp, chicken breast, andouille hot sausage, white rice, and sweet peppers along with celery and corn, then bound together in a tomato sauce.

Many home cooks can still whip up a fine **Confederate bean soup,** with onion, celery, ham stock sweetened with brown sugar, baked beans, and heavy cream cooked with bacon and chopped sausage.

HOPPIN' JOHN, RED RICE & CREAMY GRITS

Boston has its baked beans, but for Charleston and the Low Country, the soul food is **Hoppin' John.** (If you pronounce the "g" on the end of "hopping," you'll immediately be taken for a Yankee.) It's made with what the people of South Carolina call "cowpeas," also known as field peas. The dish is a blend of cowpeas and rice and is most often flavored with bacon drippings or a ham hock. Black-eyed peas are often substituted for cowpeas. A dash of dried hot peppers adds that extra kick. In the South, Hoppin' John is served on New Year's Day for good luck, but some households cook it all year long. It's a classic.

Impressions

Give me that old-timey religion but I don't want to see no wife of mine in church. When I get home from listening to some long-winded preacher rant about sin, I want my plate of Hoppin' John, along with a mess of collards cooked with hog jowl, and fresh corn bread from the oven to sop up the pot likker, the second best liquor to Bourbon.

—"Boll Weevil" Rutledge, "Hell-Raiser
of the Low Country," 1927

ROYAL RICE   Italians eat pasta, and the people of Ireland love their potatoes, but Charlestonians eat rice. In some households, rice appears at every meal, even breakfast. The Charleston rice steamer is found in most homes. The trick in serving the rice is in its side dishes: most often a gravy, a gumbo, butter beans, field peas, and—the most popular—okra and tomatoes. **Red rice** is a local favorite. It's made with vine-ripened tomatoes, chicken stock, and bacon.

Rice is also a principal ingredient in **Carolina pilau** (pronounce it *per*-loo and you'll be an instant kissin' cousin). The classic Carolina pilau is made with chicken and flavored with bacon, onion, celery, tomatoes, hot red-pepper flakes, and thyme, along with long-grain white rice. Tomato pilau, chicken pilau, shrimp pilau: If it's a pilau, Charleston serves it.

It is believed that pilaus were inspired by India back in the days when Charleston was a world-class seaport and local captains brought home recipes from the Eastern world. The best pilau we've ever had was in the private home of Mrs. Hester Demetree, who used the pilau as a stuffing flavored by fresh squab. We never could figure out what gave the squab its aromatic and delectable piquancy, and had to beg the dear Mrs. Demetree to get her to give up her culinary secret: She'd basted the squab in mustard pickle juice.

What is rare is rice pudding. Charlestonians don't like to use rice for dessert. "Rice is king here, and we take it seriously," said Ronald Savage, a local kitchen worker. "As a sweet, it doesn't make it for us."

GOOD GRITS   "Grits in the mornin', grits at noon, and grits in the evenin', cause mama's little boy can't get enough of them thar grits," went the refrain in many a poor Low Country home.

Grits, of course, are ground hominy, a white corn, as Southerners often have to explain to their visitors from some northern bog in Ohio. Charlestonians prefer whole-grain stone- or water-ground grits. **Shrimp and grits** are a Low Country classic (see below). In one restaurant, an inventive chef even serves fried grits as an appetizer topped by goat cheese and hollandaise. **Creamy grits** are also a favorite, made with milk or cream.

PORGY, FROGMORE STEW & SHRIMP 'N' GRITS

Everywhere you look, Charleston is surrounded by water, so naturally shellfish and fish are given star billing in the dining rooms of the Low Country. In the old days, blacks bearing baskets would arrive at your back door—the fish man, the oyster man, the crab man, the shrimp man. Each heralded his arrival singing a song.

SHRIMP Shrimp is ubiquitous here—just gaze out at sea most times of the year and watch the shrimp boats skimming the water. Shrimp is likely to appear in almost any dish, and is served boiled, fried, steamed, sautéed, even pickled. Nothing is more typical than shrimp and grits. It appears in countless versions, the simplest being sautéed in butter or bacon grease—a jar of which every Southern cook worth his or her salt keeps in the fridge.

Frogmore stew is said to have come from St. Helena Island near Hilton Head. It is named for the ancestral country estate outside Windsor where Queen Victoria is buried. An old Sea Island settlement adopted the name and created this savory kettle, which is prepared as a shrimp boil. Into the kettle go smoked link sausage, freshly shucked corn, and lots of shrimp.

Glorious and messy are those big bowls of **shrimp and crab gumbo.** It is the dark roux (pronounced *roo*)—invariably cooked with okra and vine-ripened tomatoes—that spells the success or failure of this dish.

CRAB Not just in the fabled she-crab soup, but also in dozens of other dishes, crab is a Low Country favorite. Even today, many young people in the Low Country grow up learning the art of "crabbing." Crabs are steamed in beer, deviled, made into some of America's greatest crab cakes, used for an intensely flavored blue-crab sauce, fashioned into a crab version of Hoppin' John, or stuffed. One local chef, John Dever, confided to us that he knew how to create 2,000 crab dishes. Alas, we can only take his word on that.

Impressions

Oh, lady, if yo' want to tas'e somethin' sweet,
Jes' take a li'l onion an' a li'l piece o' meat
An' mix 'em wid yo' tender, pure, raw swimp.

—an old shrimp vendor (Anonymous)

OYSTERS   Most often eaten raw, oysters are also typical Low Country fare. Oyster roasts, often held outdoors in the chill of early winter, are the most convivial of affairs. Oyster pie is a favorite dish, as are scalloped oysters. One of the most unusual dishes is oyster sausages, more common in kitchens of old than they are today. Made with veal or pork, with pork fat as seasoning, they are stuffed into casings derived from the intestines of hogs. Herbes de Provence add a dash of flavor. Oyster soup was called benne-oyster soup in antebellum days, when Sarah Rutledge wrote *The Carolina Housewife* in 1847. Benne was the local name for sesame seeds, although the dish was also made with peanuts.

COOTERS   Freshwater terrapin are known as "cooters" in the Low Country, and Charlestonians create any number of dishes out of them, notably a soup made with wine, bacon, and such spices as cloves and nutmeg, or else in a stew flavored with mace, cloves, red-pepper flakes, and allspice.

FISH   Most Southerners like their fish fried, especially **catfish,** and served with the ubiquitous hush puppies. Almost every Low Country cook has his or her own recipe for catfish stew, although everyone we asked made it with salted pork jowl. Grilled **porgy**—a small, bony, but nonetheless flavorful fish that's not as popular in Northern fish markets—is a dish of great renown in Charleston, evoking "Catfish Row," dramatized in the operetta *Porgy and Bess.*

Shark is less available now than before, but it still appears on some menus. Another fish whose stock has dwindled considerably is **sturgeon**—according to 18th-century accounts, the mouths of Low Country rivers were once so full of sturgeon that one could walk across the river on the backs of this species, which often grew to 12 feet long.

Shad is another popular Low Country fish, and it's common to catch roe (meaning, female) shad weighing from 3 to 5 pounds. When we were recently invited for Sunday breakfast in a Charleston home, **shad roe** was deliciously whipped into scrambled eggs. A whole shad is often baked in salt to preserve its aroma and flavor. Shad roe in cream is a favorite brunch dish, served with equally creamy grits.

In the barrier islands, crab pots often net **flounder,** a fish that appears on virtually every menu in Charleston. Flounder stuffed with crabmeat is a Low Country favorite.

BARBECUE, COUNTRY HAM & HOG-HEAD STEW

Most of the recipes for meat dishes came with the early settlers from France and England. Even today, when fish isn't the main course, oxtail stews and daubes, roasts, and steaks fill Low Country tables.

Pork became the main meat dish of the Low Country in the aftermath of the Civil War, when at times it was the only meat available.

Often, hams were salted and then cured in the smokehouse, becoming **country hams,** still in great vogue today in these days of refrigeration. **Country sausage** also became a big Southern tradition.

All the leftovers of the hog were put to use, as in **liver pudding** (a highly seasoned forcemeat), **souse** (a vinegary head cheese), and **blood pudding** (or blood sausage), inherited from Scottish or Huguenot settlers. It is illegal today to sell pig's blood, so blood pudding is confined to those Low Country homesteads that still make their own on the premises. Souse is still a traditional Christmas dish in Charleston. Sometimes called hog's head cheese, it is made with the head, pig's feet, fresh pig fat, and such flavors as white-wine vinegar, red wine, shallots, onions, bay leaves, thyme, and grated nutmeg.

Hog killin' on the Low Country farm was always a time for **hog-head stew** and **fried chitterlings.** Hog heads were cleaned, with the brains taken out to scramble with eggs for breakfast. The stew was cooked with not only the head, but also the liver, heart, spleen, kidneys, and ears.

The **Low Country barbecue** remains a Southern tradition. Pork, not beef, is the meat of choice, and the barbecue is cooked slowly over smoldering wood (hickory preferred, please). The pork is then "pulled" off the bone, if the tender meat doesn't fall off on its own.

DEERBURGERS, FROG'S LEGS & GATOR TAILS

Wild game is another Low Country culinary tradition. **Squirrel, rabbit, turtle, alligator, squab, quail,** and **deer** (venison) appear regularly in regional kitchens.

Deer is back once again (it had been threatened), and Charlestonians often fashion it into **deerburgers.** Pan-fried venison is another savory treat, especially when it's flavored with dried mixed herbs, red wine, and garlic.

Stewed **raccoon** is no longer as popular as it was in the days when it was a staple of life in the Low Country. It's still served in some homes, invariably with sweet potatoes. **Cooter soup** is really turtle soup; the diamondback turtle is used most frequently. Fried **frog's legs** and **gator tail** also appear on many tables.

Like Kentucky, Charleston also has its version of **burgoo,** originally made with squirrel but more often now based on some combination of chicken, pork, and beef. Also thrown into the pot are butter beans, potatoes, tomatoes, and corn—and everything is flavored with a *bouquet garni* (herb mixture).

Low Country people have hunted **duck** since Colonial days. **Quail** is the most popular of the game birds. Many restaurants still feature that old favorite, pan-fried quail with country ham.

3

Planning Your Trip to Charleston & Hilton Head

South Carolina's grandest and most intriguing city—in fact, one of the most spectacular cities to visit in the United States—is really a series of communities and islands centered around a historic core. First-time visitors will quickly get the hang of it, and locals are quick to make them feel at home.

This chapter provides a brief orientation to Charleston and a preview of its major neighborhoods. You'll find practical details on planning your trip, airlines that fly to Charleston, a calendar of events, visitor information, the best ways of getting around, and more.

1 NEIGHBORHOODS IN BRIEF

Charleston's streets are laid out in an easy-to-follow grid pattern. The main north-south thoroughfares are King, Meeting, and East Bay streets. Tradd, Broad, Queen, and Calhoun streets cross the city from east to west. South of Broad Street, East Bay becomes East Battery.

Two helpful city maps are distributed free at the **Charleston Visitor Center,** 375 Meeting St. (© **800/774-0006** or 843/853-8000; open daily 8:30am to 5pm).

The Historic District   In 1860, according to one Charlestonian, "South Carolina seceded from the Union, Charleston seceded from South Carolina, and south of Broad Street seceded from Charleston." The city preserves its early years at its southernmost point: the conjunction of the Cooper and Ashley rivers. White Point Gardens, right in the elbow of the two rivers, provides a sort of gateway into this area, where virtually every home is of historic or architectural interest. Between Broad Street and Murray Boulevard (which runs along the south waterfront), you'll find such sightseeing highlights as St. Michael's Episcopal Church, the Edmondston-Alston House, the Heyward-Washington House, Catfish Row, and the Nathaniel Russell House.

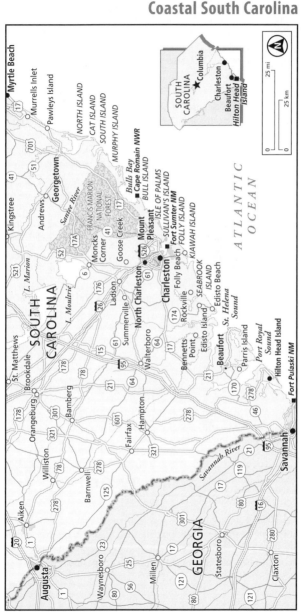

Downtown Extending north from Broad Street to Marion Square at the intersection of Calhoun and Meeting streets, this area offers noteworthy points of interest, good shopping, and a gaggle of historic churches. Just a few of its highlights include the Old City Market, the Dock Street Theatre, Market Hall, the Old Powder Magazine, Congregation Beth Elohim, the French Huguenot Church, St. John's Church, and the Unitarian Church.

Above Marion Square The visitor center is located on Meeting Street north of Calhoun. The Charleston Museum is just across the street, and the Aiken-Rhett House, Joseph Manigault House, and Old Citadel are within easy walking distance in the area bounded by Calhoun Street to the south and Mary Street to the north.

North Charleston Charleston International Airport is at the point where I-26 and I-526 intersect. This makes North Charleston a Low Country transportation hub, as well as the home of the North Charleston Coliseum. Primarily a residential and industrial community, North Charleston lacks the charm of the Historic District.

Mount Pleasant East of the Cooper River, just minutes from the heart of the Historic District, this community is worth a detour—and it's now linked by a bridge to the rest of Charleston. It encloses a Historic District along the riverfront known as the Old Village, which is on the National Register. Its major attraction is Patriots Point, the world's largest naval and maritime museum; it's also the home of the aircraft carrier USS *Yorktown*.

Outlying Areas Within easy reach of the city are Boone Hall Plantation, Fort Moultrie, and the public beaches at Sullivan's Island and the Isle of Palms. Head west across the Ashley River Bridge to pay tribute to Charleston's birth at Charles Towne Landing, and visit such highlights as Drayton Hall, Magnolia Plantation, and Middleton Place.

2 WHEN TO GO

CLIMATE

Although Charleston can be quite hot and steamy in summer (to say the least), temperatures are never extreme throughout the rest of the year, as shown in the average highs and lows noted in the accompanying chart.

	Jan	Feb	Mar	Apr	May	June	July	Aug	Sept	Oct	Nov	Dec
High (°F)	59	61	68	76	83	87	89	89	85	77	69	61
High (°C)	15	16	20	24	28	31	32	32	29	25	21	16
Low (°F)	40	41	48	56	64	70	74	74	69	49	49	42
Low (°C)	4	5	9	13	18	21	23	23	21	9	9	6
Rainfall (in.)	3.5	3.3	4.3	2.7	4.0	6.4	6.8	7.2	4.7	2.9	2.5	3.2

LOW COUNTRY CALENDAR OF EVENTS

JANUARY

Low Country Oyster Festival, Charleston. Steamed buckets of oysters greet visitors at Boone Hall Plantation. Enjoy live music, oyster-shucking contests, children's events, and various other activities. Call the Greater Charleston Restaurant Association at ℂ **843/577-4030** or go to www.charlestonrestaurantassociation. com. End of January.

FEBRUARY

Southeastern Wildlife Exposition, Charleston. More than 150 of the finest artists and more than 500 exhibitors participate at 13 locations in the downtown area. Enjoy carvings, sculpture, paintings, live-animal exhibits, food, and much more. Call ℂ **843/452-6088** or go to www.sewe.com. Mid-February.

MARCH

Festival of Houses and Gardens, Charleston. For nearly 50 years, people have been enjoying some of Charleston's most historic neighborhoods and private gardens on this tour. Call the Historic Charleston Foundation at ℂ **843/723-1623** or go to www. historiccharleston.org. Mid-March to mid-April.

Charleston Fashion Week, Charleston. This is a 5-night celebration of fashion and the city's burgeoning retail community, featuring up-and-coming designers from the Carolinas and Georgia. Special tents are set up in Marion Square, evocative of New York's Fashion Week at Bryant Park. Go to www.charlestonfashionweek. com for details. Late March.

Flowertown Festival, Summerville. More than 180 booths of arts and crafts, a road race, a "Youth Fest," and lots of entertainment are set in this historic city surrounded by brilliant azalea and dogwood blossoms. Contact the YMCA at ℂ **843/871-9622** or go to www.flowertownfestival.com. Late March to early April.

Cooper River Bridge Run, Charleston. Sponsored by the Medical University of South Carolina, this run and walk starts in Mount Pleasant, goes over the Cooper River Bridge, and ends in the center of Charleston. It's one of the best organized 10K races in the world. The participants run over the Arthur Ravenel, Jr., Bridge, which is 2.5 miles long and 200 feet high. Call ✆ **843/856-1949** or go to www.bridgerun.com. Early April.

Family Circle Cup, Charleston. Moved from Hilton Head to a modern tennis center in Charleston, the Family Circle Cup WTA tournament is one of the oldest on the women's pro tour. Call ✆ **843/856-7900** or go to www.familycirclecup.com. Mid-April.

Blessing of the Fleet, Mount Pleasant. This seafood festival, which takes place at Alhambra Hall and Park, overlooking Charleston Harbor, celebrates the historic Mount Pleasant shrimping industry and offers a host of other family activities; one highlight is an arts and crafts show with some 40 exhibitors. Call ✆ **843/849-2061** or go to www.townofmountpleasant.com. Late April.

MAY

Arts Festival, North Charleston. This is a 9-day all-encompassing cultural festival, with film presentations, theater, art workshops, street dances, concerts, performances for kids, and an outdoor sculpture competition, among other happenings. Call ✆ **843/554-5700** or go to www.northcharleston.org. Early May.

Spoleto Festival U.S.A., Charleston. This is the premier cultural event in the tri-state area. This famous international festival—the American counterpart of the equally celebrated one in Spoleto, Italy—showcases world-renowned performers in drama, dance, music, and art in various venues throughout the city. For details and this year's schedule, call ✆ **843/722-2764** or go to www.spoletousa.org. Late May to early June.

JUNE

Sweet Grass Festival, Charleston. This cultural festival celebrates the rich Gullah/Geechee heritage and provides the most extensive showcase of sweetgrass baskets in the Low Country. It also features unique handmade arts, crafts, paintings, and live performances. Visitors can enjoy classic barbecue as well as authentic Gullah cuisine. Call ✆ **843/856-9732** or go to www.sweetgrassfestival.org. Early June.

Edisto Riverfest, Walterboro. The highlight of this festival is guided trips down the blackwater Edisto River. Call (C) **843/693-3161** or go to www.edistoriver.org. Mid-June.

Charleston Harbor Fest, Charleston. From "pirates" on parade at Ansonborough Field to the "Rail Jam" demonstrations at Patriots Point, this festival is awash with activities on both sides of the harbor. The action begins with a sail of traditional tall ships and goes on to include a sail of wooden boats, a kids' village, family boat building, an education village, helicopter tours, food booths, and more. Call (C) **843/722-1030** or go to www.charlestonharborfest.org. Late June.

SEPTEMBER

Scottish Games and Highland Gathering, Charleston. This gathering of Scottish clans features medieval games, bagpipe performances, Scottish dancing, and other traditional activities. Call the Scottish Society of Charleston at (C) **843/529-1020** or go to http://charlestonscots.org. Mid-September.

Candlelight Tour of Homes & Gardens, Charleston. Sponsored by the Preservation Society of Charleston, this annual tour provides an intimate look at many of the area's historic homes, gardens, and churches. Call (C) **843/722-4630** or go to http://preservationsociety.org. Mid-September to late October.

MOJA Festival, Charleston. Celebrating the rich African-American heritage in the Charleston area, this festival features lectures, art exhibits, stage performances, historical tours, concerts, and much more. Contact the Charleston Office of Cultural Affairs at (C) **843/724-7305** or go to www.mojafestival.com. Late September to early October.

OCTOBER

A Taste of Charleston, Charleston. First held in 2004 at Boone Hall Plantation, this event offers an afternoon of food, fun, entertainment, and more. A selection of Charleston-area restaurants offers its specialties in bite-size portions, so you can sample them all. Call (C) **843/577-4030** or go to www.charlestonrestaurantassociation.com. Early October.

NOVEMBER & DECEMBER

Christmas in Charleston, Charleston. This month-long celebration features home and church tours, Christmas-tree lightings, crafts shows, artistry, and a peek at how Old Charleston once celebrated the holiday season. Call (C) **800/774-0006** or go to www.charlestoncvb.com. Early November to late December.

PLANNING YOUR TRIP

3

LOW COUNTRY CALENDAR OF EVENTS

3 GETTING THERE & GETTING AROUND

GETTING THERE

BY PLANE   **American Airlines** (© 800/433-7300; www.aa.com), **Continental Airlines** (© 800/523-3273; www.continental.com), **Delta Air Lines** (© 800/221-1212; www.delta.com), **United Airlines** (© 800/241-6522; www.united.com), and **US Airways** (© 800/428-4322; www.usairways.com) are the major airlines serving South Carolina.

You can fly into **Charleston** on Continental, Delta, United, or US Airways. **Myrtle Beach** has scheduled air service via Continental, Delta, and US Airways. If you're traveling to **Hilton Head,** you have the option of flying US Airways directly to the island or else flying into the Savannah/Hilton Head International Airport (in Georgia) via Continental or Delta, and then driving or taking a limousine to Hilton Head, which is an hour away.

Charleston International Airport is in North Charleston on I-26, about 12 miles west of the city. Taxi fare into the city runs about $25; the airport **shuttle service** (© 843/767-1100; www.chs-airport.com) charges a $12 fare. All major car-rental agencies, including Hertz and Avis, are located at the airport. If you're driving, follow the airport access road to I-26 into the heart of Charleston.

BY CAR   I-95 enters South Carolina from the north near Dillon and runs straight through the state to Hardeeville on the Georgia border. The major east-west artery is I-26, running from Charleston northwest through Columbia and on up to Hendersonville, North Carolina. U.S. 17 runs along the coast, and I-85 crosses the north-western region of the state. The main north-south coastal route, U.S. 17, passes through Charleston; I-26 runs northwest to southeast, ending in Charleston. Charleston is 120 miles southeast of Columbia via I-26 and 98 miles south of Myrtle Beach via U.S. 17.

South Carolina furnishes excellent travel information to motorists, who will find well-equipped, efficiently staffed visitor centers at the state border on most major highways. If you need help, dial © *47 (HP) for Highway Patrol Assistance. **AAA** services are available through www.aaany.com.

Remember that drivers and front-seat passengers are required by law to wear seat belts in South Carolina. Also, headlights must be on when windshield wipers are in use as a result of inclement weather.

BY TRAIN The **Amtrak** (© **800/USA-RAIL** [872-7245]; www. amtrak.com) New York–Miami and New York–Tampa runs serve Charleston and other South Carolina cities. Amtrak also offers tour packages that include hotel, breakfast, and historic-site tours in Charleston at bargain rates. Be sure to ask about the money-saving "All Aboard America" regional fares, the attractively priced rail/drive packages in the Carolinas, and any other current specials. Trains arrive at 4565 Gaynor Ave., North Charleston.

BY BUS **Greyhound** (© **800/231-2222;** www.greyhound.com) has good direct service to Charleston from out of state, with connections to almost any destination. With a 21-day advance purchase, you can get a discounted "Go Anywhere" fare (some day-of-the-week restrictions apply). Call for information and schedules, or contact the Greyhound depot in your area.

GETTING AROUND

BY BUS City bus fares are $1.50. Service is available daily from 5:35am to 10pm (until 1am to North Charleston). Between 9am and 3:30pm and after 6pm, seniors pay 75¢. The fare for persons with disabilities is 60¢ (all day). Exact change is required. For route and schedule information, call © 843/724-7420 or go to www.ridecarta.com.

BY TROLLEY The **Downtown Area Shuttle (DASH)** is the quickest way to get around the main downtown area daily. The fare is $1, and you'll need exact change. A day pass costs $4. For hours and routes, call © **843/724-7420.**

BY TAXI Leading taxi companies are **Yellow Cab** (© **843/577-6565**) and **Safety Cab** (© **843/722-4066**). Each company has its own fare structure. Within the city, however, fares seldom exceed $6. You must call for a taxi; there are no pickups on the street.

BY CAR If you're staying in the city proper, park your car and save it for day trips to outlying areas. You'll find **parking** scattered about the city, with some of the most convenient spots on Hutson Street and Calhoun Street, both near Marion Square; on King Street between Queen and Broad streets; and on George Street between King and Meeting streets. If you can't find street parking, the two most centrally located **garages** are on Wentworth Street (© **843/724-7383**) and at Concord and Cumberland streets (© **843/724-7387**); the charge is $1 per half-hour.

Leading car-rental agencies include **Avis** (© **800/331-1212** or 843/767-7030; www.avis.com), **Budget** (© **800/527-0700,** 843/767-7051 at the airport, 843/760-1410 in North Charleston, or 843/577-5195 downtown), and **Hertz** (© **800/654-3131** or 843/767-4554; www.hertz.com).

4 MONEY & COSTS

It's getting easier all the time to access your bank account while you're on the road. You won't have any problem finding ATMs all over the state that are connected to the major national networks. For specific locations of **Cirrus** machines, call ✆ **800/424-7787** or go to www.mastercard.com; for the PLUS network, go to www.visa.com.

If you run out of funds on the road, you can have a friend or relative advance you money through **MoneyGram** (www.moneygram.com). This service allows you to transfer funds from one person to another in less than 10 minutes from thousands of locations.

5 SPECIALIZED TRAVEL RESOURCES

Note that the Charleston telephone directory contains a special section of community service numbers. It's quite comprehensive and includes services for most of these groups.

What Things Cost in Charleston	US$
Taxi from Charleston airport to city center	27.00
Bus fare (exact change)	1.50
Double room at the HarbourView (expensive)	149.00
Double room at Anchorage Inn (moderate)	119.00
Double room at King George IV Inn (inexpensive)	89.00
Lunch for one at Magnolias (moderate)	18.00
Lunch for one at Jestine's (inexpensive)	14.00
Dinner for one, without wine, at Fig (expensive)	52.00
Dinner for one, without wine, at Swamp Fox (moderate)	34.00
Dinner for one, without wine, at Hyman's Seafood Co. Restaurant (inexpensive)	22.00
Bottle of beer	3.50
Coca-Cola	2.00
Cup of coffee	2.50
Admission to the Gibbes Museum of Art	9.00
Movie ticket	10.00
Ticket to a Charleston Symphony Orchestra concert	15.00–65.00

Gay & Lesbian Travelers   The major gay center in the state is the South Carolina Gay and Lesbian Pride Movement, 1108 Woodrow St., Columbia, SC 29205 (✆ 803/771-7713; www.scpride.org). It's open on Wednesday and Sunday from 1 to 6pm, Friday from 7 to 11pm, and Saturday from 1 to 8pm. On the premises are archives, a "gay pride" shop, an inventory of films, and a meeting space.

Travelers with Disabilities   South Carolina has numerous agencies that assist people with disabilities. For specific information, call South Carolina Disability Resources (✆ 866/340-7105; www.sci way.net). Two other agencies that may prove to be helpful are the South Carolina Protection & Advocacy System for the Handi-capped (✆ 800/922-2222 or 803/782-0639) and the Commission for the Blind (✆ 800/922-2222; www.sccb.state.sc.us). For trans-portation within South Carolina, individuals with disabilities can contact Wheelchair Getaways, Inc. (✆ 800/642-2042 or 864/271-3127; www.wheelchairgetaways.com).

   The America the Beautiful—National Parks and Federal Recre-ational Lands Pass—Access Pass (formerly the Golden Access Passport) gives people with visual impairments or permanent dis-abilities (regardless of age) free lifetime entrance to federal recreation sites administered by the National Park Service, including the Fish and Wildlife Service, the Forest Service, the Bureau of Land Manage-ment, and the Bureau of Reclamation. This may include national parks, monuments, historic sites, recreation areas, and national wild-life refuges. The America the Beautiful Access Pass can only be obtained in person at any NPS facility that charges an entrance fee. You need to show proof of a medically determined disability. Besides free entry, the pass also offers a 50% discount on some federal-use fees charged for such facilities as camping, swimming, parking, boat launching, and tours. For more information, go to www.nps.gov/fees_passes.htm or call the United States Geological Survey (USGS), which issues the passes, at ✆ 888/275-8747.

Family Travel   A great vacation idea is to rent a cabin in one of South Carolina's state parks, including reserves around Charleston. For details on rates, reservations, and accommodations, see "State Parks," below, or contact the South Carolina Department of Parks, Recreation & Tourism, 1205 Pendleton St., Columbia, SC 29201 (✆ 866/224-9339 or 803/734-0156; www.southcarolinaparks.com).

Senior Travel   Seniors may want to contact the Retired Senior Volunteer Program (✆ 803/252-7734; www.seniorresourcesinc. org). When sightseeing or attending entertainment events, seniors should always inquire about discounts—they're plentiful.

The U.S. National Park Service offers an **America the Beautiful— National Parks and Federal Recreational Lands Pass—Senior Pass** (formerly the **Golden Age Passport**), which gives seniors 62 years or older lifetime entrance to all properties administered by the National Park Service—national parks, monuments, historic sites, recreation areas, and national wildlife refuges—for a one-time processing fee of $10. The pass can be purchased in person at any NPS facility that charges an entrance fee. Besides free entry, the America the Beautiful Senior Pass also offers a 50% discount on some federal-use fees charged for camping, swimming, parking, and boat-launch facilities. For more information, go to www.nps.gov/fees_passes.htm or call the **United States Geological Survey** (USGS), which issues the passes, at ℂ **888/275-8747.**

6 THE ACTIVE VACATION PLANNER

BEACHES   The South Carolina coast, both north and south of Charleston, is the true gem of the state, and many of the best beaches in the South—even the country—are an easy commute from Charleston. The 280-mile coast is lined with white-sand beaches shaded by palms, stretching from the Grand Strand of Myrtle Beach to the mouth of the Savannah River. If you're looking for seclusion, head for Edisto Beach. For a luxury-resort experience, you can't beat Hilton Head. For a combination of both, check out Kiawah Island.

BIKING   The aptly named Low Country has mostly flat terrain, which makes for some of the country's best biking areas. The hard-packed sand of the beaches is particularly good for cycling. Resorts such as Hilton Head have extensive paved bike trails, and many rental outfits operate just off the beaches.

CAMPING   Many of South Carolina's lakes have lakefront camp-sites. Reservations aren't necessary, but you are strongly advised to reserve ahead for such big weekends as Memorial Day or Labor Day. Campsites are also available in South Carolina's 34 state parks, many of which lie within easy reach of Charleston. For more information, contact the **South Carolina Department of Parks, Recreation & Tourism,** 1205 Pendleton St., Columbia, SC 29201 (ℂ **866/224-9339** or 803/734-0156; www.southcarolinaparks.com).

FISHING & HUNTING   Fishing is abundant in South Carolina, especially along coastal Carolina north and south of Charleston. On the coast, fish for amberjack, barracuda, shark, king mackerel, and other species. In South Carolina's many lakes and streams, fish for

trout, bass, and blue and channel catfish. No license is required for
saltwater fishing, but a freshwater license is needed. Hunting on public lands is illegal, but many hunting clubs allow you to join temporarily if you provide references. For information, write the **South Carolina Department of Natural Resources,** P.O. Box 167, Columbia, SC 29202 (© **803/734-3883;** www.dnr.state.sc.us).

GOLF   Some of the best golf in the country is in South Carolina, at courses like the one at fabled Harbour Town in Hilton Head. Contact the **South Carolina Department of Parks, Recreation & Tourism,** 1205 Pendleton St., Columbia, SC 29201 (© **866/224-9339** or 803/734-0156; www.southcarolinaparks.com), and ask for the South Carolina Golf Guide.

THE LAKES   South Carolina's rivers feed lakes all over the state, offering plentiful opportunities for boating, fishing, and camping. With 450 miles of shoreline, the lakes are a magnet for commercial development. While lakeside resort communities are booming, 70% of the lakeshore is slated to remain in a natural state. Many operators and marinas rent boats and watercraft. For information on staying lakeside, contact the **South Carolina Department of Parks, Recreation & Tourism,** 1205 Pendleton St., Columbia, SC 29201 (© **866/224-9339** or 803/734-0156; www.southcarolinaparks.com).

STATE PARKS   Camping, fishing, boating, and extensive hiking are available in South Carolina's many state parks, including those in and around Charleston (in particular, Francis Marion National Forest). Cabin accommodations are rented year-round in 14 of the 34 parks. All cabins are heated, air-conditioned, and fully equipped with cooking utensils, tableware, and linens. Rates range from $48 to $185 per night. Cabins can accommodate anywhere from 4 to 12 people. Advance reservations are necessary for summer. For full details, contact the **South Carolina Department of Parks, Recreation & Tourism,** 1205 Pendleton St., Columbia, SC 29201 (© **866/224-9339** or 803/734-0156; www.southcarolinaparks.com).

4

Where to Stay

Charleston has many of the best historic inns in the United States, even surpassing Savannah in this regard. Hotels and motels are priced in direct ratio to their proximity to the 789-acre Historic District; if prices in the center are too high for your budget, find a place west of the Ashley River and drive into town for sightseeing. In the last decade, the restoration of inns and hotels in Charleston has been phenomenal, although it's slowing somewhat.

Bed-and-breakfast accommodations range from historic homes to carriage houses to simple cottages, and they're located in virtually every section of the city. For details and reservations, contact **Historic Charleston Bed & Breakfast,** 57 Broad St. (© **800/743-3583** or 843/722-6606; www.historiccharlestonbedandbreakfast.com; open Mon–Fri 9am–5pm).

During the Spoleto Festival and the Festival of Houses and Gardens, rates go up, and owners charge pretty much what the market will bear. Advance reservations are essential at these times.

In a city in which rooms of so many shapes and sizes are offered in the same historic building, classifying hotels by price is difficult. The rate often depends on the room itself. Some expensive hotels may in fact have many moderately priced rooms. Moderately priced hotels, on the other hand, may have special rooms that are quite pricey. When booking a hotel, also ask about package plans—deals are often granted to those who are staying 3 nights or more.

The downside of all these inns of charm and grace is that they are among the most expensive in the South. Staying at an inn or B&B in the Historic District is one of the reasons to go to Charleston and can do more to evoke the elegance of the city than almost anything else. Innkeepers and B&B owners know this all too well and charge accordingly, especially in the spring season.

1 MAKING RESERVATIONS

You may make your reservations by phone, mail, fax, or the Internet. Usually, you can cancel a reservation 1 week ahead of time and get a full refund. A few places will return your money on cancellations up to 3 days before the reservation date; others won't return any of your

> ## (Tips) Charleston's Fluctuating Room Rates
>
> Charleston's room rates are like the weather in South Caro-lina—if you wait 5 minutes, they'll change. Most establish-ments categorize their prices based on the season, as well as the type of room. High season is April to October. In addition, rates may vary depending on whether you stay during the week or over a weekend. You will find that the cheapest rates are generally on weekdays during low season—January, Feb-ruary, and, sometimes, late August.

deposit, even if you cancel far in advance. It's best to clarify this issue when you make your reservations. And always ask for a confirmation number.

If you simply can't afford a stay in one of the finer inns in the Historic District, you can confine your consumption of Charleston to dining and sightseeing in the old city. For many people, this is a sat-isfying compromise. Soak in the glamour of the city during the day, and at night retire to one of the less-expensive choices in the Historic District or one of the many clean, comfortable—and, yes, utterly dull—chain motels on the outskirts. See the most representative samples under our "Inexpensive" and "Moderate" categories below.

2 CHARLESTON'S TOP HOTELS

VERY EXPENSIVE

Charleston Place Hotel ★★★ Charleston's premier hostelry, an Orient Express Property, is an eight-story landmark in the Historic District that looks like a postmodern French château. It's big-time, uptown, glossy, and urban—at least, one former visitor, Prince Charles, thought so. Governors and prime ministers from around the world, members of Fortune 500 companies, and even visiting celebs prefer to stay here than at one of the more intimate B&Bs. Guest rooms are among the most spacious and handsomely furnished in town—stately, modern, and maintained in state-of-the-art condition. This hotel represents the New South at its most confident, a stylish giant in a district of B&Bs and small converted inns. Acres of Italian marble grace the place, leading to plush guest rooms with decor inspired by colonial Carolina. There's a deluxe restaurant, **Charleston Grill** (p. 65). A cafe provides a more casual option.

205 Meeting St., Charleston, SC 29401. © **888/635-2350** or 843/722-4900. Fax 843/722-0728. www.charlestonplacehotel.com. 440 units. $235–$590 double; $285–$880 suite. Seasonal packages available. AE, DC, DISC, MC, V. Parking $14. **Amenities:** 2 restaurants; bar; exercise room; indoor/outdoor pool; room service; sauna; spa. *In room:* A/C, TV, kitchenette (in some), minibar, Wi-Fi (free).

John Rutledge House Inn ★★   Many of the meetings that culminated in the emergence of the United States as a nation were conducted in this fine 18th-century house, now one of the most prestigious inns in Charleston. It towers over its major rivals, such as the Planters Inn and the Ansonborough Inn, which are also excellent choices. The original builder, John Rutledge, was one of the signers of the Declaration of Independence; he later served as chief justice of the U.S. Supreme Court. The inn was built in 1763, with a third story added in the 1850s. Impeccably restored to its Federalist grandeur, it's enhanced with discreetly concealed high-tech conveniences.

116 Broad St., Charleston, SC 29401. © **800/476-9741** or 843/723-7999. Fax 843/720-2615. www.johnrutledgehouseinn.com. 19 units. $300–$345 double; $375–$435 suite. Rates include continental breakfast. AE, DC, DISC, MC, V. Free parking. **Amenities:** Babysitting; concierge; access to nearby health club. *In room:* A/C, TV, fridge, Wi-Fi (free).

Market Pavilion Hotel ★   The hotel evokes old-time Charleston so effectively that virtually everyone is amazed that the structure is from 2003. With only 66 rooms, it's defined as a classy boutique hotel with a spectacularly attractive bistro, **Grill 225** (p. 69), which fills up most of its street-level entrance in a style that evokes a grandly imperious turn-of-the-20th-century bank. Accommodations are unashamedly posh, unashamedly conservative, and deeply connected to 18th-century English and colonial American (especially South Carolinian planters-style) furnishings and fabrics. There's a rooftop pool, terrace, and the Pavilion Bar; it's no surprise that this hotel attracts high-profile guests as diverse as John Kerry and Rush Limbaugh. The hotel's most visible and obvious competitor is the also-recommended and much larger and better-accessorized Charleston Place, which evokes a greater degree of European flair, more elaborate service, and even greater degrees of plush.

255 E. Bay St., Charleston, SC 29401. © **877/440-2250** or 843/723-0500. Fax 843/723-4320. www.marketpavilion.com. 66 units. $209–$329 double; from $550 suite. AE, DC, DISC, MC, V. Valet parking $20. **Amenities:** Restaurant; bar; rooftop bar/lounge and pool; exercise room; room service. *In room:* A/C, TV, Internet (free).

Planters Inn ★★★   This distinguished brick-sided inn stands next to the City Market. Renovations transformed the place into a cozy but tasteful and opulent enclave of colonial charm, turning it into one of the finest small luxury hotels of the South. The inn has a lobby filled with reproductions of 18th-century furniture and engravings, a

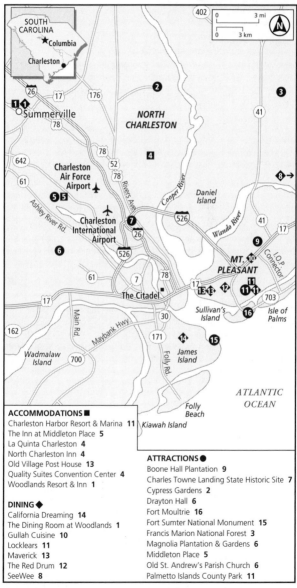

ACCOMMODATIONS ■
Charleston Harbor Resort & Marina **11**
The Inn at Middleton Place **5**
La Quinta Charleston **4**
North Charleston Inn **4**
Old Village Post House **13**
Quality Suites Convention Center **4**
Woodlands Resort & Inn **1**

DINING ◆
California Dreaming **14**
The Dining Room at Woodlands **1**
Gullah Cuisine **10**
Locklears **11**
Maverick **13**
The Red Drum **12**
SeeWee **8**

ATTRACTIONS ●
Boone Hall Plantation **9**
Charles Towne Landing State Historic Site **7**
Cypress Gardens **2**
Drayton Hall **6**
Fort Moultrie **16**
Fort Sumter National Monument **15**
Francis Marion National Forest **3**
Magnolia Plantation & Gardens **6**
Middleton Place **5**
Old St. Andrew's Parish Church **6**
Palmetto Islands County Park **11**

staff clad in silk vests, and a parking area with exactly the right number of spaces for the number of rooms in the hotel. The spacious guest rooms have hardwood floors, marble bathrooms, and 18th-century decor (the work of award-winning decorators). The suites are appealing, outfitted very much like rooms in an upscale private home. Afternoon tea is served in the lobby, and the on-site **Peninsula Grill** is an attractive dining option (p. 66).

112 N. Market St., Charleston, SC 29401. © **800/845-7082** or 843/722-2345. Fax 843/577-2125. www.plantersinn.com. 64 units. $285–$365 double; from $550 suite. AE, DC, DISC, MC, V. Parking $18. **Amenities:** Restaurant; room service. *In room:* A/C, TV, Wi-Fi (free).

Wentworth Mansion ★★★   A splendid example of America's Gilded Age, this 1886 Second Empire inn touts such amenities as hand-carved marble fireplaces, Tiffany stained-glass windows, and detailed wood and plasterwork. If it is grand accommodations that you seek, you've found them. When a cotton merchant built the property in the 1800s, it cost $200,000, an astronomical sum back then. In the mid-1990s, a team of local entrepreneurs spent millions renovating it into the smooth and seamless inn you see today. The guest rooms and suites are large enough to have sitting areas. Each unit has a king-size bed and a well-kept bathroom with a shower and whirlpool tub, and most have working gas fireplaces. The mansion rooms and suites come with a sleeper sofa for extra guests, who are charged an additional $50 per night.

149 Wentworth St., Charleston, SC 29401. © **888/466-1886** or 843/853-1886. Fax 843/720-5290. www.wentworthmansion.com. 21 units. $395–$470 double; $450–$750 suite. Each additional guest $50 extra per night. Rates include breakfast buffet and afternoon tea and cordials. AE, DC, DISC, MC, V. Free parking. **Amenities:** Restaurant; bar; babysitting; room service; spa. *In room:* A/C, TV/DVD, CD player, minibar (soft drinks only), Wi-Fi (free).

EXPENSIVE

Ansonborough Inn ★ (Kids)   This is one of the oddest hotels in the Historic District. Most visitors really like the unusual configuration of rooms, many of which are spacious enough to house families. Set close to the waterfront, the massive building, once a 1900 warehouse, has a lobby that features exposed timbers and a soaring atrium filled with plants. Despite the building's height, it has only three floors, resulting in guest rooms with ceilings of 14 to 16 feet and, in many cases, sleeping lofts. Rooms are outfitted with copies of 18th-century furniture and accessories. Breakfast is the only meal served, but many fine restaurants are located nearby.

21 Hasell St., Charleston, SC 29401. © **800/522-2073** or 843/723-1655. Fax 843/577-6888. www.ansonboroughinn.com. 37 units. Mar–Nov $159–$239 double.

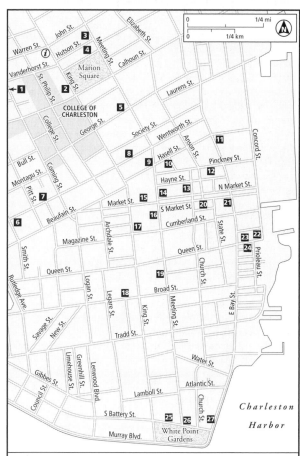

Anchorage Inn **23**
Ansonborough Inn **11**
Best Western King Charles Inn **9**
The Cannonboro Inn **1**
Charleston Place Hotel **15**
Doubletree Guest Suites **13**
1843 Battery Carriage House Inn **25**
1837 Bed and Breakfast **7**
Embassy Suites Hotel Charleston **4**
Francis Marion Hotel **2**
French Quarter Inn at Market Square **20**
Hampton Inn—Historic District **3**
HarbourView Inn **22**
Indigo Inn/Jasmine House Inn **10**
John Rutledge House Inn **18**

King George IV Inn **5**
Kings Courtyard Inn **17**
Market Pavilion Hotel **21**
Marriott Renaissance Charleston
  Historic District **8**
Meeting Street Inn **16**
Mills House Hotel **19**
Palmer Home View **27**
Palmer's Pinckney Inn **12**
Planters Inn **14**
Two Meeting Street Inn **26**
Vendue Inn **24**
Wentworth Mansion **6**

Rates include continental breakfast. Children 11 and under stay free in parent's room. AE, DISC, MC, V. Parking $12. **Amenities:** Breakfast room; babysitting. *In room:* A/C, TV, fridge, hair dryer.

1843 Battery Carriage House Inn ★ In one of the largest antebellum neighborhoods of Charleston, this inn offers guest rooms in a somewhat eccentric carriage house behind the main building. In other words, the owners use the top living accommodations for themselves but have restored the bedrooms out back to a high standard. Recent renovations added four-poster beds and a colonial frill to the not-overly-large bedrooms. Don't stay here if you want an inn with lots of public space; that, you don't get. But you can enjoy the location, which is a short walk off the Battery—a seafront peninsula where you can easily imagine a flotilla of Yankee ships enforcing the Civil War blockade.

20 S. Battery, Charleston, SC 29401. (C) **800/775-5575** or 843/727-3100. Fax 843/727-3130. www.batterycarriagehouse.com. 11 units. $159–$249 double. Rates include continental breakfast served in courtyard or room. AE, DISC, MC, V. Free parking. No children 11 and under. **Amenities:** Lounge; Wi-Fi (free). *In room:* A/C, TV.

Embassy Suites Charleston ★ One of Charleston's most interesting historic renovations is this mock-feudal pink-stucco fortress rising imperiously above a street corner in the Historic District. Today, richly appointed in a style inspired by the English colonial plantation houses of the West Indies, the courtyard houses a reception area and lobby whose artifacts, antique photographs, and displays of military memorabilia are fascinating to anyone with a military background. Even if you're not staying here, consider dropping in for a look at the sepia-toned photographs and the display cases of military and archaeological remnants dug out of the site during the building's renovations in 1995. Elevators zoom up the side of the atrium to the building's accommodations, each of which is a two-room suite with a wet bar and simple cooking facilities.

Bristling with the architectural details you'd expect in a medieval castle, the building originated in 1758 as a fort guarding the then-British-controlled city of Charleston. The structure that stands here today was in place by around 1826, when it was an arsenal storing gunpowder and weapons. In 1842, it was designated the headquarters of the Citadel Military College, where military cadets performed maneuvers every day in what is now nearby Marion Park, before the college moved to a riverfront location about 3 miles away in 1922. Listed on the National Register of Historic Places, the building was radically reconfigured in 1995 by the addition of a glass greenhouse-style roof and a hardwood floor above and below the once-open dirt-bottomed central courtyard.

337 Meeting St., Charleston, SC 29403. ℰ **800/362-2779** or 843/723-6900. Fax 843/723-6938. http://embassysuites1.hilton.com. 153 units. $199–$400 double. AE, DC, DISC, MC, V. Parking $12 per day in city lot behind hotel, or valet parking $18 per day. **Amenities:** Restaurant; bar; exercise room; outdoor pool; room service. *In room:* A/C, TV, fridge, Internet (free).

Francis Marion Hotel ★   A $14-million award-winning restoration has returned this historic hotel to its original elegance. Although the 12-story structure breaks from the standard Charleston decorative motif and has rooms furnished in traditional European style, it is not devoid of Charleston charm. Guest rooms feature a king-size, queen-size, or double bed, and the renovated bathrooms contain tub/shower combinations with brass fixtures. The hotel's restaurant, **Swamp Fox Restaurant & Bar** (p. 75), serves breakfast, lunch, and dinner, and features classic Southern cuisine.

387 King St., Charleston, SC 29403. ℰ **877/756-2121** or 843/722-0600. Fax 843/853-2186. www.francismarioncharleston.com. 233 units. $189–$279 standard double; $229–$299 deluxe double; $299–$379 suite. Children 11 and under stay free in parent's room. AE, DC, DISC, MC, V. Parking $10–$15. **Amenities:** Restaurant; bar; babysitting; exercise room; room service. *In room:* A/C, TV, minibar, Wi-Fi (free).

French Quarter Inn at Market Square ★★ (Finds)   When the designers of this boutique hotel positioned it in the midst of historic Charleston, they made sure it blended in gracefully with its surroundings. The result is a brick exterior that evokes the 18th-century town houses of Paris, and an interior with monumental staircases, elaborate wrought iron, elegant furnishings, and public areas with high ceilings and handcrafted touches. Bedrooms are relatively large and quietly dignified. Some have fireplaces and whirlpool tubs. The staff works hard to give the hotel the personal feel of a private B&B, offering champagne and pastries at check-in, afternoon wine and cheese, and elaborate bedding that's a lot more upscale than that used by many of its competitors. The hotel has an on-site restaurant, and at least 40 independently operated restaurants are within a short walk.

166 Church St., Charleston, SC 29401. ℰ **866/812-1900** or 843/722-1900. www.fqicharleston.com. 50 units. $179–$399 double. Rates include continental breakfast. AE, DC, DISC, MC, V. Valet parking $17 per day. **Amenities:** Restaurant; bar; babysitting; room service. *In room:* A/C, TV, Wi-Fi (free), iron.

Hampton Inn–Historic District   Few buildings in Charleston have been trampled over and recycled as frequently as this white-sided, five-floor testimonial to the changing nature of urban real estate. It was originally built in the 1880s as a railway station and warehouse, servicing the trains that used to rumble by along John Street. (If you look carefully, you can still see the faint indentations in the pavement where tracks were buried several decades ago.) An enclosed courtyard contains ornamental shrubbery, patios, and an outdoor swimming pool. Very few of the building's original details remain in place, having been ripped out long ago in favor of a dignified but somewhat bland replication of a late-18th-century Southern manor house. Bedrooms are conservative, comfortable, and not overly large, with flowered fabrics and a faint whiff of nostalgia for the antebellum days. The only meal served in the hotel is breakfast, although an elegant French restaurant, **39 Rue de Jean** (p. 75), is right next door.

345 Meeting St., Charleston, SC 29403. © **843/723-4000.** Fax 843/722-3725. http://hamptoninn.hilton.com. 171 units. $159–$209 double; $209–$249 suite. Children 17 and under stay free in parent's room. Rates include continental breakfast. AE, DC, DISC, MC, V. Parking $12–$15 per day in city lot next door to hotel. **Amenities:** Babysitting; outdoor pool. In room: A/C, TV, Internet (free), minibar.

HarbourView Inn ★ Spruced up and looking better than ever, this four-story inn lies in the heart of Charleston, across from the landmark Waterfront Park. From its windows you can see some of the best seascapes in the city. Known for its Old South hospitality and attentive service, this is one of the best and most comfortable inns in the historic zone. Guest rooms have an understated elegance, with plush four-poster beds, wicker chests, sea-grass rugs, and rattan chairs—decor very much in the style of an old-time Charleston sea captain's town house. Expect pampering here, from morning (when a continental breakfast is delivered to your door) to night (when turndown service comes with candy on your pillow). The beautifully maintained private bathrooms come with both tub and shower. The most elegant unit is the penthouse with its whirlpool bathroom, working fireplace, and private balcony.

2 Venue Range, Charleston, SC 29401. © **888/853-8439** or 843/853-8439. Fax 843/853-4034. www.harbourviewcharleston.com. 52 units. Double $149–$369; penthouse $299–$459. 2-night minimum weekends. Rates include continental breakfast. AE, DC, DISC, MC, V. Parking $16. **Amenities:** Babysitting; room service. In room: A/C, TV, Wi-Fi (free).

Indigo Inn/Jasmine House ★ These two hotels are set across the street from each other, with the same owners and the same reception area in the Indigo Inn. Built as an indigo warehouse in the mid–19th century, and gutted and radically reconstructed, the Indigo Inn (the larger of the two) offers rooms with 18th-century decor and comfortable furnishings. Rooms in the Jasmine House, an 1843 Greek Revival mansion whose exterior is painted buttercup yellow, are much more individualized. Each unit in the Jasmine House has a ceiling of about 14 feet, its own color scheme and theme, crown moldings, bathrooms with shower and whirlpool tubs, and floral-patterned upholsteries. Both inns serve breakfast on-site for their

respective guests. Children 17 and under are not allowed at the Jasmine House, but are welcome at the Indigo Inn.

1 Maiden Lane, Charleston, SC 29401. ℂ **800/845-7639** or 843/577-5900. Fax
843/577-0378. www.indigoinn.com. 40 units Indigo Inn, 10 units Jasmine House.
Double $139–$199 Indigo Inn, $179–$289 Jasmine House. Rates include continental
breakfast. 10% discounts available in midwinter. No children 17 and under allowed
at Jasmine House. AE, DC, DISC, MC, V. Parking $10. **Amenities:** Breakfast room;
babysitting (at Indigo Inn); Jacuzzi. *In room:* A/C, TV, Wi-Fi (in Jasmine House; free).

The Inn at Middleton Place ★★ (Finds)   It's a long way from
Tara, but if your lodging preferences south of the Mason-Dixon line
run toward strikingly modern luxury hotels, this is the place for you.
The inn is a direct counterpoint to the adjoining Middleton Place
(p. 98), an 18th-century plantation that's now a sightseeing attraction. Charles Duell, a descendant of Middleton's original owners,
wanted to offer an alternative to what he saw as "ersatz colonial" and
deliberately commissioned architects to create an inn devoid of "Scarlett and her antebellum charm." That said, the inn, with its live oaks
and setting on the bluffs of the Ashley River, still has Southern grace
and a warm and inviting interior. The guest rooms are filled with
handcrafted furniture, wood-burning fireplaces, and cypress paneling;
bathrooms have oversize tubs and private showers. Even if you're not
staying here, you can visit the inn's restaurant and enjoy classic plantation fare ranging from pan-fried quail to crawfish cakes.

4290 Ashley River Rd., Charleston, SC 29414. ℂ **800/543-4774** or 843/556-0500.
Fax 843/556-5673. www.theinnatmiddletonplace.com. 53 units. $170–$285 dou-
ble; $400–$500 suite. Rates include full breakfast. AE, DISC, MC, V. Free parking.
Amenities: Restaurant; babysitting; bike rentals; outdoor pool. *In room:* A/C, TV,
Wi-Fi (free).

Kings Courtyard Inn ★   The tiny entry to this three-story 1854
inn in the Historic District is deceiving because it opens into a brick
courtyard with a fountain. A fireplace warms the small lobby, which
is complete with a brass chandelier. Besides the main courtyard, two
courts offer fine views from the breakfast room. The owners bought
the building next door and incorporated 10 more rooms into the
existing inn. Your room might be outfitted with a canopy bed, an
Oriental rug over a hardwood floor, an armoire, or even a gas fireplace. A whirlpool is on-site. A continental breakfast is included in
the rate; a full breakfast is available for an additional charge.

198 King St., Charleston, SC 29401. ℂ **800/845-6119** or 843/723-7000. Fax 843/
720-2608. www.charminginns.com. 41 units. $175–$295 double. Rates include
continental breakfast. Children 11 and under stay free in parent's room. Off-season
3-day packages available. AE, DC, DISC, MC, V. Parking $12. **Amenities:** Breakfast
room; babysitting; Jacuzzi; room service. *In room:* A/C, TV, fridge, Wi-Fi (free).

Marriott Renaissance Charleston Historic District Hotel
Built in 2001, with a massive renovation completed in 2008, this is the most upscale member of the extended Marriott family of chain hotels in historic Charleston. It's bigger than you might have originally thought from a view of what faces Wentworth Street, thanks to a long and sprawling design that goes way, way back from the street. Bedrooms have mahogany paneling, high ceilings, and furnishings that evoke the best aspects of the genteel plantation-based South, but it's not as chic as the more appealing Charleston Place. If you opt for a stay in one of the comfortably appointed bedrooms at this hotel, expect lots of emphasis on corporate conventions, whose comings and goings are rather visible within the open spaces of this hotel's public areas.

68 Wentworth St., Charleston, SC 29401. (℃ **877/256-9840** or 843/534-0300. Fax 843/534-0700. www.marriott.com. 166 units. $249–$279 double; $269–$309 suite. AE, DC, DISC, MC, V. Parking $12–$19 per day. **Amenities:** Restaurant; bar; exercise room; rooftop outdoor pool. *In room:* A/C, TV, Wi-Fi ($13 per day).

Meeting Street Inn ★   Charming and nostalgic, and graced with the kind of expansive balconies that you'll really want to relax on, this inn originated in 1874, when a German-born entrepreneur built a saloon and beer distributorship on the site. It later became a brewery, an ice factory, a private men's club, an antiques store, and a restaurant, but its fortunes declined until 1989, when Hurricane Hugo bashed out whatever life remained in the business here. After that, the property lay rotting in the streaming sunlight until 1992, when hotel entrepreneur Frances Limehouse poured time and money into rebuilding the place into a gracious inn that's less pretentious, and less expensive, than some of its competitors.

The aforementioned balconies extend down the length of a long urban lot flanked with raised flower beds, brick walkways, fountains, and a Jacuzzi. All but about six of the accommodations lie in a modern wing that was added to the original 1870s core in the early 1980s, but the design styles between new and old are so similar that you'd need to look carefully to see the differences. Rooms contain reproduction furnishings, some with four-poster rice beds. Each has a modern bathroom that looks old-fashioned. The only meal available here is breakfast, a leisurely and relatively formal affair, although hors d'oeuvres and wine are served every day between 5:30 and 6:30pm.

Note: Do not confuse this upper-middle-bracket inn with the more expensive, more exclusive **Two Meeting Street Inn** (p. 57).

173 Meeting St., Charleston, SC 29401. (℃ **800/842-8022** or 843/723-1882. Fax 843/577-0851. www.meetingstreetinn.com. 56 units. High season $146–$299 double; low season $139–$199 double. Rates include continental breakfast and afternoon hors d'oeuvres and wine. AE, DC, DISC, MC, V. Parking $12. **Amenities:** Bar; babysitting; Jacuzzi. *In room:* A/C, TV, Wi-Fi (free).

Mills House Hotel ★★   Few hotels in Charleston can compete with the deep-rooted sense of grandeur and history that surrounds the Mills House. It was built in 1853 by entrepreneur Otis Mills, for the then-astronomical price of $200,000 (unfurnished), and received Robert E. Lee as an overnight guest during a difficult night early in the Civil War. Guests since then have included Elizabeth Taylor, Paul Newman, and George H. W. Bush, prior to his election as U.S. president. In the 1960s, its interior was gutted and reconfigured, and although the building's original height was retained, the interior was divided into seven floors (more than in the original building), and many of the building's architectural remnants were salvaged and recycled. At least two of the companies that lead walking tours of Charleston make it a point to showcase this pink-sided hotel to participants, and one company actually begins its tours in the hotel's lobby.

Today, many of the hotel's original furnishings remain as valued adornments, and an elevator hauls clients upstairs (an improvement from the early days). A concierge—a hip local resident who's meticulously trained in the nuances of the building's history—is on hand to answer questions. Operated today by InterContinental, the hotel offers small- to medium-size rooms (they're definitely not large), tastefully outfitted in antebellum manor-house style.

115 Meeting St., Charleston, SC 29401. (©) **800/874-9600** or 843/577-2400. Fax 843/722-0623. www.millshouse.com. 214 units. $219–$254 double; $269–$294 suite. AE, DC, DISC, MC, V. Parking $20–$22. **Amenities:** Restaurant (Barbados Room, p. 70); 2 bars (including First Shot Lounge, p. 121); babysitting; outdoor pool; room service. *In room:* A/C, TV, Wi-Fi (free).

Palmer Home View ★★★   This media favorite has been consistently voted one of the most outstanding B&Bs in the country by everybody from the Travel Channel to *Travel + Leisure* magazine. Now operated by the third-generation owner, the house was built in 1848 by John Ravenel, whose son designed the *Little David,* the first semi-submersible vessel and the forerunner to the submarine. A B&B since 1977, Palmer Home is beautifully decorated and furnished with antiques. Guest rooms are midsize to spacious and open onto panoramic views of Charleston Harbor and historic Fort Sumter. Many of the bedrooms contain four-poster beds. The most elegant—also the most expensive—way to stay here is to rent the on-site carriage house.

5 East Battery, Charleston, SC 29401. (©) **843/853-1574.** Fax 843/723-7983. www.palmerhomebb.net. 4 units. $165–$385 double; $420 suite. AE, MC, V. **Amenities:** Breakfast room; outdoor pool. *In room:* A/C, TV.

Two Meeting Street Inn ★   Set in an enviable position near the Battery, this house was built in 1892 as a wedding gift from a prosperous father to his daughter. Inside, the proportions are as lavish and gracious as the Gilded Age could provide. Stained-glass windows, mementos, and paintings were either part of the original decorations or collected by the present owners, the Spell family. Most guest rooms contain bathrooms with tub/shower combinations, four-poster beds, ceiling fans, and (in some cases) access to a network of balconies. A continental breakfast with home-baked breads and pastries is available.

2 Meeting St., Charleston, SC 29401. ℂ **888/723-7322** or 843/723-7322. www. twomeetingstreet.com. 9 units. $199–$479 double. Rates include continental breakfast and afternoon tea. No credit cards. No children 11 and under. **Amenities:** Breakfast room. *In room:* A/C, TV, MP3 docking station, Wi-Fi (free).

Vendue Inn ★ This three-story inn manages to convey some of the personalized touches of a B&B. Its public areas—a series of narrow, labyrinthine spaces—are full of antiques and colonial accessories that evoke a cluttered and slightly cramped inn in Europe. Guest rooms do not necessarily follow the lobby's European model, however, and appear to be the result of decorative experiments by the owners. Room themes may be based on aspects of Florida, rococo Italy, or 18th-century Charleston. Marble floors and tabletops, wooden sleigh beds, and (in some rooms) wrought-iron canopy beds, while eclectically charming, might be inconsistent with your vision of colonial Charleston. Overflow guests are housed in a historic, brick-fronted annex across the cobblestone-covered street. The inn's restaurant is called the **Kitchen House** (for dinner only). The chef here offers a menu of local favorites with unusual twists. The other restaurant, the **Roof Top Terrace,** offers a complete lunch and dinner menu in a more informal atmosphere with a panoramic view of the harbor and of the Historic District.

19 Vendue Range, Charleston, SC 29401. ℂ **800/845-7900** or 843/577-7970. Fax 843/577-2913. www.vendueinn.com. 66 units. $155–$205 double; $215–$255 suite. Rates include full Southern breakfast. AE, DC, DISC, MC, V. Parking $16. **Amenities:** 2 restaurants; bar; babysitting; free bikes; room service. *In room:* A/C, TV, kitchenette (in some), Wi-Fi (free).

MODERATE

Anchorage Inn ★★ Other than a heraldic shield out front, few ornaments mark this bulky structure, which was built in the 1840s as a cotton warehouse. The inn boasts the only decorative theme of its type in Charleston: a mock-Tudor interior with lots of dark paneling; references to Olde England; canopied beds with matching tapestries; pastoral or nautical engravings; leaded casement windows; and, in some places, half-timbering. Because bulky buildings are adjacent to the hotel on both sides, the architects designed all but a few rooms with views overlooking the lobby. (Light is indirectly filtered inside through the lobby's overhead skylights—a plus during Charleston's hot summers.)

Each room's shape is different from that of its neighbors, and the expensive ones have bona fide windows overlooking the street outside.

26 Vendue Range, Charleston, SC 29401. ℭ **800/421-2952** or 843/723-8300. Fax 843/723-9543. www.anchoragencharleston.com. 19 units. $119–$279 double; $169–$309 suite. Rates include continental breakfast and afternoon tea. AE, MC, V. Parking $12. **Amenities:** Breakfast room; babysitting. *In room:* A/C, TV, Wi-Fi (free).

The Cannonboro Inn   This buff-and-beige 1853 house was once the private home of a rice planter. The decor isn't as carefully coordinated or as relentlessly upscale as those of many of its competitors; throughout, it has a sense of folksy informality. Although there's virtually no land around this building, a wide veranda on the side creates a "sit-and-talk-a-while" mood. Each unit contains a canopy bed and formal, old-fashioned furniture.

184 Ashley Ave., Charleston, SC 29403. ℭ **800/235-8039** or 843/723-8572. Fax 843/723-8007. www.charleston-sc-inns.com. 6 units. $119–$239 double; $199–$259 suite. Rates include full breakfast and afternoon tea and sherry. AE, DISC, MC, V. Free parking. No children 9 and under. **Amenities:** Breakfast room; bike rentals. *In room:* A/C, TV, kitchenette, Wi-Fi (free).

Doubletree Guest Suites (Kids)   A somber five-story 1991 building adjacent to the historic City Market, the Doubletree offers family-friendly suites instead of rooms, each outfitted with a wet bar, refrigerator, and microwave oven. The accommodations tend to receive heavy use, thanks to their appeal to families, tour groups, and business travelers.

181 Church St., Charleston, SC 29401. ℭ **800/222-TREE** (8733) or 843/577-2644. Fax 843/577-2697. http://doubletree1.hilton.com. 212 units. $189–$209 double suite. AE, DC, DISC, MC, V. Parking $19. **Amenities:** 3 restaurants; babysitting; exercise room. *In room:* A/C, TV, Wi-Fi (free).

1837 Bed & Breakfast   Built in 1837 by Nicholas Cobia, a cotton planter, this place is called a "single house" because it's only a single room wide. Our favorite room is no. 2 in the Carriage House, which has authentic designs, exposed-brick walls, warm decor, a beamed ceiling, and three windows. All the rooms have refrigerators and separate entrances because of the layout, and all contain well-kept bathrooms and canopied poster rice beds. On one of the verandas, you can sit under whirling ceiling fans and enjoy your breakfast (sausage pie or eggs Benedict, and homemade breads) or afternoon tea. The parlor room has cypress wainscoting and a black-marble fireplace; the breakfast room is really part of the kitchen.

126 Wentworth St., Charleston, SC 29401. ℭ **877/723-1837** or 843/723-7166. Fax 843/722-7179. www.1837bb.com. 9 units. $99–$209 double. Rates include full breakfast and afternoon tea. AE, DISC, MC, V. Free off-street parking. No children 6 and under. **Amenities:** Breakfast room. *In room:* A/C, TV, fridge, hair dryer.

Palmer's Pinckney Inn ★ This is one of Charleston's most inviting B&Bs, lying in the historic market in the center of town. Run by Charleston native Francess Palamer, this charming inn offers five well-appointed bedrooms, several of which have four-poster beds. Most have king-size beds, and some even include gas fireplaces. Climbing stairs is required if you take a room on the second floor. In the Southern style, rocking chairs are placed on the veranda. Two of the units come with a Jacuzzi.

19 Pinckney St., Charleston, SC 29401. © **843/722-1733.** www.pinckneyinn.com. 5 units. $150–$300 double. Rates include breakfast. MC, V. **Amenities:** Breakfast room. *In room:* A/C, TV, Wi-Fi (free).

INEXPENSIVE

Those on tight budgets might try one of the chain motels such as **Days Inn,** 2998 W. Montague Ave., Charleston, SC 29418 (© **800/ 329-7466** or 843/747-4101; fax 843/566-0378; www.daysinn.com), near the international airport. Doubles range from $87 to $179. Children 11 and under stay free in their parent's room, and cribs are also free. **Lands Inn,** 2545 Savannah Hwy., Charleston, SC 29414 (© **843/763-8885;** fax 843/556-9536; www.landsinnsc.com), is another bargain, with doubles costing from $67 to $139, and $10 extra charged for each additional person. Children 15 and under stay free with parent. At **Red Roof Inn,** 7480 Northwoods Blvd., Charleston, SC 29406 (© **800/RED-ROOF** [733-7663] or 843/572-9100; fax 843/572-0061; www.redroof.com), doubles cost $55 to $70, and $6 is charged for each additional person; children 18 and under stay free in parent's room.

Best Western King Charles Inn (Kids) One block from the Historic District's market area, this three-story hotel has rooms that are better than you might expect from a motel and are likely to be discounted in the off season. Some rooms have balconies, but the views are limited. Although short on style, the hotel is a good value and convenient to most everything. An all-you-can-eat buffet breakfast is served in a colonial-inspired restaurant, and the hotel has a small pool and a helpful staff.

237 Meeting St. (btw. Wentworth and Hazel sts.), Charleston, SC 29401. © **866/ 546-4700** or 843/723-7451. Fax 843/723-2041. www.kingcharlesinn.com. 91 units. $139–$299 double. Children 18 and under stay free in parent's room. AE, DC, DISC, MC, V. Free parking. **Amenities:** Restaurant; outdoor pool; room service. *In room:* A/C, TV, MP3 docking station, Wi-Fi (free).

King George IV Inn This four-story 1790 Federal-style home in the heart of the Historic District serves as an example of the way Charleston used to live. Named the Peter Freneau House, it was

Kids   **Family-Friendly Hotels**

Ansonborough Inn (p. 50) This is a good value for families who want to stay in one of the historic inns, as opposed to a cheap motel on the outskirts of the city. Many of the high-ceilinged rooms in this converted warehouse have sleeping lofts.

Best Western King Charles Inn (p. 60) This is one of the best family values in Charleston. Kids stay free in a parent's room, the location is only a block from the Historic District's City Market area, and there's even a small pool.

Charleston Harbor Resort & Marina (p. 63) Some of the best children's programs in town are offered at this sprawling compound of resort facilities next to the USS *Yorktown*.

Doubletree Guest Suites (p. 59) Doubletree is a good choice for families who want extra space and a place to prepare meals. Some suites are bi-level, giving folks more privacy. The location is adjacent to the Old City Market.

La Quinta Charleston (p. 62) The sturdy, well-designed units here are tough enough for even the most spirited of kids.

Quality Suites Convention Center (p. 62) The suite accommodations and mini-kitchens make this a family favorite.

formerly the residence of a reporter and co-owner of the *Charleston City Gazette*. All rooms have wide-planked hardwood floors, plaster moldings, fireplaces, and 12-foot ceilings, and are furnished with antiques. Beds are either Victorian or four-poster (double or queen-size). All guests are allowed access to the three levels of porches on the house. The location is convenient to many downtown Charleston restaurants; tennis is a 5-minute drive, the beach is 15 minutes away, and some 35 golf courses are nearby. The continental breakfast consists of cereals, breads, muffins, pastries, and fruit.

32 George St., Charleston, SC 29401. ℂ **888/723-1667** or 843/723-9339. Fax 843/723-7749. www.kinggeorgeiv.com. 10 units, 2 with shared bathrooms. $89–$219 double. Rates include continental breakfast. AE, DISC, MC, V. Free parking. **Amenities:** Breakfast room; Wi-Fi (free). *In room:* A/C, TV.

3 OTHER AREA ACCOMMODATIONS

NORTH CHARLESTON
Moderate

Quality Suites Convention Center (Kids) This chain hotel, a 25-minute drive north of historic Charleston, isn't particularly convenient for those interested in wandering spontaneously through the old city, but the amount of space and the mini-kitchens in each unit might make up for it. Each suite has at least one bedroom and a separate living room with sleeper sofa. The layout is much like that of a clean, contemporary, albeit bland, apartment. The hotel's social center is a courtyard accented with patios and decks, a hot tub, and a pool. The culinary high point of this place is breakfast, when the staff shows its most hospitable side. Monday through Saturday from 5:30 to 8pm, the hotel offers free cocktails, beer, and wine.

5225 N. Arco Lane, North Charleston, SC 29418. (*) **800/4-CHOICE** (424-6423) or 843/747-7300. www.qualitysuitescharleston.com. 168 units. $119–$209 suite. Rates include free breakfast. AE, DC, DISC, MC, V. Free parking. **Amenities:** Restaurant; bar; exercise room; outdoor Jacuzzi; outdoor pool. *In room:* A/C, TV, fridge, Wi-Fi (free).

Inexpensive

La Quinta Charleston (Kids) This sturdy, well-designed, and childproof member of a nationwide hotel chain has an exterior that's attractively designed like a Spanish hacienda, replete with terra-cotta roof tiles, thick stucco walls, a bell tower, and references to the mission churches of California. It lies near the busy interstate and close to row upon row of shopping malls, chain restaurants, and fast-food joints. Historic Charleston is a 25-minute drive away. Each guest room is midsize and comfortably laid out with a sense of Tex-Mex whimsy.

2499 La Quinta Lane, Charleston, SC 29420. (*) **800/753-3757** or 843/797-8181. Fax 843/569-1608. www.lq.com. 122 units. $74–$79 double; $89–$99 suite. Children 17 and under stay free in parent's room. Rates include continental breakfast. AE, DC, DISC, MC, V. Free parking. **Amenities:** Outdoor pool. *In room:* A/C, TV, Wi-Fi (free).

North Charleston Inn This well-run place is hardly in the same class as the historic inns discussed earlier in this chapter, but it's kind to the frugal vacationer. An outpost for the weary interstate driver, the inn is convenient to the airport and major traffic arteries. Although you won't find charm, you will find good maintenance and proper service, and a refrigerator and microwave are available upon request.

The hotel has a lounge that features nightly entertainment. Some restaurant options (including a Red Lobster) are within walking distance.

2934 W. Montague Ave., North Charleston, SC 29418. © **877/464-2700** or 843/744-8281. Fax 843/744-6230. www.northcharlestoninn.com. 155 units. $59–$70 double. $10 each additional person. AE, DC, DISC, MC, V. Free parking. 8 miles NW of Charleston off I-26. **Amenities:** Breakfast room; lounge; outdoor pool. *In room:* A/C, TV, Wi-Fi (free).

MOUNT PLEASANT
Expensive
Charleston Harbor Resort & Marina ★ Kids Until the mid-1990s, the low-lying land on which this hotel stands was flat and marshy—an undeveloped headland jutting into Charleston Harbor, to the east of the city's historic core. Today, immediately adjacent to the USS *Yorktown* Museum, it glitters as a sprawling compound of resort facilities that to many guests is a destination in its own right and unlike anything else in Charleston. Heavily booked by conventions, but with lots of individual clients as well, it serves the hotel and dining needs of boat owners who moor their sometimes-spectacular craft in the resort's 455-slip deepwater marina. Sunbathers can loll on a beach that developers created by dumping massive amounts of sand onto the harbor's once-muddy bottom. An 18-hole golf course (under separate management) is just a 5-minute drive away, and deep-sea fishing is available. Many guests spend their days logging serious beach and pool time, but if you do want to stamp through Charleston's historic neighborhoods, a complimentary water shuttle departs at regular intervals throughout the day and evening. Bedrooms are spacious and flooded with sunlight that streams in through big windows.

20 Patriots Point, Mount Pleasant, SC 29464. © **888/856-0028** or 843/856-0028. Fax 843/856-8333. www.charlestonharborresort.com. 131 units. $169–$319 double; $299–$359 suite (year-round). AE, DC, DISC, MC, V. Free parking. **Amenities:** Restaurant; bar; children's programs; exercise room; outdoor pool; room service. *In room:* A/C, TV, Wi-Fi (free).

Moderate
Old Village Post House ★ Finds This is the best inn in the old town of Mount Pleasant, lying across the bridge from downtown Charleston. It dates from the days of the wayside inns where travelers made overnight stopovers, and today many guests prefer to stay here among the moss-draped oaks of the Old Village than in downtown Charleston. Traditional charm meets modern amenities at this well-run inn. The rooms have original hardwood floors, 10-foot ceilings, and soothing whirlpool tubs. Each of the accommodations varies in

size and decor. Room 6 is known as the Honeymoon Suite, featuring a four-poster bed, a sitting area, and an extra-large private bathroom for two. You can also dine at the on-site restaurant, Maverick (p. 81).

101 Pitt St., Mount Pleasant, SC 29464. (*C*) **843/388-8935.** www.oldvillagepost house.com. 6 units. $99–$109 double. Rates include breakfast. AE, MC, V. **Amenities:** Restaurant; bar. *In room:* A/C, TV, Wi-Fi (free).

SUMMERVILLE
Very Expensive

Woodlands Resort & Inn ★★★   This three-story 1906 Greek Revival home is one of the grandest places to stay in all of South Carolina, if not America. Standing on 42 acres, it's surrounded by moss-draped live oaks and magnolia trees, a stellar cliché of elegant Old South living. The stage is set upon your arrival, when you're presented with fresh flowers and chilled champagne. In the afternoon, you can enjoy complimentary tea, antebellum style. Sit out on the front veranda in a rocking chair and admire the Greek columns and the grounds beyond. It's definitely a luxury retreat, with prices to match.

The individually decorated bedrooms have been impeccably restored in an English-country-house style. Each has its own personality, the creation of New York designer David Eskell-Briggs. Some have sitting areas, while others are graced with fireplaces and even whirlpool tubs. The executive suites offer the most gracious accommodations of any hotel in the state, with four-poster king-size beds and all the comforts of the modern era. You won't have to go far to eat well: The **Dining Room at Woodlands** (p. 82) is among the South's most magnificent restaurants.

125 Parsons Rd., Summerville, SC 29483. (*C*) **800/774-9999** or 843/875-2600. Fax 843/875-2603. www.woodlandsinn.com. 19 units. $325 double; $390–$650 suite. AE, MC, V. **Amenities:** Restaurant; bar; babysitting; free bikes; outdoor pool; 2 tennis courts (lit). *In room:* A/C, TV, Wi-Fi (free).

5

Where to Dine

Foodies from all over the Carolinas and as far away as Georgia flock to Charleston for some of the finest dining in the tri-state area. You get not only the refined cookery of the Low Country, but also an array of French and international specialties.

1 CHARLESTON'S TOP RESTAURANTS

VERY EXPENSIVE

Charleston Grill ★★★ LOW COUNTRY/FRENCH This is the most prestigious, most formal, and most sophisticated restaurant in Charleston, with grand food, an impeccably trained staff, and one of the city's best selections of wine. In its role as the culinary showcase of the posh **Charleston Place Hotel** (p. 47), the restaurant makes absolutely no concessions to Southern folksiness—this is European and international high style at its most confident, at the top of virtually every list of superlatives in a city loaded with formidable competition. The marble-floored, mahogany-sheathed dining room is one of the city's most luxurious. Menu items change with the seasons, and you will be pleasantly surprised by how well Low Country and French cuisine meld. Main courses burst with freshness, as in the diver scallops and lobster risotto with white asparagus and a lemon vermouth sauce. Modern interpretations of Southern dishes also appear—try the duck confit with "dirty grits," baby turnips, and a bacon sage gravy.

In the Charleston Place Hotel, 224 King St. (C) **843/577-4522.** www.charleston grill.com. Reservations recommended. Main courses $25–$48. AE, DC, DISC, MC, V. Sun–Thurs 5:30–10pm; Fri–Sat 5:30–10:30pm.

Circa 1886 Restaurant ★★ AMERICAN/FRENCH Situated in the carriage house of the **Wentworth Mansion** (p. 50), this deluxe restaurant offers grand food, beautiful decor, and formal service. Begin by accepting the invitation of the concierge for a view of Charleston from the cupola. The two dining rooms are the most idyllic setting for a romantic meal in town. The chef prepares an updated version of Low Country cookery, giving it a light touch but retaining the flavors of the Old South. Menus change seasonally to take advantage of the freshest produce. For a first course, try the candied carrot soup with roasted garlic, or the spicy grilled shrimp over fried green tomatoes. Main courses are prepared with consummate skill, especially the truffle-oil fried catfish or the vanilla-glazed Berkshire pork chop. We're still smacking our lips over the strawberry shortcake soufflé hazelnut tart with lightly whipped cream and Orange Julius sherbet.

In the Wentworth Mansion, 149 Wentworth St. © **843/853-7828.** www.circa1886. com. Reservations recommended. Main courses $23–$32. AE, DC, DISC, MC, V. Mon–Sat 5:30–9:30pm.

Oak Steakhouse ★ STEAK   In 2005, chef Brett McKee opened this restaurant in a historic building dating back to 1850. With its 18-foot ceilings, mahogany paneling, and pine floors, the Brooklyn-born McKee re-creates an Italian-style steakhouse. The menu focuses on traditional items, such as New York strip or porterhouse, but infuses dishes with Italian flavor. Start with such appetizers as tuna tartare or Brett's own special meatballs with melted mozzarella. His salads are some of the best in town including his chopped salad of mixed greens that contains everything from radicchio to sweet Vidalia onions. Oak specialties include a 12-ounce burger with cottage fries or a lobster and shrimp macaroni. Vegetarian and vegan entrees are available upon request.

17 Broad St. © **843/722-4220.** www.oaksteakhouserestaurant.com. Reservations recommended. Main courses $22–$49. AE, MC, V. Mon–Sat 5–11pm; Sun 5–10pm.

Peninsula Grill ★★ CONTINENTAL/INTERNATIONAL The Peninsula Grill, in the **Planters Inn** (p. 48), manages to be quaint, historic, hip, and just a wee bit pricier than it perhaps should be—all at the same time. There's a cramped but convivial bar near the entrance that attracts a considerable crowd of prowling singles, and a warm, dimly lit interior that's posh and proudly Southern. You might start with an artfully arranged platter of three different preparations of lobster: as ravioli, as tempura, and as a sauté. Follow this with bourbon grilled jumbo shrimp, Low Country Hoppin' John (black-eyed peas and rice seasoned with ham), and lobster-basil hush puppies. A full array of steaks, chops, and seafood can be prepared any way you like, served with sides of wild-mushroom grits and bacon and cheddar fingerling potatoes. The *New York Times* and *Bon Appetit* magazine have praised "the ultimate coconut cake," based on a recipe from the chef's grandmother.

In the Planters Inn, 112 N. Market St. © **843/723-0700.** www.peninsulagrill.com. Reservations required. Main courses $28–$39. AE, DC, DISC, MC, V. Sun–Thurs 5:30–10pm; Fri–Sat 5:30–11pm.

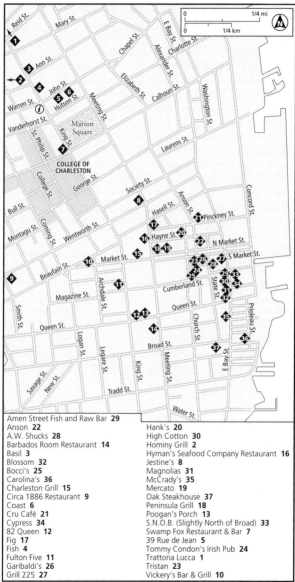

Amen Street Fish and Raw Bar **29**
Anson **22**
A.W. Shucks **28**
Barbados Room Restaurant **14**
Basil **3**
Blossom **32**
Bocci's **25**
Carolina's **36**
Charleston Grill **15**
Circa 1886 Restaurant **9**
Coast **6**
Cru Café **21**
Cypress **34**
82 Queen **12**
Fig **17**
Fish **4**
Fulton Five **11**
Garibaldi's **26**
Grill 225 **27**

Hank's **20**
High Cotton **30**
Hominy Grill **2**
Hyman's Seafood Company Restaurant **16**
Jestine's **8**
Magnolias **31**
McCrady's **35**
Mercato **19**
Oak Steakhouse **37**
Peninsula Grill **18**
Poogan's Porch **13**
S.N.O.B. (Slightly North of Broad) **33**
Swamp Fox Restaurant & Bar **7**
39 Rue de Jean **5**
Tommy Condon's Irish Pub **24**
Trattoria Lucca **1**
Tristan **23**
Vickery's Bar & Grill **10**

EXPENSIVE

Anson ★★ LOW COUNTRY/MODERN AMERICAN   Anson is simply the best. Charlestonians know they can spot local society types here; newcomers recognize it as a stylish venue with all the grace notes of a top restaurant in New York, coupled with Low Country charm. The setting is a century-old, brick-sided warehouse, decorated with salvaged Corinthian pilasters and enough rococo for anyone's taste. The food is inspired by traditions of the coastal Southeast—but this isn't exactly down-home cookery, as you'll see after sampling such appetizers as fried calamari with an apricot and shallot sauce, or cornmeal-dusted okra with chili oil and goat cheese. France meets the Deep South in the cashew-crusted grouper with Hoppin' John, green beans, and a champagne cream sauce. Our favorite is the crispy flounder, which rival chefs have tried to duplicate but have failed to equal. Some of the best meat selections include slow-roasted duck with duck confit potato cake and local peaches. A children's menu is available.

12 Anson St. ⓒ **843/577-0551.** www.ansonrestaurant.com. Reservations recommended. Main courses $18–$39. AE, DC, DISC, MC, V. Sun–Thurs 5–10pm; Fri–Sat 5–11pm.

Cypress ★ LOW COUNTRY   Some of the most imaginative Low Country food is served here, focusing on hearty platters with lots of rice and shrimp and special herbs of the region. A feature is a wood-burning grill for such main dishes as "Reconstruction lamb T-bone." For starters, treat yourself to crab cakes or almond-fried Brie with a cranberry and walnut chutney. Main course specialties include a crisp wasabi tuna with shiitake mushrooms or a filet of beef in Madeira sauce. Tableside presentations for two include a Châteaubriand with Parmesan potato gratin. James River oysters from Virginia are a feature in season, as is grilled pork belly in a butter glaze.

167 E. Bay St. ⓒ **843/727-0111.** www.magnolias-blossom-cypress.com. Reservations recommended. Main courses $20–$49. AE, DC, MC, V. Sun–Thurs 5:30–10pm; Fri–Sat 5:30–11pm.

Fig ★★ SOUTHERN/INTERNATIONAL   Mustardy deviled eggs are served while you peruse the tempting menu that ranges from the best Portuguese fish soup in Charleston (complete with salt cod, squid, and chorizo) to roast suckling pig. Charleston got lucky the day chef/owner Mike Lata hit town, coming down from Massachusetts via New Orleans and Atlanta. We like his dedication to the best local produce and have made an entire meal out of his vegetables alone, including a garlic-studded sautéed rapini and butter beans with prosciutto and basil butter. His hanger steak with caramelized shallots and an old-fashioned bordelaise sauce is a delight to the senses. The appetizers are also perfectly harmonious, including Swiss chard ravioli with walnuts and a white-corn soup with applewood-smoked bacon **69** and scallions.

232 Meeting St. ✆ **843/805-5900.** www.eatatfig.com. Reservations required. Main courses $26–$34. AE, MC, V. Mon–Thurs 5:30–10:30pm; Fri–Sat 5:30–11pm.

Fulton Five ★ NORTHERN ITALIAN   This off-the-beaten-path trattoria, tucked away on a small street off King Street, is a local favorite. The decor is traditional European, and the menu reflects some of the best dishes of the northern Italian kitchen. The best *osso buco* (braised veal shank) in Charleston is served with saffron spinach, and a half rack of lamb is aromatically roasted and served with a bean purée, asparagus, and a minty pesto. The chefs produce an admirable whole seared fish daily, and also feature a delightful caper-encrusted tuna with sun-dried tomatoes. Naturally, they pay careful attention to their pastas, as exemplified by *pappardelle* (wide noodles) with roasted rabbit.

5 Fulton St. ✆ **843/853-5555.** www.fultonfive.net. Reservations recommended. Main courses $25–$32. AE, DC, MC, V. Mon–Thurs 5:30–9pm; Fri–Sat 5:30–10pm.

Grill 225 ★ AMERICAN/INTERNATIONAL   This upscale bistro in the **Market Pavilion Hotel** (p. 48) amazes newcomers with its 21st-century setting—which you'd swear was a conversion from a century-old bank lobby (ca. 1903), ideal for a Deep South "power lunch." Choose from at least eight massive selections of grilled steaks, such as a filet mignon layered with foie gras and served with béarnaise sauce. Seafood options include "encrusted" halibut with spicy scallops, lump crabmeat, and miso-flavored lemon-grass broth. Cuba Gooding, Jr., and the Bush twins have been spotted here.

In the Market Pavilion Hotel, 225 E. Bay St. ✆ **843/723-0500.** Reservations recommended. Lunch salads, sandwiches, and platters $15–$36; dinner main courses $26–$68. AE, DC, MC, V. Daily 11:30am–3pm and 5:30–11pm.

High Cotton ★★ SOUTHERN/STEAK   This blockbuster restaurant caters to devoted locals who prefer their two-fisted drinks in an upscale macho decor, accompanied by tasty Southern-style steakhouse fare. It's also a good choice for nightlife thanks to its casual elegance and its busy but cozy bar, where live music, usually jazz, is performed nightly. Dig into the buttermilk-fried oysters with arugula in a green goddess dressing, or a homemade version of the most sophisticated platter of charcuterie in the Carolinas. With crusty bread, butter, a salad, and a glass or two of wine, it's something akin to a gift from the gods. Gourmands gravitate to the "Something Wild" section of the menu, featuring barbecue-spiced seared flounder or sliced medallions of venison *au poivre*. Most diners go for one of the juicy steaks, which are served with your choice of a half-dozen sauces ranging from bourbon to béarnaise. The chef's signature treat is a praline soufflé in chocolate sauce.

199 E. Bay St. ✆ 843/724-3815. www.mavericksouthernkitchens.com. Reservations recommended. Main courses $21–$36. AE, DC, DISC, MC, V. Daily 5:30–10pm (till 11pm Fri–Sat); Sat lunch 11am–2:30pm; Sun brunch with live music 10am–2pm.

McCrady's ★★ AMERICAN/FRENCH   Charleston's oldest eating establishment, where none other than George Washington once dined, is one of the finest kitchens in the Low Country. Praising both wine list and menu, *Esquire* named it one of the best new restaurants in the U.S. Entered via a mysterious-looking alley, it resembles an elegant wine cellar, with rough brick walls, exposed beams, and wide-plank floors. We still remember the peekytoe-crab and lobster salad; ditto for the tartare of tuna with olives, red pepper, and basil. A perfectly sautéed halibut appears with sides of spinach and cauliflower purée. Slow-roasted Moulard duck breast comes with chocolate balsamic *jus,* or you might happily settle for the herb-marinated rack of lamb.

2 Unity Alley. ✆ **843/577-0025.** www.mccradysrestaurant.com. Reservations required. Main courses $25–$32. AE, MC, V. Sun–Thurs 5:30–9:30pm; Fri–Sat 5:30–10:30pm.

Tristan ★ INTERNATIONAL   This restaurant's glossy, hipster aura stands in distinct contrast to the old Confederate look of the Market Pavilion that it faces. Inside, you'll find a seamless, postmodern, airy-looking environment. Dinners are elaborate, featuring a butternut-squash terrine, three kinds of American caviar, a sashimi made from scallops with an emulsion of sea urchins and Thai peppercorns, and hickory-smoked lamb ribs with chocolate barbecue sauce.

55 S. Market St. ✆ 843/534-2155. www.tristandining.com. Reservations recommended. Main courses $20–$29. Six-course tasting menu $75 per person. AE, MC, V. Mon–Thurs 5:30–10pm; Fri–Sat 5:30–11pm; Sun brunch 11am–2:30pm.

MODERATE

Barbados Room Restaurant ★★★ SOUTHERN   Wonderful ingredients, bountiful servings, and the panache of the chefs make this one a winner. Located in the historic **Mills House Hotel** (p. 57), this restaurant enjoys praise for the best Sunday brunch in Charleston. Few can resist the jumbo crab cakes, and the dry aged beef is the best in town. Ordering shrimp and grits will make you a local. We delight in the Low Country black-bean soup and the ginger-encrusted tuna steak.

The Mills House also offers live entertainment. For an after-dinner drink, we always gravitate to its popular rendezvous spot, the **Fountain Courtyard.** You can also enjoy cocktails in the **First Shot Lounge,** named for the first shot fired during the Civil War.

In the Mills House Hotel, 115 Meeting St. ✆ **843/577-2400.** Reservations recommended. Main courses $14–$34; Sun buffet brunch $25. AE, DISC, MC, V. Daily 7am–9pm.

Blossom ★★ MEDITERRANEAN/AMERICAN Near Waterfront Park, this contemporary cafe is a showcase for chef Randy Williams. He takes the freshest local seafood and combines it with the best regional produce to create a cuisine that has, in some cases, strong Italian overtones. Appetizers show a certain flair, especially buttermilk-fried calamari with a mango-and-ginger-laced chutney. Pizzas from a wood-burning oven are among the best in town. The chef's specialties include one of our favorite dishes, cane-sugar-encrusted salmon. Pastas, desserts, and breads are all made in-house. Their warm peach Johnnycakes (cornmeal pancakes known as "corn pones" in the Old South) are among the best in Charleston.

171 E. Bay St. ✆ **843/722-9200.** www.magnolias-blossom-cypress.com. Reservations recommended. Lunch $7–$21; dinner main courses $10–$27; Sun brunch $10–$15. AE, DISC, MC, V. Mon–Thurs 11:30am–10pm; Fri–Sat 11:30am–midnight; Sun 11am–3pm and 4–10pm. Closed Jan 1 and Dec 25.

Bocci's ★★ **Kids** ITALIAN Just a short walk from the City Market and long a local favorite, this dining room earned a mention in *USA Today* as one of the leading Italian restaurants in the South. Many of our favorites appear on the menu, including a classic minestrone and tender fried calamari in a spicy marinara sauce. The homemade pastas are full of flavor, as evidenced by the manicotti stuffed with spinach and three cheeses. Seafood dishes include seafood Alfredo with fresh shrimp and scallops. There's even a special menu for children.

158 Church St. ✆ **843/720-2121.** www.boccis.com. Reservations recommended. Main courses $15–$24. AE, DC, DISC, MC, V. Daily 11am–3pm; Sun–Thurs 4:30–10pm; Fri–Sat 4:30–11pm. Closed Thanksgiving.

Carolina's ★ **Finds** SOUTHERN Getting here is part of the fun, involving as it does a 12-minute walk from the tourist crush of the main core of historic Charleston. Amid the wharves and turned-posh town houses of Lower East Bay Street, Carolina's is a Charlestonian staple that fell out of fashion and is now fighting its way back into the city's gastronomic good graces. Since opening as Perdita's in the early 1950s—a name inspired by a local courtesan whose widely broadcast flirtations led to a duel and at least one of her suitors' deaths—it's had a revolving door of chefs and culinary styles. Today, it exerts a broad-based appeal to locals, with special value at lunch. Platters include shrimp and grits with sweet peppers and andouille gravy or pan-seared salmon with apricots, Swiss chard, and lentils. Dinners feature glazed quail with collard greens, fried flounder with peach jam, and shrimp and crab won tons with soy-lime-ginger aioli. Traditionalists will appreciate the bulk and heft of a New York strip steak perched on a mound of mashed potatoes, garnished with a red-wine and shiitake-mushroom gravy.

10 Exchange St. (C) **843/724-3800.** www.carolinasrestaurant.com. Reservations recommended. Lunch soups, salads, and platters $7–$12; dinner main courses $23–$34; 4-course tasting menu $42. AE, DC, DISC, MC, V. Mon–Fri 11:30am–2:30pm; Sun–Thurs 5–10pm; Fri–Sat 5–11pm; Sun brunch 11am–2:30pm.

Coast ★ SEAFOOD   In a former indigo warehouse, this restaurant is casual and hip, known for its menu of Charleston classics and specialties from an oak wood grill. Savvy local foodies fill up the tin-roofed booths. The chefs prepare Charleston's best seviche, one made with lobster, and you can make selections from the raw bar sampler. Appetizers are worth the trip; some diners make a meal of them like tapas. Try the cornmeal-encrusted oysters in a papaya coulis with caviar or the yellowfin tuna pan-seared with tropical salsa. Fish such as mahimahi or grouper is sizzled on the grill and served with a variety of sauces, including a pineapple chili salsa. Fish specialties include a delectable seafood paella and a Portuguese calamari stew.

39D John St. (C) **843/722-8838.** www.coastbarandgrill.com. Reservations recommended. Main courses $15–$32. AE, DC, MC, V. Daily 5:30–10pm.

Cru Café ★ (Finds) AMERICAN/INTERNATIONAL   In a small 18th-century house, this two-room cafe with its casual bench seating and open kitchen is a local favorite. Chef John Zucker has you coming back for more the following day after you taste his imaginative specialties. Start, perhaps, with his buttermilk fried oyster salad with apple smoked bacon or his duck confit arugula salad with candied pecans in a port wine vinaigrette. He makes some of the best pastas in town, including garlic scallops and angel hair pasta, or risotto, especially his Thai seafood risotto. From the a la carte grille you can try a 12-ounce jerk rib-eye, or else go for one of his tasty specialties such as seared maple leaf duck breast in a sherry thyme demi-glace.

18 Pinckney St. (C) **843/534-2434.** www.crucafe.com. Reservations recommended. Main courses $14–$24. AE, MC, V. Tues–Sat 11am–3pm; Tues–Thurs 5–10pm; Fri–Sat 5–11pm.

82 Queen ★ LOW COUNTRY   This restaurant is housed in three 18th- and 19th-century houses clustered around an ancient magnolia tree, with outdoor tables arranged in its shade. Menu items filled with flavor and flair include an award-winning she-crab soup. Some of the best Low Country meals in Charleston are served here, especially the bouillabaisse made with market-fresh seafood or the seasoned shrimp and crawfish jambalaya with tasso ham and red rice.

82 Queen St. ℰ **843/723-7591.** www.82queen.com. Reservations recommended for dinner. Main courses $10–$15 lunch, $19–$30 dinner; Sun brunch $10–$16. AE, DC, DISC, MC, V. Daily 11:30am–3pm and 5:30–11pm; Sun brunch 11:30am–3pm.

Fish ★ SEAFOOD   With a name like Fish, you know what to expect. Owners Charles and Celeste Patrick spearheaded the revitalization of North King Street when they opened a restaurant in this 1830s former private home. Now visitors flock to an area once viewed as unsafe to enjoy some of the best seafood in the Low Country. For a main course, perhaps "naked fish" is best—it's the fresh catch of the day and is prepared simply to bring out its natural flavor. Shrimp and grits with chorizo cream, peppers, and onion is a winning combination—as is the seared halibut in a cucumber yogurt sauce. The array of sides is among the city's best.

442 King St. ℰ **843/722-3474.** www.fishrestaurant.net. Reservations recommended. Main courses $10–$12 lunch, $17–$25 dinner. AE, MC, V. Mon–Fri 11am–2:30pm; Sat 11:30am–2pm and 5:30–11pm.

Hank's ★★ (Kids) SEAFOOD   In a converted warehouse overlooking the Old City Market, this has been called the quintessential Low Country seafood restaurant and saloon. It's spacious and inviting, with a friendly staff that rushes about against a backdrop of rich woods and regional artwork. Some of the finest Low Country dishes in Charleston are served here, especially the bouillabaisse and she-crab soup. Appetizers range from oyster stew to pan-fried crab cakes with a red-pepper basil sauce. Follow up some succulent oysters with any number of delectable seafood platters, including fried oysters, grouper filet, and crumb-fried shrimp, all accompanied by creamy Southern coleslaw. Most of the menu is geared toward seafood, although the chef can also whip up a grilled chicken breast, perhaps with a mushroom ragout, or a New York strip with mashed potatoes. There's a kids' menu, too.

10 Hayne St. ℰ **843/723-3474.** www.hanksseafoodrestaurant.com. Reservations recommended. Main courses $20–$29. AE, DISC, MC, V. Mon–Fri 5–10:30pm; Sat–Sun 5–11:30pm. Closed Jan 1.

Magnolias (Kids) SOUTHERN   Magnolias elevates the vernacular cuisine of the Deep South into a hip art form that's suitable for big-city trendies but even more popular with visiting families. The city's former Custom House has been redone into a sprawling network of interconnected spaces with heart-pine floors, faux-marble columns, and massive beams. The menu pairs typically Southern dishes such as blackened catfish with sides of fried green tomatoes, cheese grits, and yellow-corn salsa. At lunch, many diners fill up on soups and salads, ranging from a creamy tomato soup with lump crabmeat to a salmon BLT salad. The "Down South" main dishes are good-tasting favorites, especially the pan-seared mahimahi or the buttermilk fried chicken with cracked-pepper biscuits and collard greens.

185 E. Bay St. ℂ **843/577-7771.** www.magnolias-blossom-cypress.com. Reservations recommended. Main courses $9–$19 lunch, $19–$32 dinner. AE, DC, MC, V. Mon–Sat 11:30am–3:45pm; Sun 10am–3:45pm; Sun–Thurs 4–10pm; Fri–Sat 4–11pm.

Mercato ITALIAN   Overlooking the historic Market Pavilion is this big, airy, friendly, and informal trattoria. Start with an assortment of olives or perhaps some risotto fritters with prosciutto, mozzarella, and porcini mushrooms; then go for any of a half-dozen pizzas or pastas, such as the homemade bavette pasta with shrimp, chilies, garlic, and parsley. Well-prepared main courses include pork chops stuffed with prosciutto, capers, and sage, or a wild-mushroom risotto with white-truffle oil.

102 N. Market St. ℂ **843/722-6393.** www.mercatocharleston.com. Reservations not necessary. Pizzas and pastas $10–$19; main courses $15–$28. AE, DC, MC, V. Mon–Thurs and Sun 5–11pm; Fri–Sat 5pm–midnight.

S.N.O.B. (Slightly North of Broad) ★ ⓥalue SOUTHERN/ INTERNATIONAL   You'll find this energetic bistro in a snazzily rehabbed 18th-century warehouse with an open kitchen and exposed ventilation ducts. Winner of many culinary awards, it justifiably promotes itself as Charleston's culinary maverick, priding itself on having introduced, in the early '90s, stylishly updated versions of the vittles that kept the South alive for 300 years. Many of those innovations have since entered the mainstream, but thanks to its panache and its good value, S.N.O.B. remains a serious contender among the culinary who's who of Charleston. An array of freshly made salads, soups, sandwiches, and daily specials greet you at lunch. Main courses can be ordered in medium and large sizes—a fact appreciated by dieters. Enjoy such entrees as grilled barbecued tuna glazed with mustard sauce and topped with fried oysters, ham, and green onions; or roasted rack of lamb with green beans, pearl onions, and a rosemary cabernet sauce.

192 E. Bay St. ℂ **843/723-3424.** www.mavericksouthernkitchens.com. Reservations accepted only for parties of 5 or more at lunch, recommended for all at dinner. Main courses $9–$16 lunch, $10–$29 dinner. AE, DC, DISC, MC, V. Mon–Fri 11:30am–3pm; daily 5:30–11pm.

Swamp Fox Restaurant & Bar ★ AMERICAN   Located in the recently restored **Francis Marion Hotel** (p. 53), this restaurant offers breakfast, lunch, and dinner to discerning palates. Many locals come here to celebrate special occasions. Named for the Revolutionary War hero Gen. Francis Marion, the Swamp Fox celebrates a classic Southern cuisine featuring market-fresh ingredients. The day starts off with breakfast dishes such as grits and country ham. The lunch menu includes soups, salads, sandwiches, and appetizers, including such stalwarts as fried green tomatoes with Vidalia onion relish. The fried chicken is acclaimed by some as the best in town. The dinner menu features such delights as a peach-glazed pork chop with collards and buttermilk mashed potatoes, or pan-seared duck leg braised in brown gravy and served with greens over Hoppin' John. Among the luscious desserts are bourbon pecan pie and praline bread pudding.

In the Francis Marion Hotel, 387 King St. ✆ **843/724-8888.** www.francismarion hotel.com. Reservations recommended. Main courses $7.95–$15 breakfast, $8–$14 lunch, $17–$23 dinner. AE, DISC, MC, V. Daily 7–11am, 11:30am–3pm, and 5–10pm.

39 Rue de Jean ★ ⓥalue FRENCH/SUSHI   Transport yourself to the Left Bank at this restaurant, which pays homage to the classic brasserie cuisine of Paris. It's popular for its inexpensive French fare, traditional zinc bar, and great bottles of wine; patio dining is an added attraction. The only incongruous note is the sudden culinary departure into Japanese sushi. All of our favorite French appetizers are on the menu, including truffle potato soup and frisée lettuce with bacon lardoons. We always go for the *plat du jour,* especially the Sunday rendition of a delectable bouillabaisse. And it wouldn't be a Paris bistro without the time-honored escargots gratinée, steak *frites,* and foie gras, which the chefs do well. Special features are six preparations of mussels and a whole fish *du jour* from the marketplace that morning.

39 John St. ✆ **843/722-8881.** www.39ruedejean.com. Reservations required. Main courses $7.50–$15 lunch, $19–$25 dinner. AE, DC, DISC, MC, V. Mon–Sat 11:30am–1am; Sun 10am–3pm and 5:30–11pm.

Trattoria Lucca ★ ⓚids ITALIAN   Chef Ken Vedrinski of Siena brings Italian family dining inspired by the Tuscan city of Lucca, known for its bevy of olive oils and savory dishes, to Charleston. Unpretentious fare is served trattoria style at communal dining tables, and Sundays are marked by all-you-can-eat family suppers. The homemade pastas are among the best in town, including bucatini with goat butter, trumpet mushrooms, and homemade Italian duck sausage. Other specialties include grilled farm chicken with local fresh peas and beans or pork chop Milanese with Speck ham and arugula. One splendid dish is grilled black Angus flatiron steak with Vidalia onion fonduta and Gorgonzola macaroni.

41A Bogart St. ✆ **843/973-3323.** Reservations recommended. Main courses $19–$24. AE, MC, V. Tues–Thurs 6–10pm; Fri–Sat 6–11pm; Sun 5–8pm.

INEXPENSIVE

Amen Street Fish and Raw Bar ★ LOW COUNTRY/ SEAFOOD   One of the joys of dining in Charleston is to indulge in the rich bounty caught off the coast—oysters, clams, shrimp, fresh fish. We visit just for the raw bar, with succulent oysters, fresh daily, along with little neck clams. If you want to go more exotic, you can select the tuna tartare with wasabi. The chilled seafood cocktails are the best in town, and an array of starters await you, including lump crab cakes and fresh mussels in garlic and white wine. Ever had "lobster biscuits" with gravy? For a main dish, you can opt for the house specialty, a seafood platter with hush puppies, or else the classic shrimp and grits. Desserts are a treat as well, especially the strawberry shortcake with whipped cream.

205 E. Bay St. ✆ **843/853-8600.** Reservations not necessary. Main courses $8–$10 lunch, $12–$21 dinner. AE, DC, DISC, MC, V. Daily 11:30am–11pm.

A. W. Shuck's ★ **Value** SEAFOOD   This oyster bar is a sprawling, salty tribute to the pleasures of shellfish and the fishermen who gather them. A short walk from the Old City Market, set in a restored warehouse with rough timbers, the restaurant has a long bar where thousands of crustaceans have been cracked open and consumed, as well as a dining room. The menu highlights oysters and clams on the half shell, tasty chowders, deviled crab, shrimp Creole, and succulent oysters prepared in at least half a dozen ways. Chicken and beef dishes are also listed on the menu, but they're nothing special.

70 State St. ✆ **843/723-1151.** www.a-w-shucks.com. Main courses $14–$24. AE, DC, DISC, MC, V. Sun–Thurs 11am–10pm; Fri–Sat 11am–11pm.

Basil THAI   This is the busiest spot on North King Street, the one that's always mentioned when a newcomer asks for a recommendation in this neighborhood. It's one of only two Thai restaurants in Charleston, and as such, it's something of a gastronomic landmark. Within a somewhat cramped setting of ocher-colored walls and hardwood floors, you can order all the usual Thai curries and lemon-grass specials. Especially popular are Tom Kha Gai (chicken-coconut soup); duck salad with pineapple, carrots, ginger, and cashews; and a wide array of green, red, and yellow curries. Your hardworking host is

(Kids) **Family-Friendly Restaurants**

Bocci's (p. 71)   Known for its reliable Italian fare and affordable prices, this centrally located restaurant is a great pick for families. A children's menu is offered as well.

Hank's (p. 73)   A friendly staff, plenty of elbowroom, and a special kids' menu make this a family favorite.

Hominy Grill (p. 78)   Locally loved, this homey grill has been drawing families since 1996. Fair prices, good food, and an inviting atmosphere lure visitors to sample an array of Southern specialties at breakfast, lunch, or dinner.

Magnolias (p. 73)   Southern hospitality and charm keep this place buzzing. Lunch is the best time for families, who can opt for soups, salads, sandwiches, or pastas. But in-the-know local kids go easy on these items, saving room for the warm cream-cheese brownie with white-chocolate ice cream and chocolate sauce.

Tommy Condon's Irish Pub (p. 80)   A special menu for "little leprechauns" and spirited Irish singalongs make this a popular family spot, night and day.

Trattoria Lucca (p. 75)   At trattoria-style communal dining tables, parents and children can feast on some of the town's most succulent homemade pastas. Family suppers are offered on Sunday.

Henry Eang, an entrepreneur from Cambodia who has a tale or two to tell about the Pol Pot regime.

460 King St. ℂ **843/724-3490.** www.eatatbasil.com. Reservations not accepted. Main courses $8.95–$11 lunch, $14–$17 dinner. AE, DC, MC, V. Mon–Fri 11am– 2:30pm; Mon–Thurs 5–10:30pm; Fri–Sat 5–11pm; Sun 5–10pm.

California Dreaming ★ AMERICAN   Every table at this restaurant boasts a waterfront view. Enjoy dishes that won the West, such as homemade chili, barbecue chicken nachos, and chicken wings marinated in hot peppers. Large shrimp are steamed to order; simply peel and eat. Steaks are a specialty here, using choice aged beef— everything from a center-cut 14-ounce New York strip to an 11-ounce sirloin marinated in fruit juices, garlic, spices, and soy sauce. The chefs prepare seven different chicken dishes nightly, including one in marinara sauce. The pastry chef is known for his apple walnut cinnamon pie.

1 Ashley Point Dr. ℂ **843/766-1644.** www.centraarchy.com. Reservations recommended. Main courses $8–$26. AE, DC, DISC, MC, V. Sun–Thurs 11am–10pm; Fri–Sat 11am–11pm. Closed Thanksgiving and Dec 25.

Garibaldi's ITALIAN   Equally popular with locals and visitors, this sibling of **Anson** (p. 68) never rises to a status of grandeur—it simply succeeds admirably in what it does offer. Guests are well fed in this warm and inviting trattoria, and the chefs prepare their dishes with the best produce found at the market. The appetizers feature Italian favorites such as deep-fried artichoke hearts and stuffed mushrooms. At least a dozen succulent pastas are prepared nightly, ranging from fettuccine Alfredo to shrimp marinara. Nothing is bold or terribly creative, but oh, these dishes are good, especially the rigatoni with chicken, caramelized onions, shiitake mushrooms, and Marsala cream.

49 S. Market St. ℂ **843/723-7153.** Reservations recommended. Main courses $11–$29. AE, MC, V. Sun–Thurs 5:30–10pm; Fri–Sat 5:30–11pm. Closed Thanksgiving and Dec 25.

Hominy Grill ★ Kids LOW COUNTRY   Hominy Grill has gained a devoted following among families, who come here to feast on simply and beautifully prepared dishes inspired by the kitchens of the Low Country: barbecue chicken sandwich, avocado and Wehani rice salad and grilled vegetables, okra and shrimp beignets, and—a brunch favorite—poached eggs on biscuits with mushroom gravy. At dinner, opt for one of the down-home specials such as country-style pork ribs with red rice and pinto beans. For extra flavor, slather your

---

Ⓣips   **Packing a Picnic**

Charleston's many parks, gardens, and harborfront promenades provide ample opportunities for picnics, so if you're interested in take-away vittles that taste marvelous when consumed *en plein air,* consider a visit to the city's most comprehensive gourmet deli. Modeled after the NYC purveyor Dean & DeLuca, **Caviar & Bananas,** 51 George St. (ℂ **843/577-7757;** www.caviarandbananas.com), is the brainchild of Kris and Margaret Furniss, whose gourmet cheeses, chutneys, prepared meats, and sandwiches sometimes get consumed even before their buyers reach their picnic destination. You'll find this place in the city's historic core, a short walk from King Street. Open Monday to Friday from 7am to 8:30pm, Saturday from 8am to 8:30pm, and Sunday from 9am to 8:30pm.

chops with some blackstrap-molasses barbecue sauce. The chef likes to introduce people to new grains in the place of pasta or potatoes; many of his dishes, including salads, are prepared with barley or cracked wheat.

207 Rutledge Ave. ℂ **843/937-0930.** www.hominygrill.com. Brunch from $10; main courses $5–$11 lunch, $7–$17 dinner. AE, MC, V. Mon–Fri 7:30–9pm; Sat 9am–9pm; Sun 9am–3pm.

Hyman's Seafood Company Restaurant ★ SEAFOOD

Hyman's was established a century ago and honors old-fashioned traditions. The building sprawls over most of a city block in the heart of Charleston's business district. Inside are at least six dining rooms and a take-away deli loaded with salmon, lox, and smoked herring, all displayed in the style of the great kosher delis of New York City. One sit-down section is devoted to deli-style sandwiches, chicken soup, and salads; another to a delectably messy choice of fish, shellfish, lobsters, and oysters. We can ignore the endorsement of now-deceased Senator Strom Thurmond, but we take more seriously the praise of such big-time foodies as Barbra, Oprah, and Baryshnikov.

215 Meeting St. ℂ **843/723-6000.** www.hymanseafood.com. Main courses $11–$43. AE, DC, DISC, MC, V. Daily 11am–11pm.

Jestine's SOUTHERN

For some real Low Country flavors, try Jestine's—named after the cook and housekeeper who reared the founder of the restaurant, Shera Lee Berlin. All of Jestine's recipes have been preserved to delight a new generation of diners, who feast on country-fried steak, okra gumbo, shrimp Creole, oyster po' boys, black-eyed peas, and blueberry cobbler. There is a daily blue-plate special, and even a green-plate special for vegetarians. If you've ever wondered what "red rice" is, ask for it here. The "table wine" is actually sugary tea in tumblers.

251 Meeting St. ℂ **843/722-7224.** Reservations not accepted. Main courses $8–$15. AE, DC, DISC, MC, V. Tues–Thurs 11am–9:30pm; Fri–Sat 11am–10pm; Sun 11am–9pm. Closed Dec 25 and Jewish holidays.

Poogan's Porch ★ Finds LOW COUNTRY

If you like jamba-laya, peanut-butter pie, Carolina quail, and all those other down-home favorites, a table is waiting for you in this restored 1891 house, where the decor is appropriately antiquey Victorian. The restaurant is named after a dog that used to stand on the porch greeting guests until he died in 1979. Everyone from politicians to tourists comes here for a good country "tuck-in." Fresh local ingredients are used whenever possible to concoct a delightful repertory of dishes—sweet-potato pancakes, shrimp and grits, sweet-corn chowder, sea scallops, and grilled pork tenderloin marinated for 24 hours. For a wild finishing touch, dig into bread pudding with bourbon butter, a recipe that

(Tips) **Finding Your Way**

For the location of restaurants outside the Historic District of Charleston, see the "Charleston Area Accommodations, Dining & Attractions" map, on p. 49.

once appeared in a cookbook published by the Baptist Church—until the pastor protested.

72 Queen St. (C) **843/577-2337.** www.poogansporch.com. Reservations recommended for dinner. Main courses $15–$25; Sun brunch $6.95–$14. AE, MC, V. Mon–Fri 11:30am–2:30pm and 5–9:30pm; Sat–Sun brunch 9am–3pm.

Tommy Condon's Irish Pub (Kids) IRISH/LOW COUNTRY Ireland is a long way from Charleston, but that country's spirit is evoked every night at this big, friendly place divided into four major sections, including a 100-seat covered deck. The interior pub with its hardwood bar is where you'll find us, downing a cold Irish beer. With its wainscoted walls and antique mirrors, it's just the place for nightly singalongs. It's not so much a men's bar as a family bar, with a children's menu prepared for "little leprechauns."

Starters include crab dip and nachos, or else skip ahead to salads and sandwiches, including an excellent chargrilled burger. Fish and chips and shepherd's pie are beloved favorites. For us, the best items on the menu are the Low Country seafood dishes, especially the local oysters and the Charleston crab cakes. A scrumptious bread pudding comes with a warm caramel sauce and vanilla-bean ice cream, though it might be more Irish to opt for the Bailey's Irish Cream cheesecake.

160 Church St. (C) **843/577-3818.** www.tommycondons.com. Lunch $7–$15; dinner main courses $15–$20. AE, DC, DISC, MC, V. Sun–Thurs 11am–10pm; Fri–Sat 11am–11pm. Closed Dec 25.

Vickery's Bar & Grill CUBAN/AMERICAN When the owners turned a former tire store into this inviting restaurant, they won an award for restoration. The open patio has made it a favorite with shoppers along King Street. The black-bean cake and barbecue ribs are typical starters; more unusual is the Southern-fried squid with a wasabi marmalade. A jumbo three-cheese ravioli is tossed with crawfish and tasso ham in a garlic Parmesan cream sauce, while the pecan-crusted snapper is slathered with a creamy bourbon and brown-sugar sauce. A local favorite, the Low Country sauté, is shrimp, crabmeat, and crawfish tails in bourbon butter served over creamy grits and topped with crispy fried oysters.

15 Beaufain St. (C) **843/577-5300.** www.vickerys.com. Main courses $6.95–$14. AE, DISC, MC, V. Daily 11:30am–2am. Closed Thanksgiving and Dec 25.

2 OTHER AREA RESTAURANTS

MOUNT PLEASANT
Expensive

Maverick ★ LOW COUNTRY/AMERICAN   At the previously recommended Old Village Post House (p. 63), you can enjoy the best-prepared food in Mount Pleasant, that suburb just across the bridge from Charleston. In this classic restaurant, Low Country dining favorites are a nightly feature, including Post House crab cakes with butter beans and okra or the classic shrimp and grits flavored with scallions and garlic. Another specialty is crusted chicken breast filled with Gruyère cheese and spinach and served with a country ham gravy. Pan-seared halibut also appears on the menu, served with a gazpacho salsa, avocado salad, and savory black beans with crispy tortillas. For dessert, try the Post House's popular and velvety chocolate mousse.

101 Pitt St., Mount Pleasant. ℂ **843/388-8935.** Main courses $17–$24. AE, MC, V. Sun 10am–2pm; Sun–Thurs 5:30–10pm; Fri–Sat 5–11pm.

Red Drum ★★ AMERICAN/SOUTHWESTERN   This self-proclaimed gastropub draws visitors to Mount Pleasant, just over the Cooper River Bridge from Charleston. Winner of numerous culinary awards, the chef and owner, Ben Berryhill, maintains a constant search for the best produce South Carolina has to offer. The influence of the Southwest is seen in dishes like wood-grilled salmon with a roasted red-pepper purée and a sweet-corn pudding in corn husks. The free-range chicken won us over when it was served with barbecued sweet potatoes and caramelized pumpkin seeds. All the appetizers are full of flavor, especially the molasses-grilled quail with a cinnamon-roasted cornbread and applewood bacon.

803 Coleman Blvd., Mount Pleasant. ℂ **843/849-0313.** www.reddrumrestaurant. com. Reservations recommended. Main courses $12–$38. AE, MC, V. Tues–Sat 5:30–10pm.

Moderate

Locklears SEAFOOD   In business for 2 decades, this restaurant has won a number of prizes for its oysters, chili, and she-crab soup. It is also the area's chief promoter of heart-healthy dining. Only the freshest of produce and seafood are used in Locklears' repertoire of fine dishes, which include such appetizers as fried calamari with drawn butter or bacon-wrapped shrimp with a soy-and-ginger dipping sauce. A fried oyster salad is an unusual treat, or you can order a seafood salad of the day. At lunchtime, dig into one of the homemade sandwiches—the crab burger is delectable. Seafood plates, complete with fries and creamy coleslaw, take the prize here.

320 Coleman Blvd., Mount Pleasant. © **843/884-3346.** Reservations recommended. Lunch $7–$12; dinner main courses $10–$20. AE, DISC, MC, V. Daily 11:30am–9pm. Closed Dec 25, Jan 1, and July 4.

Inexpensive

Gullah Cuisine ★ (Finds SOUTHERN   Do you find okra slimy and shun it? That culinary prejudice will fade at this unpretentious little dive, a tribute to the cuisine of the Gullahs, among the first African Americans to live in the Low Country sea islands. The okra gumbo is a delight, as is the she-crab soup, one of the best in town. Gullah cooking is evocative of Creole flavors, and the dirty rice served here delectably comes with shrimp, chicken, and andouille sausage. Locals come from miles around to sample the Southern fried chicken served with extra-cheesy macaroni. Of course, you've got to like fried foods, at least for a day—especially the succulent fried oysters.

1717 U.S. 17, Mount Pleasant. © **843/881-9076.** Reservations not necessary. Main courses $7–$11; lunch buffet Mon–Sat $7.25; Sun brunch $14. MC, V. Mon–Sat 11am–9:30pm (buffet till 2:30pm); Sun 11am–3:30pm.

AWENDAW
Moderate

SeeWee ★ (Finds LOW COUNTRY   SeeWee makes an art of Low Country frying, serving the best fried green tomatoes—dusted with corn flour—in the Charleston area. Its perfect accompaniment is a mild horseradish sauce. The cooks also fry okra, oysters, and yellow summer squash, and you'll be hard-pressed to find fried pickles superior to theirs. Locals devour the freshest shrimp in the area with—what else?—collard greens. But you don't have to go fried all the way—it's just assumed that all diners like hush puppies. Why not try the grilled shrimp with a tomato-basil cream sauce and lump crabmeat over pasta? And for dessert, the *Post and Courier* claimed that this "arsenal of incredible cakes and pies will bring you to your knees with thanks and praise."

4808 Hwy. 17 N., Awendaw. © **843/928-3609.** Reservations not necessary. Main courses $6.95–$13 lunch, $8.95–$19 dinner. MC, V. Mon–Fri 9am–9pm; Sat 8am–9:30pm; Sun 11am–3pm.

SUMMERVILLE
Very Expensive

The Dining Room at Woodlands ★★★ LOW COUNTRY   To get a real feel for the grandeur of the South, put on your Sunday best and head for this sumptuous retreat at the **Woodlands Resort & Inn** (p. 64). How good is this place? A recent poll of *Condé Nast*

Traveler readers rated Woodlands one of the top three restaurants in North America—plus it's the only one in the state awarded AAA's coveted five diamonds. It's located in a 1906 Greek Revival home, where guests dine under 14-foot coffered ceilings, surrounded by French doors, antiques, and crystal chandeliers.

The day begins early here, and breakfast features such delights as lump-crab hash with roasted peppers and poached eggs or buttermilk pecan pancakes topped with fresh berries. At dinnertime, to truly sample the best of the cuisine here, we suggest you opt for one of the tasting menus. You may find yourself enjoying tender Kobe beef seared with foie gras; wild Maine black mussels steamed in sake and served with a black-bean sauce; or a free-form lasagna made with rock shrimp, scallops, and truffles. Desserts don't get much better than the passion-fruit mousse or the almond tart with fresh berries and apricot coulis. The best food in the entire greater Charleston area is also backed up by an award-winning wine list.

In the Woodlands Resort & Inn, 125 Parsons Rd., Summerville. ℂ **800/774-9999** or 843/875-2600. www.woodlandsinn.com. Reservations required. Breakfast $15–$30; Sun brunch $39; lunch main courses $7–$18, 3-course business lunch $19; dinner set menus $70 for 5 courses, $78 for 6 courses; 5-course vegetable menu $63. AE, DISC, MC, V. Daily 7–10am, 11am–1:30pm, and 2:30–9:30pm.

6

Exploring Charleston

Once we've settled in, we always head for the **Battery** (officially, White Point Gardens) to get the feel of this city. Right on the end of the peninsula, facing the Cooper River and the harbor, it has a landscaped park shaded by palmettos and live oaks, with walkways lined with old monuments. The view of the harbor goes out to Fort Sumter. We like to stroll along the sea wall on East Battery Street and Murray Boulevard and take in the Charleston ambience.

Before your trip, contact the **Charleston Area Convention & Visitors Bureau** (CACVB; ℭ **800/774-0006** or 843/853-8000; www.charlestoncvb.com) for information on tours, attractions, and special events.

Note: You can visit nine of the city's most visible historic attractions with the 2-day **Heritage Passport,** which costs $45 ($30 for children 6–12). This pass provides one-time admission, over the course of 2 consecutive days, to the Charleston Museum, the Heyward-Washington House, the Joseph Manigault House, Middleton Place, Drayton Hall, the Nathaniel Russell House, the Gibbes Museum, the Aiken-Rhett House, and the Edmondston-Alston House. The pass is available only from the CACVB's main downtown branch, the **Charleston Visitor Center,** 375 Meeting St. (ℭ **800/774-0006** or 843/853-8000), open daily from 8:30am to 5pm.

1 CHARLESTON'S TOP ATTRACTIONS

A CONFEDERATE FORT & A SUBMARINE

Fort Sumter National Monument ★★★   It was here, on April 12, 1861, that Confederate forces launched a 34-hour bombardment of the fort. Union forces eventually surrendered, and the Rebels occupied the federal ground that became a symbol of Southern resistance. This action, however, led to a declaration of war in Washington. Amazingly, Confederate troops held onto Sumter for nearly 4 years, though it was almost continually bombarded by the Yankees. When evacuation finally came, the fort was nothing but a heap of rubble.

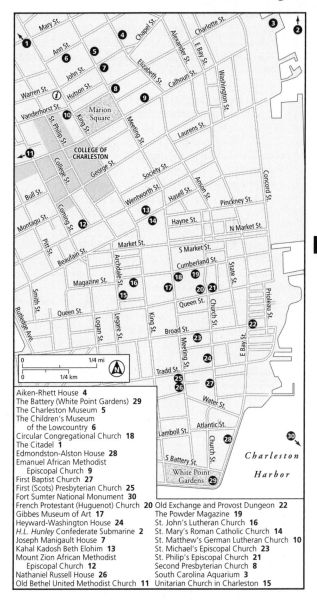

Aiken-Rhett House 4
The Battery (White Point Gardens) 29
The Charleston Museum 5
The Children's Museum
    of the Lowcountry 6
Circular Congregational Church 18
The Citadel 1
Edmondston-Alston House 28
Emanuel African Methodist
    Episcopal Church 9
First Baptist Church 27
First (Scots) Presbyterian Church 25
Fort Sumter National Monument 30
French Protestant (Huguenot) Church 20
Gibbes Museum of Art 17
Heyward-Washington House 24
H.L. Hunley Confederate Submarine 2
Joseph Manigault House 7
Kahal Kadosh Beth Elohim 13
Mount Zion African Methodist
    Episcopal Church 12
Nathaniel Russell House 26
Old Bethel United Methodist Church 11

Old Exchange and Provost Dungeon 22
The Powder Magazine 19
St. John's Lutheran Church 16
St. Mary's Roman Catholic Church 14
St. Matthew's German Lutheran Church 10
St. Michael's Episcopal Church 23
St. Philip's Episcopal Church 21
Second Presbyterian Church 8
South Carolina Aquarium 3
Unitarian Church in Charleston 15

Today, park rangers are on hand to answer your questions, and you can explore gun emplacements and visit a small museum filled with artifacts related to the siege. A complete tour of the fort, conducted daily from 9am to 5pm, takes about 2 hours.

Most visitors take the tour of the fort and harbor offered by **Fort Sumter Tours/SpiritLine Cruises,** 360 Concord St., Ste. 201 (*©* **800/ 789-3678** or 843/881-7337; www.spiritlinecruises.com). You can board at either of two locations: Liberty Square, in downtown Charleston, or Mount Pleasant's Patriots Point, the site of one of the world's largest naval and maritime museums. Sailing times vary, but from March to Labor Day, there are generally three trips per day from each location. Winter sailings are more limited; call for details. Each departure point offers ample parking, and the boats that carry you to Fort Sumter are sightseeing yachts built for the purpose—they're clean, safe, and equipped with modern conveniences.

In Charleston Harbor, 40 Patriots Point Rd., Mount Pleasant. *©* **800/789-3678** or 843/722-2628. www.spiritlinecruises.com. Admission to fort free; boat trip $16 adults, $15 seniors, $10 children 6–11; free for children 5 and under.

H. L. Hunley Confederate Submarine ★★★   One of the greatest and most sought-after artifacts in the history of naval warfare can now be viewed by the public. The Confederate submarine *H. L. Hunley,* a hand-cranked vessel fashioned of locomotive boilers, sank the Union blockade vessel USS *Housatonic* in 1864. The sinking of the Union ship launched the age of submarine warfare. But the submarine and its nine-member crew mysteriously vanished off Sullivan's Island shortly after completing the sub's historic mission. The vessel was finally located in 1995, sparking headlines across the world. It was eventually raised and brought to the old Charleston Naval Base for preservation, and the mystery of what happened to the Confederate sailors may have been solved in 2008. Scientists found that the crew had not set the pump to remove water from the crew compartment; that could have meant that crew members suffocated as they used up the available air. The bones of the crew members were buried in a historic ceremony on April 17, 2004, at the Magnolia Cemetery. The sub, which rests in a tank of 50°F water, can be visited only on weekends via 20-minute tours.

Warren Lasch Conservation Center, 1250 Supply St., Building 255, North Charleston. *©* **877/448-6539** or 843/744-2186. www.hunley.org. Admission $12, free for children 5 and under. Sat 10am–5pm; Sun noon–5pm.

HISTORIC HOMES

Aiken-Rhett House   Now deep into its decay, the Aiken-Rhett House is a mere ghost of its former self. The house was constructed in 1818 by merchant John Robinson and significantly expanded by

Governor and Mrs. William Aiken in the 1830s and 1850s. The property most likely looked glorious in 1858, before the outbreak of the Civil War. The house is decorated with crystal and bronze chandeliers, classical sculpture, paintings, and antiques, brought back from Europe by the governor and his lady. Original outbuildings include the kitchens, slave quarters, stables, privies, and cattle sheds. A major restoration is directly needed.

48 Elizabeth St. © **843/723-1159.** www.historiccharleston.org. Admission $10. Mon–Sat 10am–5pm; Sun 2–5pm.

Edmondston-Alston House ★★★   On High Battery, an elegant section of Charleston, this house—built in 1825 by Charles Edmondston, a merchant and wharf owner—was one of the first in the city to be constructed in the late Federal style. Edmondston sold it to Charles Alston, a Low Country rice planter, who modified it in Greek Revival style. The house has remained in the Alston family, which has opened the first two floors to visitors. Inside are heirloom furnishings, silver, and paintings. It was here in 1861 that General Beauregard joined the Alston family to watch the bombardment of Fort Sumter. General Robert E. Lee found refuge here when his hotel uptown caught fire in 1861.

21 E. Battery. © **843/722-7171.** www.middletonplace.org. Admission $10 adults, $8 children 7–15. Guided tours Tues–Sat 10am–4:30pm; daily 1:30–4:30pm.

Heyward-Washington House ★★★   In a district of Charleston called Cabbage Row, this 1772 house was built by Daniel Heyward, often called "the rice king," and was the setting for DuBose Heyward's *Porgy*. It was also the home of Thomas Heyward, Jr., a signer of the Declaration of Independence. President George Washington bedded down here in 1791. Many of the fine period pieces in the house are the work of Thomas Elfe, one of America's most famous cabinetmakers. The restored 18th-century kitchen is the only historic kitchen in the city that is open to the public. It stands behind the main house, along with the servants' quarters and the garden.

87 Church St. (btw. Tradd and Broad sts.). © **843/722-0354.** www.charleston museum.org. Admission $10 adults, $5 children 3–12. Combination ticket to the Heyward-Washington House, Joseph Manigault House, and Charleston Museum $22 adults. Mon–Sat 10am–5pm; Sun 1–5pm. Tours leave every half-hour until 4:30pm.

Joseph Manigault House ★   This 1803 Adams-style residence, a National Historic Landmark, was a wealthy rice planter's home. The house features a curving central staircase and an outstanding collection of Charlestonian, American, English, and French period furnishings. It's located diagonally across from the Charleston Visitor Center.

350 Meeting St. (at John St.). © **843/723-2997.** www.charlestonmuseum.org. Admission $10 adults, $5 children 3–12. Combination ticket to the Heyward-Washington House, Joseph Manigault House, and Charleston Museum $22 adults. Mon–Sat 10am–5pm; Sun 1–5pm. Last tour is at 4:30pm.

Nathaniel Russell House ★★★ One of America's finest examples of Federal architecture, this 1808 house was completed by Nathaniel Russell, one of Charleston's richest merchants. It is celebrated architecturally for its "free-flying" staircase, spiraling unsupported for three floors. The staircase's elliptical shape is repeated throughout the house. The interiors are ornate with period furnishings, especially the elegant music room with its golden harp and neoclassical-style sofa.

51 Meeting St. © **843/724-8481.** http://historiccharleston.org. Admission $10 adults, $5 children 6–16. Combination ticket to the Aiken-Rhett House and the Nathaniel Russell House $16. Guided tours Mon–Sat 10am–5pm; Sun and holidays 2–5pm.

2 MUSEUMS & GALLERIES

Charleston Museum ★★ The Charleston Museum, founded in 1773, is the oldest museum in the U.S. The collections focus on the social and natural history of Charleston and the South Carolina coastal region. The full-scale replica of the famed Confederate submarine *H. L. Hunley* standing outside the museum is one of the most-photographed subjects in the city. The museum also has the largest silver collection in Charleston, early crafts, historic relics, and hands-on exhibits for children in the "Discover Me" room.

360 Meeting St. © **843/722-2996.** www.charlestonmuseum.org. Admission $10 adults, $5 children 3–12. Combination ticket to the Heyward-Washington House, Joseph Manigault House, and Charleston Museum $22 adults. Mon–Sat 9am–5pm; Sun 1–5pm.

Gibbes Museum of Art ★ Established in 1905 by the Carolina Art Association, the Gibbes Museum contains an intriguing collection of prints and drawings spanning from the 18th century to the present. On display are landscapes, genre scenes, panoramic views of the harbor, and portraits of South Carolinians. The museum's collection of some 400 miniature portraits ranks as one of the most comprehensive in the country.

135 Meeting St. © **843/722-2706.** www.gibbesmuseum.org. Admission $9 adults; $7 seniors, students, and military; $5 children 6–18. Tues–Sat 10am–5pm; Sun 1–5pm. Closed Mon and holidays.

3 MORE ATTRACTIONS

The Citadel ★   The all-male (at that time) Citadel was established in 1842 as an arsenal and a refuge for whites in the event of a slave uprising. In 1922, it moved to its present location. Pat Conroy's novel *The Lords of Discipline* is based on his 4 years at the school. Since 1995, when the first woman notoriously enrolled, women have joined the ranks with young men. The first shot of the Civil War was fired on January 9, 1861, by Citadel cadets on the Union steamer USS *Star of the West.* Several shots were fired and three actually struck the ship. There is a monument on campus commemorating the shelling. The campus of this military college features buildings of Moorish design, with crenelated battlements and sentry towers. It is especially interesting to visit on a Friday when the college is in session and the public is invited to a precision-drill parade on the quadrangle at 3:45pm. For a history of the Citadel, stop at the **Citadel Memorial Archives Museum** (*✆* 843/953-6846).

Moultrie St. and Elmwood Ave. *✆* 843/225-3294. www.citadel.edu. Free admission. Daily 24 hr. for drive-through visits; museum Sun–Fri 2–5pm, Sat noon–5pm. Closed religious, national, and school holidays.

The Children's Museum of the Lowcountry (Kids   This is a hands-on learning place for both children and their parents, with a stated desire of sparking the love of learning in kids from 3 months to 12 years. This is done through interactive, hands-on experiences in the arts and sciences. Children can, for example, explore the life of a shrimper on the *Anna Marie,* or get lost in medieval life in a model castle. Other adventures include racing boats down rapids, boarding a pirate ship, making rain indoors, and growing vegetables in an all-organic kids' garden.

25 Ann St. *✆* 843/853-8962. www.explorecml.org. Admission $7 per person but free for kids under 1 year. Tues–Sat 9am–5pm; Sun 1–5pm.

International Center for Birds of Prey   This 152-acre attraction contains more than 80 species of birds of prey. It's located 12 miles north of Mount Pleasant and 15 miles from the center of Charleston; to get there, follow U.S. 17 north through Mount Pleasant to Awendaw and look for the signs. The collection includes eagles, hawks, owls, falcons, kites, and vultures. Guided walking tours are available, and free-flight demonstrations are staged.

4872 Seewee Rd., Awendaw. *✆* 843/971-7474. www.thecenterforbirdsofprey.org. Admission $12 adults, $10 children 6–18, free for children 5 and under. Thurs–Sat only 10am–5pm.

Old Exchange and Provost Dungeon ★ This is a stop that many visitors overlook, but it's one of the three most important Colonial buildings in the U.S. because of its role as a prison during the American Revolution. In 1873, the building became City Hall. You'll find a large collection of antique chairs, supplied by the local Daughters of the American Revolution, each of whom brought a chair here from home in 1921.

122 E. Bay St. © **843/727-2165.** www.oldexchange.com. Admission $8 adults, $4 children 7–12. Daily 9am–5pm. Closed Thanksgiving and Dec 23–25.

The Powder Magazine Used to store gunpowder in the defense of the city during the Revolutionary War, this is the oldest public building in South Carolina. It is also the only surviving building from the heyday of the Colonial governors of the state, called "Lord Proprietors." The "magazine" was constructed in 1713 to store the ammunition for the defense of the British settlement of Charles Towne. Its 32-inch-thick brick walls were designed to withstand heavy bombardment, as the town was subjected to repeated attacks from Native Americans, pirates, and Spanish and French warships. Purchased by the National Society of Colonial Dames in 1899, the building is now a museum of early Charleston history, displaying armor, costumes, antiques, and other memorabilia and artifacts of 18th-century life.

79 Cumberland St. © **843/722-9350.** www.powdermag.org. Admission $3 adults, $1 children 6–12. Mon–Sat 10am–4pm; Sun 1–4pm.

South Carolina Aquarium ★ Visitors can explore Southern aquatic life in an attraction filled with thousands of enchanting creatures and plants in amazing habitats, from five major regions of the Appalachian Watershed. Jutting into the Charleston Harbor for 2,000 feet, the focal point of this attraction is a 93,000-square-foot aquarium featuring a two-story **Great Ocean Tank.** Contained within are more than 800 animals, including deadly sharks as well as sea turtles and stingrays. One of the most offbeat exhibits in the **Coastal Plain Gallery** replicates a blackwater swamp, with atmospheric fog, a spongy floor, and twinkling lights. **Secrets of the Amazon** features the diversity of this endangered region in sights, sounds, and adventure. You'll meet such creatures as a giant green anaconda, poison dart frogs, four-eyed fish, and flesh-devouring piranhas. New in 2008 is the **Camp Carolina** exhibit, a child-friendly interactive display on how to successfully appreciate the great Carolina outdoors without leaving an ecologically destructive "footprint." Wandering around in more or less natural-looking habitats are native species of catfish, salamanders, skunks (de-scented), barn owls, and snakes, all on view and all with signage indicating their needs, preferences, and the damage they might potentially do if molested or disturbed.

100 Aquarium Wharf. ☎ **843/720-1990.** www.scaquarium.org. Admission $18 adults, $17 seniors (62 and older), $11 children 2–11. Apr 1–Aug 15 Mon–Sat 9am–6pm, Sun noon–6pm; Aug 16–Mar 31 Mon–Sat 9am–5pm, Sun noon–5pm.

4 HISTORIC CHURCHES & SYNAGOGUES

Charleston offers the greatest collection of historic churches in the South. Some keep regular visiting hours; others do not (see below for set hours, if available). Sometimes the doors will be closed, and you'll have to admire the church for its particular facade. If the doors are open, you're always welcome to step inside. Of course, everyone is welcome to attend services.

Circular Congregational Church   Founded in 1681, this is one of the oldest churches in the South, its burial grounds dating back to 1695. In 1861, a fire destroyed the building. The fourth and present church to stand here dates from 1891. The structure you see today has integrated the brick from earlier churches, one of which was leveled in an 1886 earthquake. Once called the Independent Church of Charles Towne, this church opened the first Sunday school in South Carolina.

150 Meeting St. ☎ **843/577-6400.** www.circularchurch.org. Free guided tours; call ahead to confirm times.

Emanuel African Methodist Episcopal Church   Founded in 1791 by free blacks and slaves, this is the oldest church of its type in the South. With a sanctuary holding 2,500, it has the largest black congregation south of Baltimore. The original gas lanterns hanging inside date from its founding. In 1822, Denmark Vessey urged the congregation into an insurrection, but authorities learned of the rebellion and closed the church. It was reopened in 1865, and eventually rebuilt in 1891 into the present structure you can visit today.

110 Calhoun St. ☎ **843/722-2561.** www.nps.gov and www.emanuelamechurch. org. Free admission. Mon–Thurs 9am–1pm and 2–4pm; Fri 9am–3pm.

First Baptist Church   Established in 1682, this was the first Baptist church to open in the South. In 1755, the pastor, Oliver Hart, founded the Charleston Baptist Association, the earliest organization for the education of Baptist ministers in the South. He fled from the British in 1780, never to return. The present sanctuary was designed by Robert Mills, America's first native architect. The sanctuary has been the victim of many natural disasters, including a tornado in 1885, an earthquake in 1886, and Hurricane Hugo in 1989.

61 Church St. ✆ **843/722-3896.** www.fbcharleston.org. Free guided tours Tues–Wed 10am–noon; call ahead to make arrangements.

First (Scots) Presbyterian Church This is the fifth-oldest church in Charleston, founded in 1731 by Caledonian immigrants who did not want to become members of the Anglican faith. The seal of Scotland in the windows over the main entrance can still be seen. The first congregation consisted of a dozen Scottish families who left the Independent Church of Charles Towne in 1731. The church was constructed in 1814; its design was inspired by St. Mary's Cathedral in Baltimore, whose architect, Benjamin Latrobe, also designed the U.S. Capitol. The walls of this massive brick church are 3 feet thick and covered with stucco, and twin towers rise above a pillared portico. The church bell that was donated to the Confederacy during the Civil War, to be melted down for use as cannonballs, was recently replaced by an English bell made in 1814, the same time of the church's construction. The cemetery has more than 50 tombstones from the 16th century.

53 Meeting St. ✆ **843/722-8882.** www.first-scots.org. Free admission. Open to the public, but no set hours.

French Protestant (Huguenot) Church This is the only remaining independent Huguenot church in the U.S., offering weekly church services in English as well as an annual service in French each spring. It was founded in 1681 by Huguenot refugees from Protestant persecutions in France. The first church built on this site in 1687 was destroyed in 1796 in an attempt to stop a fire. It was replaced in 1800, only to be dismantled in 1844 to make way for the present Gothic Revival building designed by Edward B. White. The church suffered heavy damage by shellfire during the Civil War and was nearly demolished in the earthquake of 1886. The original Tucker organ—one of the rarest in the country—is from 1845.

136 Church St. (at Queen St.). ✆ **843/722-4385.** www.frenchchurch.org. Free admission. Call ahead for tour times.

Kahal Kadosh Beth Elohim This is the fourth-oldest synagogue in the U.S. and the oldest Reform synagogue in the world. A congregation was formed in 1749, and the synagogue was erected in 1794, although it was destroyed by fire in 1838. The present building was constructed in 1840 as one of the country's finest examples of Greek Revival architecture. Francis Salvador, a synagogue member, signed the Declaration of Independence. He became the first known Jew to die in the Revolutionary War.

90 Hasell St. ℂ 843/723-1090. www.kkbe.org. Free 20-min. guided tours Sun–Thurs 10am–4pm; Fri 10am–noon.

Mount Zion African Methodist Episcopal Church Purchased in 1882, this was the first brick building owned by blacks in Charleston. It was purchased by members of the Emanuel A.M.E. Church when that sanctuary had become too crowded. The 54th and 55th Massachusetts Regiment worshiped here while stationed in Charleston. The church is known for offering the best choral music in Charleston, with six different choirs. Music ranges from classical hymns to original and unarranged black spirituals, many from the 18th century.

5 Glebe St. ℂ 843/722-8118. www.nps.gov and www.ame-church.com. Free admission. Mon, Wed, and Fri 11:30am–1:30pm.

Old Bethel United Methodist Church This is the third-oldest surviving church building in Charleston. Founded and paid for by both white and black citizens, it was built in 1797, with the finishing touches applied in 1807. By 1840, its black members had left to form their own congregation. In 1852, the church was moved to the western part of its lot for the black population to use, and a new church was built on the original lot for the white worshipers. After that church was given to the black members in 1880, Old Bethel moved across the street to its present location, where it currently serves the black population, many of its members descendants of the 1880s congregation.

222 Calhoun St. ℂ 843/722-3470. www.nps.gov. Free admission. Open to the public, but no set hours.

Old St. Andrew's Parish Church Founded and built in 1706 in the West Ashley area of Charleston, opening onto Hwy. 61, this is the oldest surviving church in Charleston. Part of the church was constructed from bricks used as ballast on ships arriving in the port of Charleston, and a number of historic tombs are found in the courtyard. In late March or early April—depending on flowers in bloom and the Easter holiday—the church sponsors its annual Tea Room and Gift Shop fundraiser, with waitresses dressed in period costumes serving such delicacies as magnolia pie. During the fundraiser, an onsite gift shop is open daily, selling cookbooks, jams, jellies, and crafts made by parish members.

2604 Ashley River Rd. ℂ 843/766-1541. www.oldstandrews.org. Free admission. Mon–Fri 8am–2pm.

St. John's Lutheran Church   Called the "Mother Church of Lutherans in South Carolina," this antique sanctuary celebrated its 250th anniversary in 1992. Founded by German immigrants, the congregation was established in 1742, with the first church begun in 1759. The edifice today is from 1817. Its church bell was melted down and given to the Confederacy for use as cannonballs in the Civil War. It wasn't until 1992 that the bell was replaced. After the damage wreaked by Hurricane Hugo, the church spent $1 million in repairs and restoration. A prominent member of its congregation is former U.S. Sen. Ernest F. Hollings.

5 Clifford St. ℭ **843/723-2426.** www.stjohnscharleston.org. Free admission. Tours by appointment only.

St. Mary's Roman Catholic Church   Established in 1789, this is the oldest Roman Catholic church in the state and the mother church of the diocese for South Carolina, North Carolina, and Georgia. The original church was destroyed by fire in 1838, but was rebuilt in 1839, its ceiling hand-painted by Caesare Porte of Rome. Many of the tombstones in the churchyard are in French, indicating the early French influence that prevailed at the church.

89 Hasell St. ℭ **843/722-7696.** www.nps.gov. Free admission. Mon–Fri 9:30am–3:30pm.

St. Matthew's German Lutheran Church   Intended for German-speaking settlers, this was the second Lutheran congregation formed in the city, in 1840. The building, erected in 1872 and rebuilt after a fire in 1965, is known for its 297-foot steeple, which remains the tallest in the state. The stained-glass windows in the apse under the balcony are part of the original building.

405 King St. ℭ **843/723-1611.** www.nps.gov. Free admission. Mon–Fri 8:30am–4:30pm.

St. Michael's Episcopal Church ★   A National Historic Landmark, this is one of the most impressive of America's Colonial churches, and its edifice remains the oldest in Charleston. The architect is not known, but the church was constructed between 1752 and 1761. In some respects it evokes St. Martin-in-the-Fields, a London landmark by James Gibbs. Seen for miles around, its 186-foot steeple is a Charleston landmark, its clock bell towers imported in 1764. The steeple tower was used as a compass-positioning point for artillery targets during the Revolutionary and Civil wars. Both George Washington and Robert E. Lee attended services here.

71 Broad St. ℭ **843/723-0603.** www.stmichaelschurch.net. Free admission. Mon–Fri 9am–4:30pm; Sat 9am–noon. After the 10:30am Sun service, there is an official 20-min. guided tour.

St. Philip's Episcopal Church   This impressive church is nick-named the "Lighthouse Church" because a light was once put in its steeple to guide ships into the harbor. The present building dates from 1835 to 1838 and still houses the oldest congregation in South Carolina. During the Civil War, the church bells were donated to the Confederacy to be melted down and recast into cannonballs. Buried in the churchyard are such notables as John C. Calhoun, Edward Rutledge, Charles Pinckney, and DuBose Heyward.

142 Church St. (C) **843/722-7734.** www.nps.gov and www.stphilipschurchsc.org. Free admission. Mon–Fri 10am–noon and 2–4pm (call ahead to verify times).

Second Presbyterian Church ★   Built in 1809, this is the old-est Presbyterian church in Charleston, and it's been designated by the Presbyterian Church of the United States as Historical Site Number One. When it was first constructed, it was so large and cavernous that the minister's voice couldn't be heard. Two pastors in a row died of pneumonia because of the winter chill. Remodeling in the late 1800s added a boiler beneath the church floor, thereby solving the heating problem, and architectural changes that raised the floor by 3 feet and lowered the ceiling by 16 feet eventually solved the acoustical issues.

342 Meeting St. (at Charlotte St.). (C) **843/723-9237.** www.secondpresbyterian church.org. Free admission. Call ahead if you plan to visit the church.

Unitarian Church in Charleston ★   The oldest Unitarian church in the South, this is the second-oldest church in Charleston. Its construction began in 1774 but was halted when the Revolution-ary War broke out. The site was used as a stable and as headquarters for the militia. It was restored and rededicated in 1787, and remod-eled and enlarged in 1852. Francis Lee designed the fan-vaulted ceil-ing, nave, and chancel, using the Chapel of Henry VII in Westminster Abbey in London for his inspiration. Designated a National Historic Landmark, the church is one of the country's most stellar examples of the Perpendicular Gothic Revival style, and was the first to incorpo-rate this type of architecture.

4 Archdale St. (C) **843/723-4617.** www.charlestonuu.org. Free admission. Call ahead to reserve a tour.

---

5 PARKS & GARDENS

See also the listing for **Magnolia Plantation** under "Nearby Planta-tions," below. Another park of great interest lies on the northern periphery of Charleston, **Palmetto Islands County Park** (p. 104).

Charles Towne Landing State Historic Site ★★   This 663-acre park is located on the site where English settlers first landed in 1670, thereby establishing the birthplace of the Carolina colony and the plantation system that eventually spread throughout the American South. The park's infrastructure and pathways have been upgraded, and a visitor center contains interactive exhibits describing the history of the first permanent English settlement in the Carolinas. A history trail, with the option of listening to a prerecorded audio tour, enables visitors to experience the reality of those early settlers. Interpretive park rangers in 17th-century dress tend heirloom crops, fire cannons and muskets, and deliver information about the daily life of the era's indentured servants. You can wander through informal English gardens and an Animal Forest, home to species that were native to the area at the time of the original settlement. There's absolutely no flashy theme-park atmosphere here: just a commitment to natural beauty, archaeology, and history.

500 Old Towne Rd. (S.C. 171, btw. U.S. 17 and I-26). ℭ **843/852-4200.** www. charlestowne.org and http://southcarolinaparks.com. Admission $7.50 adults, $3.50 children 6–15, free for children 5 and under, free for those with disabilities. Daily 9am–5pm. Closed Dec 24–25.

Cypress Gardens ★★   This 163-acre swamp garden was used as a freshwater reserve for Dean Hall, a huge Cooper River rice plantation, and was given to the city in 1963. Today, the giant cypress trees draped with Spanish moss provide an unforgettable setting for flat-bottom boats that glide among their knobby roots. Footpaths wind through a profusion of azaleas, camellias, daffodils, and other colorful blooms. Visitors share the swamp with alligators, pileated woodpeckers, wood ducks, otters, and barred owls. The gardens are worth a visit at any time of year, but they're at their most colorful in March and April. Also on-site are a reptile center, aquarium, aviary, and butterfly house.

3030 Cypress Gardens Rd. (off U.S. 52), Moncks Corner. ℭ **843/553-0515.** www. cypressgardens.info. Admission $10 adults, $9 seniors, $5 children 6–12. Daily 9am–5pm. Closed major holidays. Take U.S. 52 some 24 miles north of Charleston.

6 NEARBY PLANTATIONS

Boone Hall Plantation & Gardens ★★★   This unique plantation is approached via a famous **Avenue of Oaks ★★★**, lined with huge old moss-draped trees planted in 1743 by Captain Thomas Boone. The first floor of the plantation house is elegantly furnished and open to the public. Outbuildings include the circular smokehouse and slave cabins constructed of bricks made on the plantation.

A large grove of pecan trees lies behind the house. Note that Boone Hall is not an original structure, but a replica; history purists may be disappointed in the plantation house, but the grounds are stunning and worth visiting. **Boone Hall Farms** sells produce grown on the plantation and offers seasonal pick-your-own crops. Also see p. 104 for details on the family-friendly **Palmetto Islands County Park.**

1235 Long Point Rd. (U.S. 17/701), Mount Pleasant. ✆ **843/884-4371.** http://boonehallplantation.com. Admission $18 adults, $15 seniors 65 and over, $7.50 children 6–12. Apr to Labor Day Mon–Sat 8:30am–6:30pm, Sun 1–5pm; day after Labor Day to Mar Mon–Sat 9am–5pm, Sun 1–4pm. Take U.S. 17/701 9 miles north of Charleston.

Drayton Hall ★★ This is one of the oldest surviving plantations, built in 1738 and owned by the Drayton family until 1974. Framed by majestic live oaks, the Georgian-Palladian house is a property of the National Trust for Historic Preservation. Its hand-carved woodwork and plasterwork represent new-world craftsmanship at its finest. Because such modern elements as electricity, plumbing, and central heating have never put in an appearance, the house is much as it was in its early years; in fact, it is displayed unfurnished. You can visit an African-American cemetery and take self-guided walks along the river.

3380 Ashley River Rd. (S.C. 61). ✆ **843/769-2600.** www.draytonhall.org. Admission $15 adults, $8 children 12–18, $6 children 6–11. Mar–Oct daily 8:30am–5pm, with tours on the hour; Nov–Feb daily 9:30am–4pm. Closed Thanksgiving and Dec 25. Take U.S. 17 S. to S.C. 61; it's 9 miles northwest of Charleston.

Magnolia Plantation & Gardens ★★★ Ten generations of the Drayton family have lived here continuously since the 1670s. They haven't had much luck keeping a roof over their heads; the first mansion burned just after the Revolution, and the second was set afire by General Sherman. But you can't call the replacement modern: A simple pre-Revolutionary house was barged down from Summerville and set on the foundations of its unfortunate predecessors. The house has been filled with museum-quality Early American furniture; an art gallery has been added to the house as well.

The flower gardens—among the most beautiful in the U.S.—reach their peak bloom in March and April, but are colorful year-round. You can tour the house, the gardens (including an herb garden, horticultural maze, topiary garden, and biblical garden), a petting zoo, and a waterfowl refuge, or walk or bike the wildlife trails.

Other sights include a restored antebellum cabin, a rice barge on display beside the Ashley River, and a Nature Train that carries guests on a 45-minute ride around the plantation's perimeter. Low Country wildlife is visible in marsh, woodland, and swamp settings. The **Audubon Swamp Garden,** also on the grounds, is an independently operated 60-acre cypress swamp that offers a close look at egrets, alligators, wood ducks, otters, turtles, and herons.

3550 Ashley River Rd. (S.C. 61). ✆ **800/367-3517** or 843/571-1266. www. magnoliaplantation.com. Admission to garden and grounds $15 adults, $14 seniors, $10 children 6–12. Tour of plantation house additional $7 for ages 6 and up; children 5 and under not allowed to tour the house. Admission to Audubon Swamp Garden $7 adults, $6 seniors, $5 children 6–12. Magnolia Plantation and Audubon Swamp Gardens summer daily 8am–5:30pm; call for winter hours.

Middleton Place ★★★   This was the home of Henry Middleton, president of the First Continental Congress, whose son, Arthur, was a signer of the Declaration of Independence. Today, this National Historic Landmark includes America's oldest landscaped gardens, the Middleton Place House, and the Plantation Stableyards.

The gardens, begun in 1741, reflect the elegant symmetry of European gardens of that period. Ornamental lakes, terraces, and plantings of camellias, azaleas, magnolias, and crape myrtle accent the grand design.

The Middleton Place House itself was built in 1755, but in 1865, all but the south flank was ransacked and burned by Union troops. The house was restored in the 1870s and today houses collections of fine silver, furniture, rare first editions by Mark Catesby and John James Audubon, and portraits by Benjamin West and Thomas Sully. In the stable yards, craftspeople demonstrate life on a plantation of yesteryear. There are also horses, mules, hogs, cows, sheep, and goats.

A plantation lunch is served daily from 11am to 3pm at the **Middleton Place Restaurant,** a replica of an original rice mill. *American Way* magazine cited this restaurant as one of the top 10 representing American cuisine at its best. Specialties include she-crab soup, Hoppin' John and ham biscuits, okra gumbo, Sea Island shrimp, and corn pudding. Dinner, offered daily from 5 to 9pm, is likely to include panned (pan-seared) quail with ham, sea scallops, or broiled oysters. For dinner reservations, call ✆ **843/556-6020.**

4300 Ashley River Rd. (S.C. 61). ✆ **800/782-3608** or 843/556-6020. www.middleton place.org. Admission to gardens and stable yard $25 adults, $5 children 7–15. Tour of house additional $10 adults, $6 children 6–12. Gardens and stable yards daily 9am–5pm; house Mon noon–4:30pm, Tues–Sun 10am–4:30pm. Take U.S. 17 W. to S.C. 61 (Ashley River Rd.) 14 miles northwest of Charleston.

---

6

7 ESPECIALLY FOR KIDS

For more than 300 years, Charleston has been the home of pirates, patriots, and presidents. Your child can see firsthand the **Great Hall at the Old Exchange,** where President Washington danced; view the

Provost Dungeons, where South Carolina patriots spent their last days; and touch the last remaining structural evidence of the **Charleston Seawall.** Children will take special delight in **Charles Towne Landing** and **Middleton Place.** At **Fort Sumter,** they can see where the Civil War began. They'll also enjoy **Magnolia Plantation,** with its Audubon Swamp Garden.

Kids and Navy vets alike will love the aircraft carrier **USS *Yorktown,*** at **Patriots Point,** 2 miles east of the Cooper River Bridge. Its World War II, Korean, and Vietnam exploits are documented in exhibits, and general naval history is illustrated through models of ships, planes, and weapons. You can wander through the bridge wheelhouse, flight and hangar decks, chapel, and sick bay, and view the film *The Fighting Lady,* which depicts life aboard the carrier. Also at Patriots Point are the World War II destroyer *Laffey,* the World War II submarine *Clamagore,* and the cutter *Ingham.* Patriots Point is open daily from 9am to 6pm April through October, until 5pm November through March. Admission is $18 for adults, $15 for seniors 62 and over and military personnel in uniform, and $11 for kids 6 to 11. Adjacent is the fine 18-hole public Patriots Point Golf Course. For further information, call © **866/ 831-1720** or visit **www.patriotspoint.org**.

8 ORGANIZED TOURS

BY HORSE & CARRIAGE The **Old South Carriage,** 14 Anson St. (© **843/723-9712;** www.oldsouthcarriagetours.com), offers narrated horse-drawn carriage tours through the Historic District, daily from 9am to dusk. A 1-hour carriage tour spans a distance of 2½ miles, covering 30 blocks of the Historic District. The cost is $21 for adults, $13 for children 3 to 11.

BY MULE TEAM **Palmetto Carriage Tours,** 40 N. Market St., at Guignard Street (© **843/723-8145;** www.carriagetour.com), uses mule teams for its guided tours of the old city. Tours originate at the Big Red Barn behind the Rainbow Market, daily from 9am to 5pm. The cost is $20 for adults, $12 for children 4 to 11.

BY BOAT **SpiritLine Cruises,** 360 Concord St., Ste. 201 (© **800/ 789-3678** or 843/722-2628; http://spiritlinecruises.com), offers a **Fort Sumter Tour** by boat, departing daily from two locations: downtown Charleston's Liberty Square and Mount Pleasant's Patriots Point Naval & Maritime Museum. This is the only harbor tour to stop at Fort Sumter, target of the opening shots of the Civil War. There's also a **Charleston Harbor Tour,** with departures from Patriots Point. The

2-hour cruise passes the Battery, Charleston Port, Castle Pinckney, Drum Island, Fort Sumter, and the aircraft carrier USS *Yorktown,* sailing under the Cooper River Bridge and on to other sights. Rates for both tours are $16 for adults, $15 for seniors, $10 for children 6 to 11, and free for children 5 and under.

WALKING TOURS   Charlestonians are proud to discuss the historical quirks of their city, and as such, several tour operators compete for your walking-tour business. The well-recommended **Charleston Strolls** (© **843/766-2080;** www.charlestonstrolls.com) conducts a 2-hour tour that touches on the salient points of the city's sometimes-bloody history, every day beginning at 10am. The cost is $18 for adults, $10 for kids 7 to 12; reservations are a good idea.

Also recommended is the **Charleston Tea Party Walking Tour** (© **843/722-1779;** http://charlestongateway.com). This guided stroll through historic Charleston lasts 2 hours and costs $25 for adults and $10 for children 12 and under. Departing Monday through Saturday at 9:30am and 2pm year-round, tours originate at the Kings Courtyard Inn, 198 King St., and explore the nooks and crannies of Charleston, including secret courtyards and gardens. At the end, you get that promised tea. Reservations are required.

Genteel, erudite, well-informed tours that stress the city's role as a centerpiece for art and architecture are conducted by **Architectural Walking Tours of Charleston** (© **800/931-7761** or 843/893-2329; www.architecturalwalkingtoursofcharleston.com). Tours depart from a point in front of the Meeting Street Inn, 173 Meeting St., twice a day except Tuesday and Sunday, at 10am and 2pm. Morning tours highlight the city's legacy of 18th-century (mostly Georgian-style) architecture; afternoon tours focus on 19th-century (mostly Federal and Victorian) architecture. Participation in either tour costs $20 for adults, $15 for children 9 and under. Fern Williams Tuten, a dyed-in-the-wool Charlestonian with links to many previous generations of Charleston-based Huguenots, also arranges weekend packages, complete with accommodations, for out-of-towners interested in specialty themes (such as Charleston silver as showcased by the Gibbes Museum).

Walking tours that emphasize the ghostlier side of Charleston's sometimes-tormented history are conducted with panache by **Bulldog Tours,** 40 N. Market St. (© **843/722-TOUR** [722-8687]; www. bulldogtours.com). Four different options, priced at $18 each and lasting between 45 and 90 minutes, focus on haunted houses, haunted jails, unfair court trials and seizure of antebellum real estate, and the vendettas from the afterlife that followed. One of them, the Dark Side of Charleston Tour, reveals in breathy detail the scandals

involving prostitution, blackmail, gambling, gunrunning, and all
manner of corruption that over the decades has been associated with
Charleston and its surrounding lowlands.

9 BEACHES & OUTDOOR PURSUITS

BEACHES   Three great beaches are within a 25-minute drive of the
center of Charleston.

In the West Islands, **Folly Beach,** which had degenerated into a
funky Coney Island–type amusement park, is making a comeback
following a multimillion-dollar cleanup, but it remains the least pristine beach in the area. The best bathroom facilities are located here,
however. At the western end of the island is the **Folly Beach County
Park,** with bathrooms, parking, and shelter from the rain. To get here,
take U.S. 17 E. to S.C. 171 S. to Folly Beach.

In the East Cooper area, both the **Isle of Palms** and **Sullivan's
Island** offer miles of public beaches, mostly bordered by beachfront
homes. Windsurfing and jet-skiing are popular here. Take U.S. 17 E.
to S.C. 703 (Ben Sawyer Blvd.). S.C. 703 continues through Sullivan's Island to the Isle of Palms.

Kiawah Island has the area's most pristine beach—far preferable to
Folly Beach, to our tastes—and draws a more upmarket crowd. The
best beachfront is at **Beachwalker County Park,** on the southern end
of the island. Get here before noon on weekends; the limited parking
is usually gone by then. Canoe rentals are available for use on the
Kiawah River, and the park offers not only a boardwalk, but also
bathrooms, showers, and a changing area. Take U.S. 17 E. to S.C.
171 S. (Folly Beach Rd.), and turn right onto S.C. 700 SW (Maybank Hwy.) to Bohicket Road, which turns into Betsy Kerrison
Parkway. Where Betsy Kerrison Parkway dead-ends, turn left on
Kiawah Parkway, which takes you to the island.

For more details on Kiawah Island, Sullivan's Island, and the Isle of
Palms, see chapter 9.

BIKING   Charleston is mostly flat and free of traffic congestion
except on its main arteries at rush hour. Biking is a popular local
pastime, and most of the city parks have biking trails. The most
popular run is across the 2.5 mile, eight-lane Arthur Ravenel, Jr.,
Bridge, which links downtown Charleston to the suburb of Mount
Pleasant. For the best bike rentals, contact **Bike the Bridge** at 6 Vendue Range (© **843/853-BIKE** [853-2453]; www.bikethebridge
rentals.com). Rentals begin at $15 for 3 hours or $25 per day.

Another deal is offered by **Charleston Cruiser Rentals** (© 843/ 754-0176), which will deliver a rental bike to your hotel door. This outfitter offers a half-day rental for $20 and an 8-hour rental for $30.

The **Bicycle Shoppe,** 280 Meeting St. (© 843/722-8168; www. thebicycleshoppecharleston.com), open Monday to Friday 9am to 6pm, Saturday 9am to 6pm, and Sunday 1 to 5pm, offers a selection of cruisers and hybrids, which range in price from $28 to $32 per day.

BOATING   A true Charlestonian is as much at home on the sea as on land. Sailing local waters is a popular family pastime. One of the best places for rentals is **Isle of Palms Marina,** Isle of Palms (© 843/ 886-0209; www.iop.net), where 18-foot boats, big enough for seven people, rent for around $240 for 4 hours, plus fuel. A larger boat, big enough for 10, goes for $375 to $450 for 4 hours, plus fuel.

DIVING   Several outfitters provide rentals and ocean charters, as well as instruction for neophytes. At **Atlantic Coast Diving,** 426 W. Coleman Blvd., Mount Pleasant (© 843/884-1500; www.charleston diving.com), you can rent diving equipment for $50 per day. Snorkel gear is also available. It's open Monday through Saturday from 10am to 6pm.

FISHING   Freshwater fishing charters are available year-round along the Low Country's numerous creeks and inlets. The waterways are filled with flounder, trout, and spot-tail and channel bass. Some of the best striped-bass fishing in the United States can be found at nearby Lake Moultrie.

Offshore-fishing charters for reef fishing (where you'll find fish such as cobia, black sea bass, and king mackerel) and for the Gulf Stream (where you fish for sailfish, marlin, wahoo, dolphin, and tuna) are also available. Both types of charters can be arranged at the previously recommended **Isle of Palms Marina,** Isle of Palms (© 843/ 886-0209; www.iop.net). A fishing craft holding up to 10 people rents for $875 for 6 hours, including everything but food and drink. Reservations must be made 24 hours in advance.

Folly Beach Fishing Pier, at Folly Beach (© 843/588-3474; www.ccprc.com), is a 25-foot-wide wooden pier that extends 1,045 feet into the Atlantic Ocean. Facilities include restrooms, a tackle shop, and a restaurant. It's accessible to people with disabilities.

GOLF   Charleston is said to be the home of golf in America. Charlestonians have been playing the game since the 1700s, when the first golf clubs arrived from Scotland. With 26 public and private courses in the area, Charleston has a golf game waiting for every buff.

For local golf courses, contact **Charleston Golf, Inc.** (© **800/774-4444;** www.charlestongolfguide.com; Mon–Fri 8:30am–5pm). The company represents 17 golf courses, offering packages that range from $100 to $205 per person March through August. Off-season packages go for $75 to $150 per person. Prices include greens fees on one course, the use of a golf cart, a hotel room based on double occupancy, and taxes. Travel pros here will customize your vacation with golf-course selections and tee times; they can also arrange rental cars and airfares. Reserve at least 1 week in advance.

HIKING The most interesting hiking trails begin around Buck Hall in **Francis Marion National Forest** (© **843/887-3257;** www.fs.fed.us/r8/fms), some 40 miles north of the center of Charleston via U.S. 17 N. The site consists of 250,000 acres of swamps, filled with towering oaks and pines. Within the national forest is **Buck Hall Recreation Area,** with 15 campsites that cost $15 to $25 per night, plus a boat ramp and fishing. Other hiking trails are at **Edisto Beach State Park,** State Cabin Road, on Edisto Island (© **843/869-2156**).

TENNIS Charlestonians have been playing tennis since the early 1800s. Your best bet is the **Family Circle Tennis Center,** 161 Seven Farms Dr., Daniel Island (© **843/849-5300;** www.familycirclecup.com), which charges hourly rates of $10 to $15 per person. Hours are Monday through Thursday 8am to 8pm, Friday 8am to 7pm, Saturday 8am to 5pm, and Sunday 9am to 5pm. The location is northeast of the center of Charleston, about a 10-minute drive from the airport.

10 A SIDE TRIP TO MOUNT PLEASANT

Directly north of Charleston and linked by a bridge, Mount Pleasant is where locals first began retreating from the city's summer heat around the turn of the 18th century. Since that time the community has grown and grown, now containing hotels, restaurants, and strip malls. Many of the most popular Charleston seafood restaurants are found here. To reach them and also to see the shrimp-boat fleet, turn right off U.S. 17 just beyond the bridge onto S.C. 703.

Boone Hall Plantation & Gardens See p. 96 for a full review of this unique plantation.

1235 Long Point Rd. (U.S. 17/701), Mount Pleasant. © **843/884-4371.** http://boonehallplantation.com. Admission $18 adults, $15 seniors, $7.50 children 6–12. Apr to Labor Day Mon–Sat 8:30am–6:30pm, Sun 1–5pm; day after Labor Day to Mar Mon–Sat 9am–5pm, Sun 1–4pm. Take U.S. 17/701, 9 miles north of Charleston.

Palmetto Islands County Park (Kids)   At the site of Boone Hall Plantation is this 983-acre family-friendly park in a tropical setting. It features a playground, picnic sites with grills, nature trails, and the Splash Island Waterpark. You can also rent bikes and pedal boats for summer fun. Recreational opportunities abound, including crabbing and fishing from floating docks along tidal creeks and lagoons.

444 Needlerush Pkwy., Mount Pleasant. (✆ **843/795-4386.** http://ccprc.com. Admission $1. May–Aug daily 9am–7pm; Nov–Feb daily 10am–5pm; Mar–Apr and Sept–Oct daily 9am–6pm. Located off Long Point Rd. (U.S. 17/701), 9 miles north of Charleston.

Charleston Shopping

The densest and most appealing collection of upscale shops in the Carolinas is on **King Street,** which Charleston's mayor has called "the longest shopping street in the world." If you have a materialistic bone in your body, you will almost certainly be tempted by some of the objects glinting (some say, winking) at you from behind plate glass. The latest shopaholic destination is a short stretch of trendy, youth-conscious boutiques known as the **Upper King Street Design District** (http://littleworksofheart.typepad.com/upperkingcharleston), where about a dozen avant-garde artisans sell jewelry, millinery, and crafts. The **Shops at Charleston Place,** at 130 Market St. (© **888/635-2350;** www.charlestonplaceshops.com), is an upscale complex of designer labels—Gucci, St. John, Ralph Lauren, and so on.

1 TOP SHOPS FROM A TO Z

ANTIQUES

George C. Birlant & Co. ★ If you're in the market for 18th- and 19th-century English antique furnishings, this is the place for you. This Charleston staple prides itself on its Charleston Battery Bench, which is seen (and sat upon) throughout the Battery. The heavy iron sides are cast from the original 1880 mold, and the slats are authentic South Carolina cypress. It's as close to the original as you can get, but be warned that this high-style garden ornament doesn't come cheap. Open Monday to Saturday 9am to 5:30pm. 191 King St. © **843/722-3842.** www.birlant.com.

Livingston Antiques For nearly a quarter of a century, discriminating antiques hunters have patronized the showroom of this dealer. Both authentic antiques and fool-the-eye reproductions are sold. Hours are Monday to Saturday 10am to 5pm. 2137 Savannah Hwy. © **843/556-3502.** www.livingstonantiques.com.

Roumillat's Antiques Mall & Auctions ★★ The Roumillats are one of the oldest antiques-selling families in Charleston, having been in business since 1779. Two centuries later, they established

Roumillat's Auction House, where regular public auctions of local estate wares are staged on the first and third Saturdays of each month at 10am. In addition to their auctions, the Roumillats offer a 15,000-square-foot antiques mall featuring a little bit of everything, but specializing in American, French, and English furnishings dating from the early 19th century to pre–World War II. Open Monday to Saturday 10am to 6pm, Sunday 1 to 5pm. 2241 Savannah Hwy. (Hwy. 17 S.). ✆ 843/766-8899. www.antiquesandauctions.com.

ART

Audubon Gallery Serious "birdies" flock to this shop in the Historic District, which offers high-quality Audubon prints along with both original paintings and reproductions of such birds as the ruffed grouse or the bald eagle. It also sells hand-carved decoys and other wildlife work, such as bronze sculptures and antique prints. Open Monday to Saturday 10am to 5pm. 190 King St. ✆ 843/853-1100. www.audubonart.com.

Gallery Chuma With some 2,900 square feet of exhibition space, this is the largest African-American art gallery in the South. The original pieces change every 2 months. On permanent display are the works of prominent artists, including Dr. Leo Twiggs and historical artist Joe Pinckney (prints only). Hours are Monday to Saturday 10am to 6pm. 43 John St. ✆ 843/722-7568. www.gallerychuma.com.

Helena Fox Fine Art ★ Savvy and well connected, Helena Fox is on the short list of everybody's favorite and best-respected Charleston art dealers. From a base in the city's French Quarter, she represents about a dozen successful, widely publicized artists that include West Fraser, a painter who wades hip-deep into swamp water in his efforts to capture what he calls "the luminosity of the Carolina wetlands"; Donald Demers, known for his maritime scenes; and Kent Ullberg, who creates monumental sculptures. Open Monday to Saturday 10am to 5pm. 12 Queen St. ✆ 843/723-0073. www.helenafoxfineart.com.

Lowcountry Artists In a former book bindery, this gallery is operated by eight local artists, who work in oil, watercolor, drawings, collage, woodcuts, and other mediums. Hours are Monday to Saturday 10am to 5pm, Sunday noon to 5pm. 148 E. Bay St. ✆ 843/577-9295. www.lowcountryartists.com.

Museum Store at the Gibbes Museum of Art This is the official outlet of reproductions whose originals are on display within the Gibbes Museum of Art, and as such, you'll find a lot of emphasis on the artistic movement of the 1920s and 1930s known as the Charleston Renaissance. Especially prominent are reproductions of works by early-20th-century Charleston artists such as Alice Ravenel

Huger and Elizabeth O'Neill Verner. Many visitors fall in love with the pastels of their cityscapes and still lifes on display within the museum, then end their visit at this shop with a purchase of one or more of the reproductions. Open Tuesday to Saturday 10am to 5pm, Sunday 1 to 5pm. 135 Meeting St. ℂ **843/722-2706.** www.gibbesmuseum.org.

Smith-Killian Fine Art ★ (Finds) The more you know about this gallery, "a focal point for contemporary realism and color," the more intriguing it becomes—even before you scan any of its artwork. It's owned by an artist whose children—triplets, actually—are acknowledged and acclaimed artists in their own right. There's a wealth of South Carolina landscapes inside, most of them produced by Betty Anglin Smith and her children: Shannon Smith, Jennifer Smith Rogers, and photographer Tripp Smith. The awards and publicity that each has generated independent from the others is staggering. If you don't believe that talent sometimes runs in the family, think again, and drop into this antique masonry building in Charleston's historic core. The works of other accomplished artists are also represented, including Kevin Beers, Darrell Davis, and Kim English. Open Monday to Saturday 10am to 5pm, Sunday noon to 5pm. 9 Queen St. ℂ **843/853-0708.** www.smithkillian.com.

Waterfront Gallery Facing Waterfront Park, this gallery is the premier choice for the work of South Carolina artists. The works of 21 local artists are presented, in mediums ranging from sculpture to oils. Hours are Monday to Thursday 11am to 6pm, Friday and Saturday 11am to 10pm, and Sunday noon to 5pm. 215 E. Bay St. (across from the Custom House). ℂ **843/722-1155.** www.waterfrontartgallery.com.

Wells Gallery Works by artists from the Low Country and all over the Southeast are on display at this Charleston gallery. It specializes in Low Country landscapes, but also represents artists from all over the U.S. Prices range from $600 to $12,000. Hours are Monday to Saturday 10am to 5pm. 125 Meeting St. ℂ **843/853-3233.** www.wellsgallery.com.

BOOKS

Blue Bicycle Books Near John Street in the city center, this long, narrow, independent bookstore buys, sells, and trades a roster of carefully screened and often very unusual books, offering some 50,000 previously owned titles, most sold at half-price. The store also carries popular reading material and has a collection of rare books, along with collectibles, Low Country memorabilia, and gifts. Because its owners and staff actually read many of the books they stock, it's viewed as a cut above most of the larger chain-operated bookstores in the region. Open Monday to Saturday 10am to 7:30pm, Sunday 1 to 6pm. 420 King St. ℂ **843/722-2666.** http://bluebicyclebooks.com.

The Basket Ladies of the Low Country

Greatly diminished, but not lost, is the art of **sweetgrass basketry,** a living symbol of the antebellum plantation heyday in the Low Country. A tradition for 3 centuries, the art of basket weaving was brought to the Low Country when slaves were shipped here from the western coast of Africa, bringing their time-tested basket-weaving skills with them. The skill had been passed down to them by their own mothers for generation after generation.

Originally, male slaves wove baskets used in agriculture, including the harvesting of rice. The women slaves wove a more functional but also decorative basket for the home, and these were used for storage of non-perishable items, such as rice or beans, sewing material, and the like. Sometimes if a plantation master took a liking to one of the more artfully executed baskets, he'd pass it along to a friend as a gift or else sell it for profit.

Low Country coil basketry remains one of the oldest crafts of African origin in the United States. Pine needles, bulrush, and fiber strips from palmetto trees are used for binding. A basket can take anywhere from 12 hours to several months to make, depending on the design. Artisans refer to their craft as "basket sewing," not "weaving." Those that are true

Historic Charleston Foundation Shop & Bookstore Near Chalmers Street in the Historic District, this shop stocks books on the preservation and restoration of buildings. Its strong suit is a collection of coffee-table books whose topics range from creating Southern gardens to selecting house colors popular during the reign of Queen Victoria. The shop also has a fine selection of gift items such as miniatures, reproductions in brass and china, textiles, and handicrafts. Open Monday to Saturday 10am to 5pm. 108 Meeting St. © 843/723-1623. www.historiccharleston.org.

Preservation Society of Charleston Bookstore This shop in the Historic District features a collection of books about Charleston and the Low Country. It also sells art books, Southern literature, and even early recordings of Low Country lore told in the Gullah dialect. Local handicrafts, art prints, and the acclaimed architectural works of art command high prices and are often secured for exhibition in museums, including the Smithsonian.

The sweetgrass itself is a perennial, warm-season grass that grows in the coastal dunes from North Carolina to Texas. Unfortunately, coastal development has greatly harmed the raw material used to produce these baskets, and sweetgrass has become rarer and rarer. The Historic Charleston Foundation, hoping to save the industry, is sponsoring a test project on James Island to cultivate the native grass as a crop.

Today, the number of families engaged in making sweetgrass baskets is estimated at around 300, a significant decline in the basket-making community. Most of the basket makers are from Mount Pleasant, north of Charleston. To purchase a sweetgrass basket for yourself, you can visit the Old City Market or else drive from Charleston along Route 17 N., where you'll see basket vendors in makeshift wooden stalls hawking their wares along the roadside, as they have for centuries. You can easily obtain a fine basket for $65 and up. In public markets where the prices seem wildly outrageous, we strongly recommend bargaining, and hard: Often the salesperson suddenly remembers that baskets are "on sale," and prices come down substantially.

drawings of Jim Polzois are featured among the merchandise. Hours are Monday to Saturday 10am to 5pm. 147 King St. (near Queen St.). ✆ 843/722-4630. www.preservationsociety.org.

CARPETS

Khoury Oriental Rugs This outlet has the best collection of hand-knotted Oriental carpets in town—you'll find your "magic carpet" here. The vast collection features Persian designs—handwoven or else reproductions—as well as rugs from China and India. In addition to these carpets, there is a tasteful selection of hand-painted Indian furniture and handcrafted Indonesian teakwood furniture. Open Monday to Saturday 9:30am to 5pm. 71 Wentworth St. ✆ 843/720-7370. www.khouryorientalrugs.com.

Visiting the Old City Market

The area around Market Hall, just south of the old residential suburb of Ansonborough, may never be what it was in its mid-19th-century prime when the Charleston Hotel stood here. One of America's grandest hotels, it attracted everyone from Jenny Lind to William Thackeray, Daniel Webster to Queen Victoria.

But Market Hall and the surrounding Charleston City Market are still going strong, on land willed by the wealthy Pinckney family to be used as a market for merchandise and slaves. The main building, from 1841, is a bastardized version of the Grecian Doric temple of "Wingless Victory" in the city of Athens, Greece. It represented the finest achievement of Edward B. White, a leading architect and engineer of the mid-1800s. Made for the Confederacy in 1861, the cannon in the upper portico was the first manufactured in the United States.

Today, the Old City Market sprawls across four rambling buildings stretching from Meeting Street to East Bay Street.

CIVIL WAR ARTIFACTS

CSA Galleries   This is one of the busiest and best-stocked Civil War shops in the South. Its main specialty is Civil War prints, and it offers a full framing department as well. It also peddles gifts and collectibles, clothing, glassware, videos, books, music boxes, and a collection of specialty foods. Based in North Charleston, it happens to be owned by one of South Carolina's state senators, Glenn McConnell. Open Monday to Friday 10am to 6pm, Saturday 10am to 5pm. 5605 Rivers Ave., North Charleston. ✆ **800/256-1861** or 843/747-7554. www.csa galleries.com.

CRAFTS & GIFTS

Charleston Crafts   This is a permanent showcase for Low Country crafts artisans who work in a variety of mediums, including metal, glass, paper, clay, wood, and fiber. Handmade jewelry is also sold, along with basketry, leather, traditional crafts, and even homemade soaps. Hours are Monday to Saturday 10am to 5:30pm. 87 Hasell St. ✆ 843/723-2938. www.charlestoncrafts.org.

Indigo Home   Across from Waterfront Park, this store sells an eclectic variety of items ranging from folk to funk. Inventories and

Hundreds of vendors hawk their wares within these precincts. The market has a hard-to-shake reputation as a flea market, but interspersed with the tacky, you'll find occasional samplings of high-quality merchandise, the most famous product being sweetgrass baskets (haggle aggressively over basket prices, as you're likely to get a deal). You can also purchase paintings, rugs, dolls, afghans, costume jewelry, local candies and cookies, and even rice and beans if you so desire.

This is the most historically evocative place to shop in South Carolina, with just a whiff or two of the tragedies that have unfolded over the centuries within its perimeter. It's open daily 9am to 6pm.

If you're looking for more upscale merchandise sold in a more stylish setting, consider walking a short distance to boutique-jammed King Street or to the air-conditioned mall-like premises of Charleston Place, on nearby Meeting Street, less than a block from Market Hall.

even the theme of what's featured here are likely to change with the whims of the owners. You may find various versions of carved wooden animals, local art from South Carolina artists made from polymer clays or metal, table linens, lamps, clocks, rugs, door knockers, lanterns, fountains, jewelry, mirrors, and wine accessories. Some of the sculptural depictions of birds and insects are especially appealing. Open Monday to Saturday 10am to 9pm, Sunday 10am to 7pm. 4 Vendue Range. ℂ 843/723-2983. www.indigohome.com.

Max Jerome   Punky, funky, and irreverent, this is a good example of the kind of whimsical and ultra-eclectic boutique for which Upper King Street is becoming famous. Named after the dog (Max Jerome) of the owner (Cassie Walsh), it focuses on clothing, accessories, and furnishings for the countercultural home—everything from stained glass to Lazy Susans like you've never seen before. You might get the feeling that you're shopping within a small-scale museum dedicated to pop culture. Open Monday to Saturday 10am to 5:30pm. 46 John St. ℂ 843/853-6299. www.maxjeromecharleston.com.

People, Places & Quilts ★   This is the most comprehensive quilt-making shop in Charleston, with enough patterns, fabric, thread, and inspiration for many generations of crafts enthusiasts. It also sells a limited array of quilts, when they're available, and folk art made on-site. The store was chosen by *Better Homes & Gardens* as one of the top 10 quiltmaking supply shops in North America. Open Monday to Saturday 10am to 5pm. 1 Henrietta St. ✆ **843/937-9333.** www.ppquilts.com.

The Silver Puffin The Silver Puffin is unique in Charleston in that it seeks odd and interesting pieces from artists around the globe. You might find glass and jewelry from Finland, collectibles from Austria, and maybe even a hand-carved wooden sculpture from Zimbabwe. The shop is strong on a charming selection of gifts for animal fanciers. Open daily 10am to 6pm. 329 King St. (near George St.). ✆ **888/723-7900** or 843/723-7900. www.silverpuffin.com.

FASHION
For Men
Ben Silver This is the best place to get yourself dressed like a member of Charleston's finest society. Ben Silver specializes in blazers and buttons; it has a collection of more than 600 blazer-button designs that are unique in the city. The store features house names and designs only, so don't go looking for Ralph Lauren here. Hours are Monday to Saturday 9am to 6pm. 149 King St. ✆ **843/577-4556.** www. bensilver.com.

Grady Ervin & Co. ★★★ By some accounts, this is the best, most meticulous, and most labor-intensive menswear store in America's Southeast. Established in 1995, with an astonishingly comprehensive tailoring staff on its second floor, it focuses on suits, dress shirts, business attire, sportswear, and formalwear for men. Garments are sold either off-the-rack, with the possibility of extensive alterations, or made-to-measure in ways rarely seen this side of London. Brand names include Oxxford, Hickey Freeman, Samuelsohn, and Polo. Open Monday to Saturday 9am to 6pm. 313 King St. ✆ **843/722-1776.** www.gradyervin.com.

For Women
Anne's Downtown This is a woman's clothier with a history going back to 1942, when it was established by a matriarch of the Friedman and Snyder families, who continue to operate it today. As such, hundreds of Charlestonian women make it one of their regular shopping stops during their pilgrimages up and down King Street. There's something here for women from 25 to 60, but the typical shopper is a well-heeled, relatively conservative mover and shaker in her early 40s. Come here for everything from sportswear to that gown you might wear to any of the city's most important charity balls.

Among the designers represented are Yansi Fugel, Elliott Lauren, and Piece of Cloth. Open Monday to Saturday 9:30am to 5:30pm. 312 King St. © **843/577-3262.** www.annesdowntown.com.

Nancy's On the main shopping street, Nancy's specializes in clothing for the woman who wants to be both active and stylish. Complete outfits in linen, silk, and cotton are sold, along with such accessories as belts and jewelry. Hours are Monday to Saturday 10am to 5:30pm. 342 King St. © **843/722-1272.** www.nancyscharleston.com.

FOODSTUFFS & SWEETS

Cupcake No, it isn't just an affectionate name for one's significant other. Cupcakes are the only confection sold within this pervy-pink homage to sugar fixes and junk food. In this case, each is as artfully decorated as an edible version of a Fabergé egg. It's even been proposed that a gift of a half-dozen of these will get a philandering man back into the good graces of his girlfriend. Open Monday to Saturday 10am to 7pm. 433 King St. © **843/859-8181.** www.freshcupcakes.com.

Lucas Belgian Chocolate ★ This is one of the truly fine chocolatiers in South Carolina, in business for more than 2 decades. In the Historic District near Market Street, it sells imported Belgian chocolates, chocolate truffles, turtles, and clusters, among other mouthwatering confections. Your purchases, incidentally, will be beautifully wrapped. Hours are Tuesday to Saturday 10am to 6pm, Sunday 12:30 to 5:30pm. 73 State St. © **843/722-0461.**

Market Street Sweets Following the success of a parent store in Savannah, this outlet opened in the Historic District next to the Old City Market. It's most famous for its pralines, although it also makes bear claws, chocolates, and other homemade candies. Samples of fudge, pralines, and other goodies are given out all day, and you can also watch candy being made and even talk to the chefs. The shop ships sweets anywhere. Open daily 9am to 10pm. 100 N. Market St. © **800/793-3876.** www.riverstreetsweets.com.

Paolo's Gelato Italiano Charleston can get just as hot and just as sweaty as the southern tier of Italy, so it's only natural that a penchant for gelato should have arrived here recently with a flourish. This might be the most appealing of the new horde of sugar shacks in town, any of which might send even robust physicalities into something approaching diabetic shock. You'll face a choice of more than 60 flavors, any of which is guaranteed to kill your appetite if you indulge before a meal. Open Monday to Friday 11am to 10pm, Saturday and Sunday 10am to 11pm. 41 John St. © **843/577-0099.** www. paolosgelato.com.

FURNISHINGS

Historic Charleston Reproductions Shop ★★   It's rare that a store with so much to offer could be not-for-profit, but that's the case here. All items are approved by the Historic Charleston Foundation, and all proceeds benefit the restoration of Charleston's historic projects. Licensed-replica products range from furniture to jewelry (inspired by the iron designs you'll see around town) to a collection of china from Mottahedeh. The pride of the store is its home-furnishings collection by Baker, an esteemed American furniture company. What makes this collection unusual is the fact that the pieces are adaptations of real Charleston antiques, made of mahogany, a rich dark wood with an authentic feel. Hours are Monday to Saturday 10am to 5pm. The store also operates shops in several historic houses; for slightly more than basic souvenirs, see its Francis Edmunds Center Museum Shop, at 108 Meeting St. (② **843/724-8484;** www.heritage federation.org). 135 Meeting St. ② **843/722-2706.**

HANDBAGS

Mary Norton Handbags   This is the flagship store for chic handbags personally designed by Charleston-based designer Mary Norton. Celebrities are often photographed carrying these luxurious accessories, which initially became famous for the array of different materials used to make them—everything from exotic skins and feathers to semi-precious stones and the most elegant of fabrics. Most of the bags are made in Italy. Other merchandise carried here includes high-style women's shoes. Open Monday to Saturday 10am to 6pm. 318 King St. ② **843/724-1081.** www.marynorton.com.

JEWELRY

Croghan's Jewel Box   Here you'll find gift ideas for any situation, from baby showers to weddings. Estate jewelry and some contemporary pieces are featured. This store also sets diamonds for rings and pendants, and can even secure the diamond for you, with the price depending on the type of stone and grade that you choose. Hours are Monday to Friday 9:30am to 5:30pm, Saturday 10am to 5pm. 308 King St. ② **843/723-3594.** www.croghansjewelbox.com.

Dazzles   One-of-a-kind jewelry is sold here, along with the finest collection of handmade 14-karat-gold slide bracelets in town. Some of the pieces are of heirloom quality. The staff will also help you create jewelry of your own design from a choice of stones. Hours are Monday to Wednesday 10am to 6pm, Thursday to Saturday 10am to 7pm, and Sunday noon to 5pm. In Charleston Place, 226 King St. ② **843/722-5951.** www.dazzlesjewelry.com.

Felice Designs ★ (Finds) It's small, it's artful, and its inventory consists entirely of the kind of portable objects you can smuggle into your undergarments in case you have to run quickly from a relationship in the middle of the night. Don't expect rubies and sapphires, however: Everything here is crafted from Murano-style blown glass and hot-fired ceramic beads, strung onto filaments in ways that might have suited Carmen Miranda. Based partly on the fact that they have the most fun body ornaments in town, this place and its gewgaws have joined the ne plus ultra of Charlestonian chic. If you're intent on exploring the new bohemia of local counterculture shopping, this intensely original boutique on Upper King Street might be an excellent beginning point. Felice Vigueria Killian, a South Carolinian by way of New Orleans, is the much-publicized inspiration behind this place. Open Monday to Friday 10am to 5:30pm, Saturday 10am to 5pm. 424 King St. ✆ **843/853-3354.** www.felicedesigns.com.

Joint Venture Estate Jewelers ★ (Finds) This is an unusual and, in some ways, wonderful jewelry store in that its major focus is jewelry placed here on consignment. The pieces come from some 2,000 consignors of estates, as well as from select private individuals and dealers. Because it doesn't own the inventory, Joint Venture sells at prices much lower than those of a traditional jewelry store. Open Monday to Saturday 10am to 5:30pm. 185 King St. ✆ **800/722-6730** or 843/722-6730. www.jventure.com.

JOGGLING BOARDS

Old Charleston Joggling Board Co. Since the early 1830s, joggling boards have been a Charleston tradition. These boards are the creation of Mrs. Benjamin Kinloch Huger, a native who sought a mild form of exercise for her rheumatism. Mrs. Huger's Scottish cousins sent her a model of a joggling board, suggesting that she sit and gently bounce on the board. The fame of the device spread, and the board soon turned up in gardens, patios, and porches throughout the Charleston area. After World War II, joggling boards became rare due to the scarcity of timber and the high cost of labor, but the tradition was revived in 1970. The company also produces a joggle bench, a duplicate of the joggling board, but only 10 feet long (as opposed to the original 16 ft.) and 20 inches from the ground. Hours are Monday to Friday 8am to 5pm. 652 King St. ✆ **843/723-4331.** www.old charlestonjogglingboard.com.

LINGERIE

Bits of Lace This lingerie boutique is the best of the town's chic and demurely erotic boutiques. Its owner infuses it with the romance and beauty of a Harlequin novel. You'll find every type of merchandise here, from a "diamond tea" cashmere robe to Lise Charmel bras. The staff is justifiably proud of its lace slip collection, as well as its wide range of clothing items in silk, lace, and soft cotton. Bra sizes range from 32A to 44H. Open Monday to Saturday 10am to 6pm. 302 King St. ✆ 800/842-3999 or 843/577-0999. www.bitsoflace.com.

PERFUME

Scents of Charleston   Favorite fragrances, some of them original and unique to this store, are found here, and prices (for the most part) are relatively reasonable. A fragrance that has endured virtually since the store was established in the 1980s is Southern Rain, evocative of lily of the valley, magnolias, and violets. The glycerine body cream is a bestseller, and the store is also the exclusive sales outlet in Charleston for every Crabtree & Evelyn scent, soap, and cream. Open Sunday to Thursday 10am to 9pm, Friday and Saturday 10am to 10pm. 92 N. Market St. ✆ 800/854-8804 or 843/853-8837. www.scentsofcharleston. com.

PHARMACY

Pitt Street Pharmacy ★★   This time-honored old-fashioned pharmacy is pretty much as it was more than 7 decades ago. You can still get thick malted milk shakes like your grandfather enjoyed, or else mortar-and-pestle ground prescriptions (called "compounds" here). It's like wandering back in time to when you ordered a cherry Coke float from the old soda fountain. If you drop in for lunch, you might order a grilled cheese sandwich. You can also get almost any prescription filled here. Hours are Monday to Saturday 9am to 6pm. The pharmacy is located in the suburb of Mount Pleasant, across the bridge from downtown Charleston. 111 Pitt St., Mount Pleasant. ✆ 843/884-4051. www.pittstreetpharmacy.com.

SHOES

Bob Ellis ★   Established in 1950, this is the most famous shoe store in Charleston, with a roster of anecdotes ("fashion divas from Atlanta buying 50 pair of shoes at a time") known to virtually everyone in town. In this shop on the corner of King and George streets, Bob Ellis provides an extensive selection of high-fashion and high-quality durable shoes, even featuring hard-to-find sizes for both women and men. The store also sells an assortment of women's handbags. Most of the goods here are from Italy, England, France, and Spain. Open Monday to Saturday 9am to 6pm. 332 King St. ✆ 843/722-2515. www.bobellisshoes.com.

SMOKE SHOP

The Smoking Lamp   This is Charleston's oldest smoke shop, with the most complete array of tobacco products in the city, and a relatively new address adjacent to the Frances Marion Hotel. You'll find an assortment of pipes, tobacco, cigars, and even walking canes and other paraphernalia. Open Monday to Wednesday 10am to 10pm, Thursday to Saturday 10am to 11pm, and Sunday 11am to 8pm. 401 King St. ✆ 843/577-7339. www.smokinglamp.com.

SPORTING GOODS

Half-Moon Outfitters   Launched in 1993, this store is staffed by New Age folks who take their outdoor pursuits seriously. Surfers, climbers, paddlers, windsurfers, and backpackers are waiting to serve you and advise on the staggering number of sporting goods available here. Open Monday to Saturday 10am to 7pm, Sunday noon to 6pm. 280 King St. ✆ 877/846-7589. www.halfmoonoutfitters.com.

STATIONERY

Dulles Designs ★   Since the advent of the computer age, the art of letter writing has been in decline—but if correct penmanship on cream-colored stationery in blue, black, or blue-black ink is important to you, this shop is a must. It reigns as one of the most elegant and most comprehensive stationery stores along the Eastern Seaboard, thanks to Normandy, France–born owner Martine Dulles and her daughter, Emily. Many of the clients come for engraved wedding invitations or important announcements (births, deaths, graduations). The selection of writing supplies, including pens, is staggering. Open Monday to Saturday 10am to 5:30pm. 89 Church St. ✆ **866-DULL-ESD** (385-5373) or 843/805-7166. www.dullesdesigns.com.

TEXTILES

Lulan Artisans ★★ (Finds)   This is the showcase of Eve Blossom, a specialist in modern textile design fused with Southeast Asian weaving techniques. Moving to Charleston from San Francisco, she opened this chic showcase for her products. Her weavers are master artisans, working in such countries as Cambodia, Vietnam, Thailand, even Laos, using centuries-old techniques to create intricate handwoven textiles. Hours are Tuesday to Saturday 10am to 5pm. 469 King St. ✆ 843/722-0118. http://lulan.com.

8

Charleston After Dark

Not surprisingly, Charleston offers more nighttime diversions than any other city in South Carolina. It has a rich cultural scene, and also features a number of bars for good times and often live music.

1 THE PERFORMING ARTS

Charleston Stage (© 843/577-7183 for tickets; www.charleston stage.com) is a local not-for-profit theater company whose season runs from mid-September to May. Performances range from Shakespeare to *My Fair Lady* to kid-friendly comedies such as *A Year with Toad and Frog*. The company is most active during the Spoleto Festival U.S.A., in May and June.

The **Charleston Ballet Theatre,** 477 King St. (© 843/723-7334; www.charlestonballet.com), is one of the South's best professional ballet companies. The season begins in late October and continues into April. Tickets are $22 to $50.

The **Robert Ivey Ballet,** 1910 Savannah Hwy. (© 843/556-1343; http://robertiveyballet.org), offers both classical and contemporary dance as well as children's ballet programs. The group performs at various venues throughout the Charleston area, with general-admission prices of $25 for adults and $15 for children.

The **Charleston Symphony Orchestra,** 145 King St. (© 843/723-7528; www.charlestonsymphony.com), performs throughout the state, but its main venues are the Gaillard Auditorium, 77 Calhoun St., and Memminger Auditorium, 56 Beaufain St. The season runs from September through May.

A major cultural venue for theater and drama is the **Dock Street Theatre,** 133 Church St. (© 843/577-7183). The original was built in 1736, but burned down in the early 19th century, and the Planters Hotel (not related to the Planters Inn) was constructed around its ruins. In 1936, the theater was rebuilt in a new location on Church Street. In 2010 the 463-seat theater reopened after a $19-million renovation.

2 THE CLUB & MUSIC SCENE

Blind Tiger Pub This artfully battered and very charming pub occupies a historic location, a bar having operated here since 1803. The name comes from the days when Charlestonians opened up illegal "parlors of (liquor) consumption," before the days of speakeasies; these parlors were known as "blind tigers." The legend was that admission fees were paid to see the mythical beast known as a Blind Tiger, with "complimentary" cocktails served. The tiger never showed up, of course, and the drinks weren't really free. These days, lawyers and businessmen in suits frequent the on-site restaurant during the lunch hour, but at night more casual attire is worn by the 30- to 40-year-old crowd that comes to hear live jazz and other kinds of music. Out back, sheltered by a labyrinth of old moss-encrusted brick walls, is an outdoor patio with subdued lighting, a fountain, and a bar of its own. The Blind Tiger is open as a bar Monday to Saturday 11:30am to 2am, with food served until 11pm. 38 Broad St. (near E. Bay St.). © 843/577-0088. www.btpub.com.

Chai's ★ Chai's is the most consistently crowded, most talked-about, and most intriguing bar on Upper King Street. As such, it's a nocturnal centerpiece of a neighborhood that insiders refer to as Charleston's version of New York City's SoHo. The most popular night here, other than Friday and Saturday (when it's packed), is Wednesday, when reggae is the theme and all things Jamaican help the evening rock 'n' roll along. The color scheme is terra cotta, and there's an enlarged mural of Angkor Wat on one wall, but other than that, the main visual focus is on the rambling wooden bar, where tapas are available. Management does its best to keep out rowdies, so despite the crowd (especially after 10pm), things remain unusually civilized here. *Hint:* The mojitos here are big. Open Monday to Saturday 5pm to midnight. 462 King St. © 843/722-7313. www.eatatchais. com.

Henry's One of the best places for jazz in Charleston, this club features a live band on Friday and Saturday nights. Otherwise, you get taped Top 40 music for listening and dancing. If you're a single man or woman with a roving eye, this is defined by locals as either one of the hottest pickup bars in town, or its most dehumanizing meat market, depending on who you talk to. It attracts a mainly over-30 crowd. Happy hour, with drink discounts and free appetizers, is Monday to Friday 4 to 7pm. Open Monday to Saturday 4pm to 2am and Sunday noon to 2am. 54 N. Market St. © 843/723-4363. http://henryshouse charleston.com.

Music Farm ★★ This place describes itself as "Charleston's premier music venue." It covers nearly every taste in music, from country to rock. You're as likely to hear funkster George Clinton as you are country legend George Jones. The club hosts local and regional bands, as well as national acts. Music is present anywhere from 2 to 6 nights a week, from 8pm to 2am. With the right crowd, and when the music is right, the place can be a lot of fun. Call ✆ **843/577-7996** for schedules and information. 32 Ann St. ✆ **843/577-6989.** www.music farm.com. Cover $10–$25.

Tommy Condon's Irish Pub Located in a restored warehouse in the City Market area, this fun and irreverent Irish pub and family restaurant is full of Old Ireland memorabilia. The bartender turns out a leprechaun punch, a glass of real Irish ale, and most definitely Irish coffee. The menu offers Irish food, along with Low Country specials such as shrimp and grits or jambalaya (p. 80 for the full dining review). Happy hour is Monday to Friday 5 to 7pm. Live Irish entertainment is featured Wednesday to Sunday 8:30pm until closing. Pub hours are Sunday to Thursday 11am to 10pm, Friday and Saturday 11am to 2am. 160 Church St. ✆ **843/577-3818.** www.tommycondons.com.

Trio Club This high-energy live-music venue in the Historic District has often been cited for attracting a higher percentage of hip expat New Yorkers than any other bar in town. If the crowd gets to be too much for you, you can flee to the outdoor patio for some air. The club features Latin, blues, folk, jazz, and rock performances, usually enjoyed by a crowd in its 20s and 30s. Open Thursday to Saturday 8pm to 2am. 139 Calhoun St. (near Meeting St.). ✆ **843/965-5333.** Cover $10–$25.

3 THE BAR SCENE

The Brick Set in what was built in the 19th century as a warehouse, this neighborhood bar is lined with handmade bricks and capped with heavy timbers. Although at least some of its clientele has migrated in recent years to the also-recommended Squeeze (see below), it still receives a wide medley of drinkers, everyone from college students to local dockyard workers, as well as a scattering of travelers from out of town. Appetizers and burgers are the only food served, but at least a dozen beers are on tap. Live music begins at 9:30pm Wednesday to Saturday. The tavern is open daily 5pm to 2am. 213 E. Bay St. ✆ **843/720-7788.**

Club Habana With the ambience of a private club, this second-floor lounge in an 1870 house is where the Ernest Hemingway of today would head if he were in Charleston. Relax in one of three Gilded Age salons, each evocative of the Reconstruction era of the Old South. You pass through a well-stocked tobacco store downstairs to reach the club. In fact, it's famous for being the only bar in Charleston where smoking is still legal. While filming *The Patriot,* Mel Gibson made Habana his second home in the city. The house specializes in exotic cigars and martinis, and also serves appetizers, desserts, fruit and cheese plates, and even miniature beef Wellingtons. Open Sunday to Thursday 4:30pm to midnight, Friday and Saturday 4:30pm to 2am. 177 Meeting St. ℭ 843/853-5900. www.clubhabana.com.

First Shot Lounge ★   Our preferred watering hole is this old standby in the Mills House Hotel (p. 57), where over the years we've seen such visiting celebs as Gerald Ford and Elizabeth Taylor (not together, of course). The bar is one of the most elegant in Charleston, a comfortable and smooth spot for a drink. If you get hungry, the kitchen will whip you up some shrimp and grits. Open daily 4 to 10:30pm. In the Mills House Hotel, 115 Meeting St. ℭ 843/577-2400. www.millshouse.com.

The Griffon   Much Scotch and beer is consumed at this popular English-style pub. A full array of home-cooked specials from the old country is served as well, including such pub-grub favorites as steak pies, bangers and mash (English sausage and mashed potatoes), and the inevitable fish and chips. Open daily 11am to 2am; happy hour is Monday to Friday 4 to 7pm. 18 Vendue Range. ℭ 843/723-1700. www.griffoncharleston.com. Cover varies.

Mad River   Immediately adjacent to the gritty historicity of the Market Pavilion, this is a loud, animated, and occasionally raucous sports pub. If you appreciate big-screen TVs—there are about 27 of them here—and a wide choice of beer and liquor, you can have a lot of fun at this place. But what makes it distinct from virtually every other bar in town is that it's housed within a church (deconsecrated in 1947) that's replete with stained-glass windows, a very high trussed ceiling, and enough religious trappings to evoke just a twinge of guilt. (Indeed, you might get the feeling that it would be better to keep your sordid jokes to a minimum within these once-hallowed walls.) A simple menu lists a short selection of "Wraps and Sandwiches" and "Burgers and Breasts" for $8 to $11 each. Reduced prices kick in frequently, bringing the cost of most draft beers down to as low as $2 a glass. Open daily 11am to 2am. 32 N. Market St. ℭ 843/723-0032. www.madrivercharleston.com.

Pavilion Bar ★   To reach this bar, you'll pass through the paneled lobby of the Market Pavilion Hotel and ride an elevator to the building's rooftop. Here, hemmed in by rhythmic rows of faux-baroque ironwork, you'll find a tiny swimming pool, an open-air bar, and a view that stretches from the historic core of Charleston out over the rivers and flatlands around it. You're also likely to see such in-town celebrities as the Bush twins or else hard-partying, recently disgraced scions of the upper-crust Ravenel family on a binge. The most popular cocktail is a Pavilion-tini ($9), made from Absolut Citron, pineapple juice, and orange juice. The place is open Sunday to Thursday 11:30am to 12:30am, Friday and Saturday 11:30am to 2am. During daylight hours until sundown, it remains relatively low-key. But in the cool of the evening, when the lights from the faraway Ravenel Bridge begin to glitter, the joint can get a whole lot rowdier. In the Market Pavilion Hotel, 225 E. Bay St. © **877/440-2250.** www.marketpavilion.com.

Peninsula Grill Bar ★★   Attached to a deluxe restaurant in the swanky Planters Inn (p. 48), this upscale and rather cramped champagne bar has received national acclaim. It is a lavish setting for drinking, with velvet-paneled walls, oil paintings, and antique lamps, all of which create a 1930s supper-club ambience. The crowd tends to be middle-aged, and dress is business casual to stylish. You can order champagne by the glass to accompany such delights as fresh oysters, lobster, and crab. The bar is open daily 4pm to 1am; the restaurant is open Sunday to Thursday 5:30 to 10pm, Friday and Saturday 5:30 to 11pm. In the Planters Inn, 112 N. Market St. © **843/723-0700.** www.peninsulagrill.com.

Rooftop at the Vendue Inn   If you like your drinks with a view, there is none more awesome and panoramic than the rooftop of the previously recommended Vendue Inn (p. 58). As you down your cocktails, you can take in a sweeping vista of Charleston that includes Waterfront Park, the Cooper River Bridge, and embattled Fort Sumter. Patronize this upmarket bar for your "sundowner" (while you watch the sun set). From Sunday to Wednesday, you can listen to live music, including jazz, reggae, and bluegrass. There's never a cover. Hours are daily 11:30am to 11pm. In the Vendue Inn, 19 Vendue Range. © **843/845-7900.** www.vendueinn.com.

Social Restaurant + Wine Bar ★   Housed in a warehouse from the 1800s, this is the leading wine bar in Charleston. Its display cellar features some 4,000 bottles, including many exclusive vintages. Come here to taste the grape, but stick around to order from the menu, which features modern American cuisine with a wood-burning oven as its focal point. The thin-crust pizzas are delectable. Open Monday to Saturday 4pm to midnight. 188 E. Bay St. © **843/577-5665.** www.social winebar.com.

Squeeze It's hip, sexy, and permissive, and its scads of 20- and 30-something clients describe it as either "cozy" or "sensually claustrophobic," depending on their individual preferences and pickup techniques. Open daily 4pm till very late, this smoke-free spot perhaps intentionally fosters the image of a Deep South version of television's *Cheers* bar, as evidenced by photos of happy singles emoting—sometimes manically—on camera. Don't even try calling this bar; the ringing likely won't be heard over the background noise. 213 E. Bay St. ✆ **843/937-6210.**

Vickery's Bar & Grill This is one of the most popular—and consistently fun—gathering places in Charleston for the younger crowd, especially students. Known for serving dinner later than virtually anywhere else in town, it's also a good restaurant choice, with an international menu that includes jerk chicken and gazpacho (p. 80 for the full dining review). But the real secrets of the place's success are its 16-ounce frosted mugs of beer for $3.50 and its convivial atmosphere. Open daily 11:30am to 1am. 15 Beaufain St. ✆ **843/577-5300.** www.vickerys.com.

4 GAY & LESBIAN BARS

Déjà Vu II Some people say this is the coziest and warmest "ladies' bar" in the Southeast. The owners (Laura and Rita) have transformed what used to be a supper club into a cozy enclave with two bars, weekend live entertainment (usually by "all-girl bands"), and a clientele that's almost exclusively gay and 75% lesbian. The ambience is unpretentious and charming, and definitely does not exclude sympathetic patrons of any ilk. Open Thursday to Saturday nights; call ahead for exact hours. 4628 Spruill Ave., North Charleston. ✆ **843/554-5959.** Cover $5–$11 after 11pm.

Dudley's If you happen to be gay, over 35, a wee bit jaded, and without any real interest in disco madness, Dudley's is the kind of mellow, laid-back gay bar that might appeal to you. Nobody dances, and there's a pool table in case you feel like challenging somebody. Open nightly 4pm to 2am. 42 Ann St. ✆ **843/577-6779.**

Pantheon This is the biggest and probably the most high-energy gay venue in town. Located in the Historic District, it used to be known as Avalon's and was patronized by virtually every gay man in all of South Carolina. It is basically a bar with a dance floor and DJs spinning tunes. On Friday and Sunday, that retro form of entertainment, female impersonation, is presented. Open Friday to Sunday 10pm to 2am. 28 Ann St. (near Meeting St.). ✆ **843/577-2582.** Cover varies.

Patrick's Pub & Grill   If you like your men in leather, chances are you'll find Mr. Right here. A gay pub and grill right outside Charleston, this is a late-night venue attracting some of the hottest men in town. Levi's take second place to leather. Open daily 6pm to 2am. 1377 Ashley River Rd. (Hwy. 61). ℭ 843/571-3435.

5 LATE-NIGHT BITES

Kaminsky's Most Excellent Café   Following a night of jazz or blues, Kaminsky's is a good spot to rest your feet and order the power boost (read: anything loaded with sugar) that you'll need to make it through the rest of the evening. The handsome bar offers a wide selection of wines and is ideal for people-watching. Most of the food items sold here are desserts; many are worth-going-out-of-your-way-for sinful, especially the Italian cream cake and the mountain of chocolate cake. Open daily noon to 2am. 78 N. Market St. ℭ 843/853-8270. www.tbonz.com.

9

Nearby Islands

For their summer fun, the people of Charleston head southeast to a series of islands in the Atlantic Ocean. The most popular of these are the **Isle of Palms, Sullivan's Island,** and **Kiawah Island.** In July and August, these breeze-swept islands are the place to be.

Some of the islands now contain upscale resorts, and all have long sandy beaches. This chapter is for sun worshipers, surf fishermen, boaters, and beachcombers in general. White-tailed deer and bobcats live in the maritime forests in the area, and the endangered small tern and loggerhead turtles still nest and lay their eggs on some of these islands.

There are no tourist information offices on these islands except at Kiawah. For information, contact the **Charleston Area Convention & Visitors Bureau (CACVB),** 375 Meeting St., Charleston (© **800/ 774-0006** or 843/853-8000; www.charlestoncvb.com).

1 ISLE OF PALMS

10 miles NE of Charleston

A residential community bordered by the Atlantic and lying 10 miles north of Charleston, this island of salt marshes has been turned into a vacation retreat, albeit one that is more downscale than Kiawah Island (discussed later in this chapter). The attractions of Charleston are close at hand, but the Isle of Palms is also self-contained, with shops, dining, accommodations, and two championship golf courses.

Charlestonians have been flocking to the Isle of Palms for holidays since 1898. The first hotel opened here in 1911. Seven miles of wide, white sandy beach are the island's main attraction, and sailing and windsurfing are popular. The more adventurous go crabbing and shrimping in the creeks.

GETTING THERE From Charleston, take U.S. 17 N. to S.C. 517, then S.C. 703 to Isle of Palms. I-26 intersects with I-526 heading directly to the island via the Isle of Palms Connector (S.C. 517).

OUTDOOR PURSUITS

BEACHES The beach is often the center of activity on the Isle of Palms. You can rent a bodyboard from a nearby stand, play a friendly game of volleyball, or comb the beach for shells like sand dollars, whelks, and angel wings.

BOATING A true Charlestonian is as much at home on the sea as on land. Sailing local waters is a popular family pastime. One of the best places for rentals is **Isle of Palms Marina** (© 843/886-0209; www.iop.net), where 18-foot boats, big enough for seven people, rent for around $240 for 4 hours, plus fuel. A larger pontoon boat, big enough for 10, goes for $395 to $475 for 4 hours, plus fuel.

FISHING Freshwater fishing charters are available year-round along the Low Country's numerous creeks and inlets. The waterways are filled with flounder, trout, and spot-tail and channel bass.

Offshore-fishing charters for both reef fishing (where you'll find fish such as cobia, black sea bass, and king mackerel) and Gulf Stream fishing (where you fish for sailfish, marlin, wahoo, dolphin, and tuna) are also available. Both types of charters can be arranged at **Isle of Palms Marina** (© 843/886-0209). A fishing craft holding up to three people rents for $375 to $525 inshore, including everything but food and drink. Offshore 12-hour rentals are also available for $1,995. Reserve 1 week in advance.

GOLF **Wild Dunes Resort** (© 843/886-6000; www.wilddunes.com) offers two championship courses designed by Tom Fazio. The **Links Course ★★★** is a 6,387-yard, par-70 layout that takes the player through marshlands, over or into huge sand dunes, through a wooded alley, and into a pair of oceanfront finishing holes once called "the greatest east of Pebble Beach." The **Harbor Course** offers 6,402 yards of Low Country marsh and Intracoastal Waterway views. This par-70 layout is considered target golf, challenging players with 2 holes that play one island to another across Morgan Creek. Greens fees at these courses range from $95 to $175. Clubs can be rented at either course for $50 for 18 holes, and instruction costs $85 for a 1-hour session. Both courses are open daily 7am to 6pm year-round.

WHERE TO STAY

Wild Dunes Resort ★★ Kids A bit livelier than Kiawah Island, its major competitor, this complex is set on landscaped ground on the north shore. The resort sits on 1,600 acres of private, gated land. The award-winning hotel has two widely acclaimed golf courses, plus an array of other outdoor attractions, including kayaking, a kids' camp, and more. Guests have a wide choice of options for accommodations, including the 93-room Boardwalk Inn, plus the Village at Wild Dunes, with some 160 quality rooms and suites with AAA's four-diamond rating. The rest of the compound is formed by homes and villas ranging from 1 bedroom to 11, many of them oceanfront. All

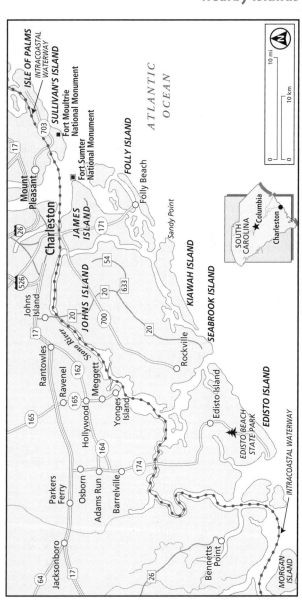

accommodations are just steps from the beach. The family recreation program is designed for ages 8 to 88.

5757 Palm Blvd., Isle of Palms. 𝒞 **888/778-1876** or 843/886-6000. Fax 843/886-2916. www.wilddunes.com. 600 units. $149–$339 double; 1-bedroom villas from $200. Golf packages available. AE, DC, DISC, MC, V. Free parking. Amenities: 4 restaurants; 3 bars; babysitting; exercise room; 2 18-hole golf courses; room service; sauna; 17 tennis courts (5 lit). In room: A/C, TV, Wi-Fi (in some; free).

WHERE TO DINE

The Boathouse at Breach Inlet ★ SEAFOOD   Starting out as a ramshackle bait shop, this Low Country beach-style structure is now one of the finest seafood restaurants in the area. The decor, as might be expected, is nautical, with artifacts taken directly from hand-built wooden boats. Diners can select from a half-dozen different types of the freshest fish in the area, and they can also choose an equal number of preparation styles, ranging from blackened to pesto. At lunchtime, feast on some of the best sandwiches in the area, ranging from a shrimp or oyster po' boy to crab cake with chipotle aioli. At night the menu expands, featuring everything from crab fritters with a green Tabasco to a Low Country egg roll with andouille, chicken, collards, and shrimp. The chef's specialties are Parmesan-crusted tilapia seared in brown butter and local fresh fish roasted with basil and lemon. Also look for nightly specialties.

101 Palm Blvd., Isle of Palms. 𝒞 **843/886-8000.** Reservations recommended. Main courses $17–$29. AE, DC, DISC, MC, V. Tues–Sat 11am–2pm; daily 5–10pm.

2 SULLIVAN'S ISLAND

15 miles SE of Charleston

Lying between the Isle of Palms to its east and historic Fort Sumter to its west, Sullivan's Island is the site of Fort Moultrie, the oldest fortification around Charleston, which dates back to the Revolutionary War. The island is steeped in history: On June 28, 1776, the Battle of Sullivan's Island became the first Patriot victory in the Revolutionary War. The fort also saw some of the earliest action of the Civil War. Even during World War II, its sea-facing bunkers and battlements were used by U.S. forces to spot German submarines.

Today, this quiet residential community east of Charleston is visited mainly for its sandy beaches. Along with the Isle of Palms, Sullivan's Island has for years been one of the favored retreats of Charleston families. Large houses constructed on stilts line the dunes.

Sullivan's Island has more or less bounced back from the massive devastation caused by Hurricane Hugo in 1989. Still, beach erosion can be an issue, especially at high tide when the silvery, hard-packed sands run a bit thin.

GETTING THERE   From Charleston, take U.S. 17 N. to S.C. 703.

OUTDOOR PURSUITS

In the **East Cooper** area, Sullivan's Island offers miles of public sandy beaches, mostly bordered by beachfront homes. Windsurfing and jet-skiing are popular here.

SEEING ONE OF AMERICA'S OLDEST FORTS

Fort Moultrie   Only a palmetto-log fortification at the time of the American Revolution, the half-completed fort was attacked by a British fleet in 1776. Colonel William Moultrie's troops repelled the invasion in one of the first decisive American victories of the Revolution. The fort was subsequently enlarged into a five-sided structure with earth-and-timber walls 17 feet high. The British didn't do it in, but an 1804 hurricane ripped it apart. By the War of 1812, it was back and ready for action. Osceola, the fabled leader of the Seminoles in Florida, was incarcerated and eventually died at the fort. During the 1830s, Edgar Allen Poe served as a soldier here; he set his short story "The Gold Bug" on Sullivan's Island. The fort also played roles in the Civil War, the Mexican War, the Spanish-American War, and even in the two World Wars, but by 1947, it was retired from action.

1214 Middle St., Sullivan's Island. ✆ **843/883-3123.** www.nps.gov/fosu. Admission $3 adults, $1 seniors 62 and over, free for children 11 and under; $5 per family. Federal Recreation Passes honored. Daily 9am–5pm. Closed Jan 1 and Dec 25. Take S.C. 703 from Mount Pleasant to Sullivan's Island.

WHERE TO STAY

There are no hotels or multifamily housing units on Sullivan's Island, but rental properties are available through both **Dunes Properties** (✆ 843/886-5600; www.dunesproperties.com) and **ResortQuest** (✆ 800/870-4078; www.resortquestisleofpalms.com).

WHERE TO DINE

Atlanticville ★ ASIAN   Many Charleston residents make the 20-minute drive from the city to dine here at night in a relaxed setting or to sit on the patio for their "sundowner." It's a romantic atmosphere—and the food's good, too. The chefs range the world for culinary inspiration, offering, for example, a Thai Tuesday, featuring specialties from Southeast Asia. The appetizers are the most imaginative in the area, including a slow-roasted duck mole burrito with a smoked apple salsa. They cook a lamb shank here so tender that the meat falls off the bone, and the deviled-crab-stuffed pork loin is sheer delight. The Sunday brunch is a well-attended event.

2063 Middle St., Sullivan's Island. (€) **843/883-9452.** www.atlanticville.net. Brunch $9–$15; dinner main courses $25–$29. AE, MC, V. Daily 5:30–10pm; Sun 10am–2pm. Closed Dec 24–25.

---

3 KIAWAH ISLAND

21 miles S of Charleston

This eco-sensitive private residential and resort community sprawls across 10,000 acres. Named for the Kiawah Indians who inhabited the islands in the 17th century, it consists of two resort villages today: East Beach and West Beach. The community fronts a lovely 10-mile stretch of Atlantic beach; magnolias, live oaks, pine forests, and acres of marsh characterize the island.

Kiawah boasts many challenging golf courses, including the Ocean Course, designed by Pete Dye. *Tennis* magazine rates Kiawah as one of the nation's top tennis resorts, with its 28 hard-surface or Har-Tru clay courts. Anglers are also attracted to the island, especially in spring and fall.

GETTING THERE　From Charleston, take U.S. 17 E. to S.C. 171 S. (Folly Beach Rd.); turn right onto S.C. 700 (Maybank Hwy.) southwest to Bohicket Road, which turns into Betsy Kerrison Parkway. Where Betsy Kerrison Parkway reaches a traffic circle, turn left on Kiawah Parkway, which takes you to the island.

VISITOR INFORMATION　The **Kiawah Island Visitor Center,** 21 Beachwalker Dr. ((€) **843/768-9166;** www.kiawahisland.org), is open Monday through Friday 9am to 3pm.

OUTDOOR PURSUITS

BEACHES　Kiawah has the area's most pristine beach—far preferable to nearby Folly Beach, at least according to our tastes—and draws a more upmarket crowd. The best beachfront is at **Beachwalker County Park,** on the southern end of the island. Get here before noon on weekends; the limited parking is usually gone by then. Canoe rentals are available for use on the Kiawah River, and the park offers not only a boardwalk, but also bathrooms, showers, and a changing area.

GOLF　Designed by Jack Nicklaus, **Turtle Point Golf Course** ((€) **843/768-2121;** www.kiawahresort.com) is an 18-hole, par-72, 7,054-yard course. Greens fees are $212 for Kiawah Island Golf

Resort, open March to June and September to December. In the off season, fees are $111 for resort guests, $139 for non-guests.

The **Ocean Course** (© 843/768-2121), designed by Pete Dye, was home of the 1991 Ryder Cup, 1997 World Cup, 2001 U.S. Warburg Cup, 2003 World Cup, and 2007 Senior PGIA championship. It's an 18-hole, par-72, 7,296-yard course, the finest in South Carolina. It was even featured in the 2000 movie *The Legend of Bagger Vance.* High season is March to June and September to December, when greens fees are $257 for Kiawah Island Golf Resort guests. Call for off-season rates.

TENNIS One of the greatest tennis resorts in the South is found at the **Kiawah Island Golf Resort** (© 843/768-2121), with 28 hard-surface or Har-Tru clay courts in two tennis complexes. The per-hour cost is $27 for Kiawah Island Golf Resort guests and $37 for non-guests. Open daily, from 8am to 8pm in summer, 8am to 7pm in spring and fall, and 9am to 5pm in winter.

WHERE TO STAY

The Sanctuary at Kiawah Island ★★★ The Sanctuary, one of the greatest resorts in the Southeast, opened in the summer of 2004. With its sweeping views of the Atlantic, this $125-million ultra-luxury resort and spa lies just south of Charleston. It is nestled among majestic live oaks and stretches along the island's 10-mile beachfront. It was constructed in the grand tradition of a seaside mansion, offering guests preferred tee times at the island's five championship golf courses. The sprawling resort features some of the largest and most luxurious guest rooms in America, with 90% of the rooms opening onto the water. In addition, the resort offers two oceanfront restaurants, plus other dining choices. The entrance to the resort is lined with some 150 transplanted live oak trees.

One Sanctuary Beach Dr., Kiawah Island, SC 29455. © **800/654-2924** or 843/576-1570. Fax 843/768-2736. www.kiawahresort.com. 255 units. $490–$860 double; from $1,300 suite. AE, DC, DISC, MC, V. Amenities: 12 restaurants; 4 bars; babysitting; exercise center; 5 18-hole golf courses; room service; sauna; spa; 28 tennis courts (lit as needed). In room: A/C, TV, minibar, Wi-Fi (free).

WHERE TO DINE

Ocean Room ★★★ AMERICAN/STEAK One of the premier restaurants in greater Charleston, the Ocean Room is as luxurious as the hotel in which it's nestled. As you pass through grand wrought-iron gates framing the entrance, you'll see a mahogany-paneled bar with an equestrian decor. From your table, you can enjoy a panoramic ocean view. The menu reveals global culinary influences, as in the tantalizing salad lyonnaise, featuring a poached egg, duck confit, and foie gras with hollandaise. Delectable main courses include pan-seared Carolina triggerfish with wasabi peas. There's always something new and exciting on the ever-changing tasting menu. You can dine more casually at the resort's **Jasmine Porch,** where the dishes are less expensive and the portions more generous.

In the Sanctuary at Kiawah Island Golf Resort, 1 Sanctuary Beach Dr., Kiawah Island. © **843/768-6253** or 768-6007 (Kiawah Island Resort Concierge). Reservations required. Main courses $25–$48; tasting menu $75. AE, DC, DISC, MC, V. Sun–Wed 6–10pm; Thurs–Sat 5:30–10pm.

4 SEABROOK ISLAND

21 miles SW of Charleston

Seabrook Island as the "gated community" we know today originated in the 1970s, when a group of investors added electrical, water, and sewage lines to an isolated barrier island, connected it to the South Carolina mainland via causeway, and hauled in construction teams for the erection of a wide array of houses and villas.

The flat 2,200-acre island is now dotted with carefully planned clusters of private homes, each with its own architectural style, but each corresponding to the demands imposed by the site and the island's role as a resort and retirement community. Seabrook's social centerpiece is a country club-inspired restaurant and bar, where many of the full-time residents catch up on the goings-on of their community. Other dining choices, in many price ranges—including some that are downright honky-tonk—lie on the South Carolina mainland, just across the causeway.

Your Own Private Seabrook Condo

If the Seabrook lifestyle appeals to you, consider renting an apartment or house. Contact **ResortQuest,** one of the region's premier rental services, at 1001 Landfall Way, Seabrook Island (© **800/742-2532** or 843/768-0880; www.resortquestseabrook.com). You can also book villas through **Seabrook Resort,** 3772 Seabrook Island Rd., Seabrook Island (© **866/586-6380;** www.discoverseabrook.com). Rates begin as low as $150 per day, going up to $450 and beyond.

GETTING THERE   From Charleston, take U.S. 17 E. to S.C. 171 S. (Folly Beach Rd.); turn right onto S.C. 700 (Maybank Hwy.) southwest to Bohicket Road, which turns into Betsy Kerrigan Parkway. Turn right on Seabrook Island Road, then right on Persimmon Pond Court.

OUTDOOR PURSUITS

On the island, you'll find 3½ miles of unspoiled beaches, along with championship golf courses and other recreational activities. **Bohicket Marina** has 20 slips available for all sizes of boats; rentals and charters for deep-sea fishing are also offered.

HORSEBACK RIDING   Contact the **Seabrook Equestrian Center,** 1001 Landfall Way (© **843/768-7541**), at least 1 week in advance of your trip (even further in advance around the holidays). The center offers both trail rides and beach rides; a 1-hour ride costs $65. It also gives lessons and can be used by non–resort guests who make reservations; your pass will be available at the security gate at the entrance to the island.

---

5 EDISTO ISLAND ★

---

49 miles SW of Charleston

Isolated, and offering a kind of melancholy beauty, Edisto lies some 45 miles south of Charleston (take U.S. 17 W. for 21 miles; then head south along Hwy. 174 the rest of the way). By the late 18th century, Sea Island cotton had made the islanders wealthy, and some plantations from that era still stand. Today the island attracts families from Charleston and the Low Country to its white sandy beaches. Watersports include shrimping, surf-casting, deep-sea fishing, and sailing.

Edisto Beach State Park, State Cabin Road, sprawls across 1,255 acres, opening onto 2 miles of beach. There's also a signposted nature trail. Enjoy a picnic lunch under one of the shelters. The park has 75 campsites with full hookups and 28 with no hookups. Campsites cost $25 to $30 per night (the price is the same for RV hookups). Tent sites are $17 to $22 per night. Two restaurants are within walking distance of the campsite. Call © **843/869-2756** for reservations.

You can also stay in a hotel in Charleston and commute here during the day.

Barbecue fanciers—and what Southerner isn't one?—flock to **Po-Pigs BBQ Restaurant,** 2410 Hwy. 174 (© **843/869-9003**), for the finest barbecue on the island, with all the Southern fixin's. An all-you-care-to-eat barbecue buffet is a daily feature for only $7.50 for adults and $3.50 for children. In addition to the barbecue, you get grilled or fried chicken, liver hash, red rice, and an assortment of vegetables served the long-cooked Southern way, including turnip greens, field peas, and squash casserole. Hours are Wednesday to Saturday 11:30am to 9pm; no credit cards.

The Old Post Office SOUTHERN   This is the most prominent building that you're likely to see as you drive through the forests and fields across Edisto Island. About 5 miles from the beach, the restaurant was once a combination post office and general store, as its weathered clapboards and old-time architecture imply. Partners David Gressette and Philip Bardin, who transformed the premises in 1988, prepare a worthy compendium of Low Country cuisine and serve it in copious portions. Try island corn and crabmeat chowder, Orangeburg onion sausage with black bean sauce, scallops and grits with mousseline sauce, fried quail with duck-stock gravy, and "fussed-over" pork chops with hickory-smoked tomato sauce and mousseline.

Hwy. 174 at Store Creek. © **843/869-2339.** Reservations recommended. Main courses $15–$29. MC, V. Mon–Sat 5:30–10pm.

Hilton Head

Much more commercial than Charleston is Hilton Head
Island ★★, home of wealthy Northerners (mostly retired) and vacationers from all parts of the country. With myriad contemporary
beachfront restaurants and rows of hotels, timeshare villas, and cottages, the island has recently sprouted boutiques and upscale shopping areas. Although the traffic is horrendous (there is only one main
thoroughfare both on and off the island), development hasn't obliter-
ated nature on Hilton Head, and you can still find solitude at the
north end of the beach.

On the positive side, Hilton Head has become more socially and
culturally oriented, playing host to presidents and world leaders and
also supporting its own symphony orchestra and ballet company. **Sea
Pines** is one of the country's premier golf resorts, located on a 605-
acre Wildlife Foundation preserve that's home to birds, squirrels,
dolphins, and alligators. The island also has 15 miles of bike paths
and 5 miles of pristine beaches.

The largest sea island between New Jersey and Florida and one of
America's great resort meccas, Hilton Head is surrounded by the Low
Country, where much of the romance, beauty, and graciousness of the
Old South survives. Broad white-sand beaches are warmed by the
Gulf Stream and fringed with palm trees and rolling dunes. Those
palms mingle with live oaks, dogwood, and pines, and everything is
draped in Spanish moss. Graceful sea oats, anchoring the beaches,
wave in the wind. The subtropical climate makes all this beauty the
ideal setting for fantastic golf and for some of the Southeast's finest
saltwater fishing. Far more sophisticated and upscale than Myrtle
Beach and the Grand Strand, Hilton Head's "plantations" (as most
resort areas here call themselves) offer visitors something of the traditional leisurely lifestyle that's always held sway here.

Although it covers only 42 square miles (it's 12 miles long and 5
miles wide at its widest point), Hilton Head feels spacious, thanks to
judicious planning from the beginning of its development in 1952.
And that's a blessing, because about 2.3 million resort guests visit
annually (the permanent population is around 35,000). The broad
beaches on its ocean side, sea marshes on the sound, and natural
wooded areas of live and water oak, pine, bay, and palmetto trees in
between have all been carefully preserved amid commercial explosion.
This lovely setting attracts artists, writers, musicians, theater groups,

and craftspeople. The only city (of sorts) is Harbour Town, at Sea Pines Resort, a Mediterranean-style cluster of shops and restaurants.

1 ESSENTIALS

GETTING THERE   Visitors fly into either **Hilton Head Airport** or **Savannah/Hilton Head International Airport** (in Georgia). From Savannah, it's easy to rent a car and drive to Hilton Head, about an hour away. See chapter 3 for details on airlines that serve the area. If you're driving from other points south or north, exit I-95 to reach the island (Exit 28 off I-95 S., exit 5 off I-95 N.). U.S. 278 leads over the bridge to the island, which is located directly on the Intracoastal Waterway.

VISITOR INFORMATION   The **Welcome Center** of the **Hilton Head Island–Bluffton Chamber of Commerce and Visitor & Convention Bureau** (© **800/523-3373** or 843/785-3673; www.hilton headisland.org) is located at 100 William Hilton Pkwy. and is open daily from 8:30am until 5:30pm. You can pick up free vacation guides and maps of the area (or order them online in advance of your trip). The staff can assist you in arranging activities and finding places of interest; video tours in several languages are also available. The main Chamber of Commerce office is located at 1 Chamber Dr.

GETTING AROUND   U.S. 278 is the divided highway that runs the length of the island.

   Yellow Cab (© **843/686-6666;** www.yellowcabhhi.com) has two-passenger flat fares determined by zone, with an extra $2 charge for each additional person.

SPECIAL EVENTS   Scattered cultural events in February, including basket-weaving classes, art exhibitions, and storytelling, showcase the island's mysterious Gullah heritage as part of the annual **Gullah Celebration** (© **843/689-9314;** www.gullahcelebration.com). During the first week of March, the **Winefest** (© **800/424-3387;** www.hilton headhospitalityassociation.com), an outdoor wine-tasting event—and the largest of its kind on the East Coast—transforms even the most devoted beer drinkers into oenophiles. Outstanding PGA golfers descend on the island in mid-April for the **Verizon Heritage PGA Tournament,** at the Harbour Town Golf Links at the Sea Pines Resort (© **800/243-1107;** www.verizonheritage.com). The **Hilton Head Celebrity Golf Tournament** (© **843/842-7711;** www.hhcelebritygolf. com) is held on Labor Day weekend at various island golf courses. For 3 days straddling Halloween, Hilton Head's **Concours d'Elegance & Motoring Festival** (© **843/785-7469;** www.hhiconcours.com) provides a venue for some of the most sought-after antique automobiles in the world.

2 BEACHES, GOLF, TENNIS & OTHER OUTDOOR PURSUITS

You can have an active vacation here any time of year; Hilton Head's subtropical climate ranges in temperature from the 50s (10°–15°C) in winter to the mid-80s (around 30°C) in summer. And if you've had your fill of historic sights in Savannah or Charleston, don't worry—the attractions on Hilton Head mainly consist of nature preserves, beaches, and other places to play.

Make time to stop at the **Coastal Discovery Museum,** 70 Honey Horn Dr./100 William Hilton Pkwy. (© **843/689-6767** or 689-3033; www.coastaldiscovery.org). In 1990, the Town of Hilton Head bought 68 acres of landlocked flatlands (Honey Horn) that were historically used to grow cash crops such as rice and indigo, as a means of protecting them from development into a shopping center. The site contains about a dozen historic buildings, a few of them dating from before the Civil War. Today, as administered by the museum, the site is used for municipally sponsored picnics, concerts, charity drives, and sporting events. The museum itself celebrates the history and culture of Low Country South Carolina with both adults' and children's education programs and lecture series. It sponsors guided tours that go along island beaches and salt marshes or stop at Native American sites and the ruins of old forts and plantations. Children can search for sharks' teeth with an identification chart. The nature, beach, and history tours generally cost $12 per adult and $7

The Gullah Heritage of Hilton Head

Take a journey back in time with **Gullah Heritage Trail Tours** (© **843/681-7066;** www.gullaheritage.com), which will introduce you to this West African–based system of traditions, art forms, customs, and beliefs. A 2-hour narrated tour takes you through the hidden paths of Hilton Head, where you'll meet a fourth-generation Gullah family who tell stories of their traditions and even speak Gullah for you. The tour also visits the Hilton Head of yesterday, including stops at a one-room schoolhouse, plantation tabby ruins, and a historic marker of the First Freedom Village. Tours depart from the Coastal Discovery Museum, 70 Honey Horn Dr., Wednesday to Saturday at 10am and 2pm, and Sunday at 2pm. The cost is $32 for adults, $15 for children 11 and under.

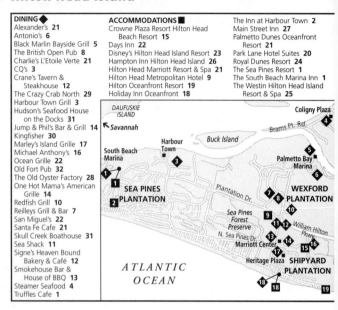

DINING◆
Alexander's **21**
Antonio's **6**
Black Marlin Bayside Grill **5**
The British Open Pub **8**
Charlie's L'Etoile Verte **21**
CQ's **3**
Crane's Tavern & Steakhouse **12**
The Crazy Crab North **29**
Harbour Town Grill **3**
Hudson's Seafood House on the Docks **31**
Jump & Phil's Bar & Grill **14**
Kingfisher **30**
Marley's Island Grille **17**
Michael Anthony's **16**
Ocean Grille **22**
Old Fort Pub **32**
The Old Oyster Factory **28**
One Hot Mama's American Grille **14**
Redfish Grill **10**
Reilleys Grill & Bar **7**
San Miguel's **22**
Santa Fe Cafe **21**
Skull Creek Boathouse **31**
Sea Shack **11**
Signe's Heaven Bound Bakery & Café **12**
Smokehouse Bar & House of BBQ **13**
Steamer Seafood **4**
Truffles Cafe **1**

ACCOMMODATIONS■
Crowne Plaza Resort Hilton Head Beach Resort **15**
Days Inn **22**
Disney's Hilton Head Island Resort **23**
Hampton Inn Hilton Head Island **26**
Hilton Head Marriott Resort & Spa **21**
Hilton Head Metropolitan Hotel **9**
Hilton Oceanfront Resort **19**
Holiday Inn Oceanfront **18**

The Inn at Harbour Town **2**
Main Street Inn **27**
Palmetto Dunes Oceanfront Resort **21**
Park Lane Hotel Suites **20**
Royal Dunes Resort **24**
The Sea Pines Resort **1**
The South Beach Marina Inn **1**
The Westin Hilton Head Island Resort & Spa **25**

per child 4 to 12. The dolphin and nature cruise costs $19 per adult, $13 per child, while a kayak trip goes for $32 per adult and $28 per child. Museum hours are Monday to Saturday from 9am to 4:30pm, Sunday from 11am to 3pm.

BEACHES ★★★ *Travel + Leisure* ranked Hilton Head's beaches among the most beautiful in the world, and we concur. The sands are extremely firm, providing a sound surface for biking, hiking, jogging, and beach games. In summer, watch for the endangered loggerhead turtles that lumber ashore at night to bury their eggs.

All beaches on Hilton Head are public, but land bordering the beaches is private property. Most beaches are safe, although there's sometimes an undertow at the northern end of the island. Lifeguards are posted only at major beaches, and rental beach chairs, umbrellas, and watersports equipment are available.

Most frequently used are the **North** and **South Forest** beaches, adjacent to Coligny Circle (enter from Pope Ave. across from Lagoon Rd.). You'll have to use the parking lot opposite the Holiday Inn, paying a $4 daily fee until after 4pm. The adjacent beach park has

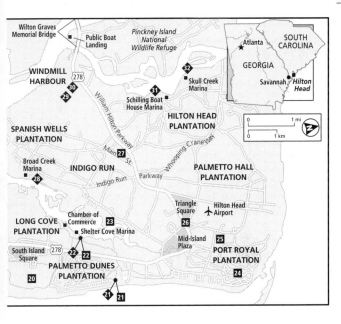

toilets and a changing area, as well as showers, vending machines, and phones. It's a family favorite.

There are a number of public-access sites at popular beach areas. **Coligny Beach,** at Coligny Circle at Pope Avenue and South Forest Beach Drive, is the island's busiest strip of sand with toilets, sand showers, a playground, and changing rooms. **Alder Lane,** entered along South Forest Beach Road at Alder Lane, offers parking and is less crowded. Toilets are also available here. Off the William Hilton Parkway, **Dreissen Beach Park,** at Bradley Beach Road, has toilets, sand showers, a playground, picnic tables, and plenty of parking. Of the beaches on the island's north shore, we prefer **Folly Field Beach,** which has toilets, changing facilities, and parking.

BIKING Hilton Head has 25 miles of bicycle paths. There are even bike paths running parallel to U.S. 278. Beaches are firm enough to support wheels, and every year, cyclists delight in dodging the waves or racing fast-swimming dolphins in the nearby water.

Most hotels and resorts rent bikes to guests. If yours doesn't, try **Hilton Head Bicycle Company,** off Sea Pines Circle at 112 Arrow

Rd. (© **800/995-4319** or 843/686-6888; www.hiltonheadbicycle. com). Its inventory includes cruisers, BMXs, mountain bikes, tandems, and bikes for kids. The cost starts at $27 per week. Baskets, child carriers, locks, and headgear are supplied. Hours are daily from 9am to 5pm. The company also offers free delivery and pickup.

Pelican Cruisers (© **843/785-3546;** www.pelicancruiser.com) also offers beach cruisers, tandems, child carriers, and bikes for kids, with free delivery to any area hotel or resort. The cost is $15 for a full day, or $25 for 3 days. Hours are daily from 9am to 6pm.

BOATING   Advanced Sail, Inc., Palmetto Bay Marina (© **843/686-2582;** www.hiltonheadisland.com/sailing), is a charter operator piloted by Captain John and his mate, Jeanne. Pack a picnic lunch and bring your cooler aboard for a 2½-hour trip—sometimes in the morning, but more often in the afternoon or at sunset. The cost for an excursion aboard the 53-foot *Pau Hana* is $35 for adults and $20 for children 11 and under. The 30-foot *Flying Circus* offers private 2-hour trips for up to six people, priced at $250. Call for special daytime rates for fewer than six people.

H2O Sports, Harbour Town Marina (© **843/671-4386;** www. h2osportsonline.com), offers jet-skiing, parasailing, water-skiing, and more. We especially recommend its eco-tours (or "enviro tours"), which take passengers out on Zodiac inflatable boats for close encounters with wildlife, including dolphin sightings and bird-watching. Parasailing costs adults $65 per hour; groups of five can go water-skiing for 2 hours for $275; sailing lessons cost $30 per person hourly; kayak tours are $40 for adults, $35 for teenagers, and $25 for kids 12 and under.

CRUISES & TOURS   To explore Hilton Head's waters, contact **Adventure Cruises, Inc.,** Shelter Cove Harbour, Dock C, Business Hwy. 278 (© **843/785-4558;** www.hiltonheadisland.com/adventure). Outings include a 1¾-hour dolphin-watch cruise, which costs $20 for adults and $15 for children.

Another outfitter, **Drifter & Gypsy Excursions,** 232 S. Sea Pines Dr., South Beach Marina (© **843/363-2900;** www.hiltonheadboat tours.com), takes its 65-foot *Gypsy,* holding 89 passengers, on dolphin-watches, sightseeing cruises, and nature cruises. Call for information on what's happening at the time of your visit.

FISHING ★   No license is needed for saltwater fishing, although freshwater licenses are required for the island's lakes and ponds. The season for fishing offshore is April through October. Inland fishing is good between September and December. Crabbing is also popular; crabs are easy to catch in low water from docks, from boats, or even right from the banks.

Off of Hilton Head, you can go deep-sea fishing for amberjack, barracuda, shark, and king mackerel. Many rentals are available; we've recommended only those with the best track records. The previously recommended **Drifter & Gypsy Excursions,** 232 S. Sea Pines Dr., South Beach Marina (© **843/363-2900;** www.hiltonheadboattours. com), features a 50-passenger, 60-foot drifter vessel that offers 3- to 5-hour offshore and inshore fishing excursions ranging in price from $54 to $64. The 32-foot *Boomerang* fishing boat is available for private offshore and inshore custom fishing charters lasting up to 8 hours.

Harbour Town Yacht Basin, Harbour Town Marina (© **843/671-2704;** www.harbourtownyachtbasin.com), has five boats of various sizes and prices, each available for rental. The *Hero* and the *Echo* are 32-foot ships. Their rates for a group of six are $495 for 4 hours, $750 for 6 hours, and $990 for 8 hours. A smaller four-passenger inshore boat is priced at $425 for 4 hours, $650 for 6 hours, and $850 for 8 hours. Two six-passenger boats are also available for rent, costing $550 for 4 hours, $800 for 6 hours, and $1,050 to $1,150 for 8 hours.

GOLF ★★★ With more than 20 highly challenging golf courses on the island itself, and an additional 16 within a 30-minute drive, Hilton Head is heaven for both professional and novice golfers. Some of golf's most celebrated architects—including George and Tom Fazio, Robert Trent Jones, Pete Dye, and Jack Nicklaus—have designed championship courses on the island. Wide, scenic fairways and rolling greens have earned Hilton Head the reputation of being the resort with the most courses on the "world's best" lists. To receive a copy of the island's *Golf Planner,* a guide to the golf courses and golf packages on Hilton Head Island, call © **888/465-3475.** For additional information about golf on Hilton Head, go to www.golfisland. com or www.hiltonheadgolf.net.

Most of Hilton Head's championship courses are open to the public, including those at the **Palmetto Dunes Oceanfront Resort** (© **843/785-1130;** www.palmettodunes.com). Its **George Fazio Course ★,** an 18-hole, 6,534-yard, par-70 course that *Golf Digest* ranked among the top 75 American resort courses, has been cited for its combined length and keen accuracy. Greens fees are $58 to $130 for 18 holes. Its **Robert Trent Jones Oceanfront Course** is an 18-hole, 6,710-yard, par-72, with greens fees of $65 to $98. Hours are daily from 7am to 6pm.

On Hwy. 278, 1 mile west of the bridge leading to Hilton Head, is **Old South Golf Links ★★★,** 50 Buckingham Plantation Dr., Bluffton (© **800/257-8997** or 843/785-5353; www.oldsouthgolf. com). This 18-hole, 6,772-yard, par-72 course was recognized upon its completion in 1992 as one of the "Top 10 New Public Courses" by *Golf Digest,* which cited its panoramic views and settings that range from an oak forest to tidal salt marshes. Greens fees are $55 to $120; hours are daily from 7:30am to 7pm.

Also on Hwy. 278 is the **Hilton Head National Golf Club,** 60 Hilton Head National Dr., Bluffton (© **843/842-5900;** www.golfhilton headnational.com), a Gary Player signature design. The 27-hole, 6,779-yard, par-72 course has gorgeous scenery that evokes Scotland. Facilities include a full-service pro shop, driving range, and a grill. Greens fees range from $55 to $125; hours are daily from 7am to 6pm.

Farther west on Hwy. 278 is **Island West Golf Club,** 40 Island West Dr., Bluffton (© **843/689-6660;** www.islandwestgolf.net). With its backdrop of oaks, elevated tees, and rolling fairways, it's a challenging but playable 18-hole, 6,803-yard, par-72 course. Greens fees are $70; hours are daily from 7am to 6pm.

HORSEBACK RIDING   Riding through beautiful maritime forests and nature preserves is reason enough to visit Hilton Head. We like **Lawton Stables,** 190 Greenwood Dr., Sea Pines Resort (© **843/671-2586;** www.lawtonstableshhi.com), which offers trail rides for adults and children through the Sea Pines Forest Preserve. The cost is $60 per person for a ride that lasts a bit over an hour. Riders must weigh under 250 pounds; kids 7 and under ride ponies instead of horses. The stables are open Monday to Saturday from 7:30am to 5:30pm. Reservations are necessary.

JOGGING   Our favorite place for a jog is Harbour Town at the Sea Pines Resort. Go for a run through the settlement just as the sun is going down. Later, you can explore the marina and have a refreshing drink at one of the many outdoor cafes. In addition, the island offers lots of paved paths and trails that cut through scenic areas. However, jogging along U.S. 278, the main artery, can be dangerous due to heavy traffic.

KAYAKING   Kayaking is one of the few ways to get an up-close view of the flora and fauna of the salt marshes. **Outside Hilton Head** (© **800/686-6996** or 843/686-6996; www.outsidehiltonhead.com) offers well-orchestrated kayak tours of various Low Country waterways and salt marshes from at least two locations on the island. Its busiest location is at 32 Shelter Cove Lane, near the Shelter Cove Marina. The 2-hour guided nature tour costs $40 for adults, $20 for children 12 and under. After getting instructions on how to control your boat, you'll go through the salt-marsh creeks of the Calibogue Sound or Pinckney Island National Wildlife Refuge.

A worthy competitor is **Marshgrass Adventures** (© **843/684-3296;** www.marshgrassadventures.com), featuring sailing and kayaking tours from a base at Broad Creek Marina. Every day between

April and October, an experienced guide takes participants out on 2-hour kayak tours for sightings of egrets, herons, fish, crabs, and all manner of crawling critters. There's even the occasional dolphin. The cost is $35 for adults, $20 for children 12 and under.

NATURE PRESERVES The **Audubon-Newhall Preserve ★★**, Palmetto Bay Road (www.hiltonheadaudubon.org/outings.htm), is a 50-acre preserve on the south end of Hilton Head Island. Here you can walk along marked trails to observe wildlife in its native habitat. Guided tours are available when plants are in bloom. Except for a scattered handful of public toilets, there are no amenities. The preserve is open from sunrise to sunset; admission is free, and it's likely that your entire time within these laissez-faire acres will be unsupervised.

Also on the south end of the island is **Sea Pines Forest Preserve ★★**, Sea Pines Resort (© **843/363-4530** or 866/561-8802; www.seapines. com), a 605-acre public wilderness with marked walking trails. Nearly all the birds and animals known to live on Hilton Head can be seen here. Yes, there are alligators, but there are also less fearsome creatures, such as egrets, herons, osprey, and white-tailed deer. All trails lead to public picnic areas in the center of the forest. The preserve is open from sunrise to sunset year-round. Maps and toilets are available.

Pinckney Island National Wildlife Refuge ★★ (© **912/652-4415;** www.fws.gov/pinckneyisland) is protected land with 115 prehistoric and historic sites. French and Spanish settlers inhabited Pinckney Island back in the 1500s, with the first permanent settlement formed in 1708. The island is named for General Charles Cotesworth Pinckney, a signer of the U.S. Constitution. By 1818, more than 200 slaves were used to harvest sea-island cotton here. In 1975, the refuge was donated to the U.S. Fish and Wildlife Service. Today, it comprises four islands, including Corn, Little Harry, Big Harry, and Pinckney, the latter the largest of the islands with 1,200 acres. The islands are riddled with hiking and biking trails, and are home to large concentrations of white ibis, herons, and egrets; you may even spot osprey nests. Two of the island's freshwater ponds were ranked among the top 20 wading bird colony sites of the South Carolina coastal plain. Alligators are also a common sight. To get here, take I-95 to S.C. exit 8; go east on Hwy. 278 toward Hilton Head for 18 miles to the refuge entrance. From Hilton Head itself, exit the island via Hwy. 278 W. The refuge, which can be visited during daylight hours, will be on your right after a 30-minute drive.

TENNIS ★★★ *Tennis* magazine included Hilton Head in its "50 Greatest U.S. Tennis Resorts." No other domestic destination can boast such concentration of tennis facilities: more than 300 courts that are ideal for beginner, intermediate, and advanced players. The

HILTON HEAD

10

OUTDOOR PURSUITS

(Moments) Hilton Head's Wonderful Wildlife

Hilton Head has preserved more of its wildlife than almost any other resort destination on the East Coast.

Hilton Head's **alligators** are a prosperous lot—in fact, the South Carolina Department of Wildlife and Marine Resources uses the island as a resource for repopulating state parks and preserves in which alligators' numbers have greatly diminished. The creatures represent no danger if you stay at a respectful distance.

Many of the large **water birds** that regularly grace the pages of nature magazines are natives of Hilton Head. The island's Audubon Society reports around 200 species of birds every year in its annual bird count, and more than 350 species have been sighted on the island during the past decade. The snowy egret, the large blue heron, and the osprey are among the most noticeable. You may also see the white ibis, with its strange beak that curves down, plus the smaller cattle egret, which first arrived on Hilton Head in 1954 from a South American habitat. These birds follow the island's cows, horses, and tractors to snatch grasshoppers and other insects.

A big part of the native story includes **bobcats, deer, otter, mink,** and a few **wild boars.** The bobcats are difficult to spot, lurking in the deepest recesses of the forest preserves and in the undeveloped parts of the island. The deer, however, are easier to encounter. One of the best places to watch these timid creatures is the Sea Pines Resort, on the southern end of the island. The resort planners had the

island has 19 tennis clubs, seven of which are open to the public. A wide variety of tennis clinics and daily lessons are also available.

Sea Pines Racquet Club ★★★, Sea Pines Resort (© **843/363-4495;** www.seapines.com), was selected by the *Robb Report* as the best tennis resort in the United States. The club has been the site of more nationally televised tennis events than any other location. The club has 23 clay courts, two lit for night play. Hotel guests get 2 hours of complimentary tennis time; after that, they pay $25 per hour.

Sea Pines's most visible competitor is the **Van Der Meer Shipyard Tennis Resort,** 116 Shipyard Dr. (© **800/845-6138** or 843/785-8388;

foresight to set aside areas for a deer habitat back in the 1950s, when the island's master plan was conceived.

The **loggerhead turtle,** an endangered species, nests extensively along Hilton Head's 12 miles of wide, sandy beaches. Because the turtles choose the darkest hours of night to crawl ashore and bury eggs in the soft sand, few visitors meet these 200-pound giants.

Ever-present is the **bottle-nosed dolphin,** usually called a porpoise by those unfamiliar with the island's sea life. In summer, they feed on small fish and sea creatures very close to shore. The waters off Port Royal Plantation, adjacent to Port Royal Sound, are good places to meet up with the playful dolphins, as are Palmetto Dunes, Forest Beach, and all other oceanfront locations. Island beaches are popular among bikers, and this often offers a real point of interest for curious dolphins, who sometimes seem to swim along with the riders. The waters immediately adjacent to shrimp boats as they're hauling in their catch are a guaranteed point of congregation for the hungry guys as well. Or consider participating in one of the kayak tours described under "Kayaking," above.

The Sea Pines Forest Preserve, the Audubon-Newhall Preserve, and the Pinckney Island National Wildlife Refuge, just off the island between the bridges, are all of interest to nature lovers. The **Coastal Discovery Museum** (© **843/689-6767;** www.coastaldiscovery.org) hosts several guided nature tours and cruises; see p. 137 for information.

www.vandermeertennis.com). It has an equivalent number of courts, equivalent prices, and a long history of teaching tennis techniques.

Port Royal Racquet Club, Port Royal Plantation (© **843/686-8803;** www.portroyalgolfclub.com), offers 10 clay and 4 hard courts. The fee is $25 per hour, and reservations should be made a day in advance. Clinics are $23 per hour for adults and $15 for children. Private lessons are also available for $58 per hour.

Palmetto Dunes Tennis Center, Palmetto Dunes Resort (© **843/785-1152;** www.palmettodunes.com), has 23 clay and 2 hard courts (some lit for night play). Hotel guests pay $25 per hour; otherwise, the charge is $30 per hour.

3 SHOPPING & SPA TREATMENTS

Hilton Head is browsing heaven, with more than 30 shopping centers spread around the island. Chief shopping sites include **Pineland Station** (Matthews Dr. and Hwy. 278), with more than 30 shops and half a dozen restaurants; and **Coligny Plaza** (Coligny Circle), with more than 60 shops, food stands, and several good restaurants.

We've found some of the best bargains in the South at **Tanger Outlet Centers I and II** (© 843/837-4339; www.tangeroutlet.com), on Hwy. 278 at the gateway to Hilton Head. Tanger has more than 45 factory outlets, including Ralph Lauren, Brooks Brothers, and J. Crew. Most shops are open Monday to Saturday from 10am to 9pm and Sunday from 11am to 6pm.

Another desirable gaggle of upscale boutiques is the **Village at Wexford,** 1000 William Hilton Pkwy. (www.villageatwexford.com), at Hilton Head's south end. One of its tenants, **Le Cookery** (© 843/785-7171; www.lecookeryusa.com), is among the most comprehensive purveyors of kitchen tools and tableware in the Low Country.

If you're ready for some pampering, you're in luck: Hilton Head boasts a denser concentration of spas than virtually anywhere else in South Carolina. As such, you might be confronted with a barrage of brochures touting various health-and-beauty farms, each offering a staggering array of treatments. They don't come cheap—we urge you to compare prices and treatment options, and then, if possible, to pre-reserve your spa session as far in advance as possible.

Your best choices are the **Heavenly Spa by Westin,** at the Westin Hilton Head Island Resort (© 843/681-4000; www.starwoodhotels. com); and the **Spa Soleil,** at the Hilton Head Marriott Resort (© 843/686-8400; www.hiltonheadmarriott.com). You need not be a hotel guest in order to book spa treatments.

Spas more geared to in-and-out traffic include **Faces Day Spa,** Village at Wexford (© 843/785-3075; www.facesdayspa.com), and the **Sanctuary,** Park Plaza (© 843/842-5999; www.sanctuaryeuro spa.com).

4 AN EXCURSION TO SLEEPY BUT HISTORIC BLUFFTON

Despite the appeal of the area's outdoor activities, history buffs might want a morning's diversion at a Low Country destination that's older and more historic than what can be found within the relatively modern resorts of Hilton Head. If that's the case, consider spending a few hours in a 19th-century riverfront community that time has almost literally passed by: historic Bluffton, a town perched on the South Carolina mainland within a short drive of Hilton Head.

Bluffton's historic core still looks about the way it looked in 1901. Don't expect palatial, aristocratic homes open to the public. Some of those were burned in the wartime aggressions of 1863. Most of those that remain are private, relatively small, and closed to the public; they collectively reflect the mercantile society of river traders who once occupied them. The most impressive of the buildings is the much-weathered, Carpenter Gothic–style **Episcopal Church of the Cross,** 110 Calhoun St., at the edge of the May River.

Calhoun Street also has the community's densest concentration of historic homes. But for a deeper insight into just how slow and sleepy this town really is, drop into the **Heyward House,** 70 Boundary St., at Bridge Street (© **843/757-6293;** www.heywardhouse.org). The low-slung farmhouse design of Heyward House, originally built in 1840 and later enlarged prior to 1900, was inspired by earlier plant-ers' homes in the British West Indies. It's open for guided tours Monday to Friday from 10am to 3pm, Saturday from 11am to 2pm. It's recommended that adults donate $5 and students $2 for the upkeep of the place; ages 9 and under enter free.

For more information, contact the **Bluffton Old Town Merchant Society** (© **843/815-9522;** www.oldtownbluffton.com).

5 WHERE TO STAY

Since its debut, Hilton Head has tended to specialize in the rental of mostly upscale, oceanfront luxury homes and villas, and prices are higher than in other parts of South Carolina. In recent years, however, the roster of lodgings has expanded to offer a wider variety of options. The island now boasts more than 6,000 villas, 3,000 hotel and motel rooms, and at least 1,000 timeshare units. Most facilities offer dis-counted rates between November and March; golf and tennis pack-ages are available year-round.

VERY EXPENSIVE

Hilton Head Marriott Resort & Spa ★★ Set on 2 acres of landscaped grounds and bordering the oceanfront, this supremely comfortable hotel is surrounded by the much more massive acreage of the Palmetto Dunes Oceanfront Resort (p. 153) and is just 10 min-utes from the Hilton Head Airport. But the hotel's 10-story tower of rooms dominates everything around it. Rooms are smaller and less opulent than you might expect of such a well-rated hotel, but all are

HILTON HEAD

10

WHERE TO STAY

comfortably furnished. Most open onto small balconies overlooking the garden or the ocean. The hotel's program of sports and recreation is among the best on the island, and its state-of-the-art spa (Spa Soleil) is the largest on Hilton Head.

In the Palmetto Dunes Oceanfront Resort, Hilton Head Island, SC 29938. ☎ **800/ 228-9290** or 843/686-8400. Fax 843/686-8450. www.marriott.com. 513 units. $179–$219 double; $324–$725 suite. AE, DC, DISC, MC, V. Valet parking $20; self-parking $11. **Amenities:** Restaurant; 2 bars; babysitting; 3 18-hole golf courses; health club; room service; 25 tennis courts; coffee shop. In room: A/C, TV, minibar, Wi-Fi ($9.95 per day).

The Inn at Harbour Town ★★★   Set within the boundaries of the Sea Pines Resort, this postmodern and upscale inn provides the only conventional hotel accommodations within a resort that's otherwise devoted to rentals of villas or condominiums. In their development of this inn, Sea Pines demanded an exceptionally high staff-to-client ratio. The building's exterior (ca. 2001) is high style, buff colored, and postmodern. Inside, there's a richly upholstered, lushly paneled replica of an English-inspired country house, with heart pine floors. Although the inn isn't positioned directly beside the sea, shuttle buses haul guests back and forth, and its location within a very short walk from the waterways, restaurants, shops, and entertainment of Harbour Town and its marina more than make up for it. The hotel is proud of its four-diamond rating from AAA.

7 Lighthouse Lane, in the Sea Pines Resort, Hilton Head Island, SC 29928. ☎ **800/ 732-7463** or 843/363-8100. Fax 843/363-8155. www.seapines.com. 60 units. $139–$249 double. AE, DC, DISC, MC, V. **Amenities:** Bike rentals; concierge; exercise room; outdoor pool; room service; spa; 23 tennis courts (5 lit). In room: A/C, TV, fridge, Wi-Fi (free).

The Inn at Palmetto Bluff ★★★ (Kids)   A jewel in the crown of the world-renowned Auberge Resorts, the Inn at Palmetto Bluff is an elegant, peaceful, relentlessly upscale resort on the May River. Guests can walk through the beautiful gardens, play golf on the Jack Nicklaus signature course, relax in the full-service spa, enjoy watersports like kayaking and fishing, enroll their children in the kids' camp, take art classes, or enjoy a beach excursion. There is a $25-per-day service fee per guest room to be able to use the fitness center, kayaks, canoes, and outdoor lap pool. Accommodations include cottages, cottage suites, and village homes. Exquisitely appointed, the cottages and cottage suites have vaulted ceilings, hardwood pine floors, fireplaces, screened porches, and water views. With two to four bedrooms, full kitchens, screened porches, and luxury bed linens, the village homes are ideal for families. The Inn at Palmetto Bluff offers four dining options: the elegant **River House Restaurant,** with river views; the **May River**

Grill at the May River Golf Club; **Buffalo's,** in the Village; or dining in your own cottage.

476 Mount Pilla Rd., Bluffton, SC 29910. ℂ **866/706-6565** or 843/706-6500. Fax 843/706-6550. www.palmettobluffresort.com. 77 units, 42 cottages, 8 cottage suites, 27 village homes. $475–$950 cottage; $700–$1,100 cottage suite; from $1,100 village home. AE, DC, DISC, MC, V. **Amenities:** 3 restaurants; exercise room; outdoor pool; spa; children's camp. *In room:* A/C, TV, fridge, kitchen (in village home), Wi-Fi (free).

Main Street Inn ★★★ Ⓕinds Don't expect cozy Americana from this small, luxurious inn, as it's grander and more European in its motifs than its name would imply. Designed like a small-scale villa that you might expect to see in the south of France, it was built in 1996 in a format that combines design elements from both New Orleans and Charleston, including cast-iron balustrades and a formal semitropical garden where guests are encouraged to indulge in afternoon tea. Inside, you'll find artfully clipped topiary, French Provincial furnishings, and accommodations that are more luxurious than those of any other hotel in Hilton Head. Overall, despite a location that requires a drive to the nearest beach, the hotel provides a luxe alternative to the less-personalized megahotels that lie nearby.

2200 Main St., Hilton Head Island, SC 29926. ℂ **800/471-3001** or 843/681-3001. Fax 843/681-5541. www.mainstreetinn.com. 33 units. $139–$199 double. Additional person $35 extra. Rates include breakfast. AE, DISC, MC, V. Free parking. **Amenities:** Breakfast room; outdoor pool; spa. *In room:* A/C, TV, minibar, Wi-Fi (free).

The Westin Hilton Head Island Resort & Spa ★★ Set near the relatively isolated northern end of Hilton Head Island on 24 landscaped acres, this hotel stands out as the most child- and pet-friendly blockbuster hotel on the island. Its Disneyesque design, including cupolas and postmodern ornamentation that looks vaguely Moorish, evokes fanciful Palm Beach hotels. If there's a drawback, it's the fact that it's so obviously geared to families with children that romantically inclined couples without children in tow might not necessarily thrill to the family-friendly sweep of it all. Fortunately, there's an active and much-respected children's camp on-site for the care and attention of young'uns. Most of the guest rooms have ocean views, and are outfitted in modernized interpretations of the Low Country plantation style. The hotel is also home to the new Heavenly Spa by Westin, a full-service spa.

2 Grasslawn Ave., Hilton Head Island, SC 29928. ℂ **800/937-8461** or 843/681-4000. Fax 843/681-1096. www.starwoodhotels.com. 412 units. $169–$429 double; $450–$1,900 suite. Children 17 and under stay free in parent's room; children 4 and under eat free. Special promotions offered. AE, DC, DISC, MC, V. **Amenities:** 3 restaurants; bar; 3 18-hole golf courses; Jacuzzi; room service. *In room:* A/C, TV, minibar, Wi-Fi ($13 per day).

Crowne Plaza Hilton Head Island Beach Resort ★   Tucked away in the Shipyard Plantation and designed as the centerpiece of that plantation's 800 acres, this five-story inn gives the Westin stiff competition. The golf course associated with the hotel has been praised by the National Audubon Society for its respect for local wildlife. Guest rooms are simple, yet the sheer beauty of the landscaping, the attentive service, and the well-trained staff (dressed in nautically inspired uniforms) go a long way toward making your stay memorable. The most glamorous restaurant is **Portz,** and a good middle-bracket choice is **Brella's,** serving both lunch and dinner. Certain nights in the premier bar, **Signals,** feature line dancing and shag dancing.

130 Shipyard Dr., Shipyard Plantation, Hilton Head Island, SC 29928. ℭ **800/334-1881** or 843/842-2400. Fax 843/785-8463. www.cphiltonhead.com. 340 units. $199–$399 double; from $299 suite. AE, DC, DISC, MC, V. Free parking. **Amenities:** 2 restaurants; bar; bike rentals; exercise room; 2 pools (1 indoor); room service. *In room:* A/C, TV, minibar, Wi-Fi ($9.95 per day).

Disney's Hilton Head Island Resort ★★   This medium-scale, family-conscious resort is on a 15-acre island, inland from the coast, that rises above Hilton Head's widest estuary, Broad Creek. About 20 woodsy-looking buildings are arranged into a compound. Expect lots of pine trees and fallen pine needles, garlands of Spanish moss, plenty of families with children, and an ambience that's several notches less intense than that of hotels in Disney theme parks. Characters include Shadow the Dog (a golden retriever that is the resort's mascot) and Blue Crab, a storyteller, fisherman, and musician. Part of the fun is the many summer-camp-style activities for kids with or without their parents. Guest rooms usually contain mini-kitchens, suitable for feeding sandwiches and macaroni to the kids. **Tide Me Over** is a walk-up window serving Carolina cookery for breakfast and lunch. The resort runs a shuttle bus to and from a nearby beach at 15-minute intervals daily between 10am and 5pm.

22 Harbourside Lane, Hilton Head Island, SC 29928. ℭ **800/500-3990** or 843/341-4100. Fax 843/341-4130. http://dvc.disney.go.com. 123 units. $165–$350 studio; $260–$1,100 villa. AE, DC, DISC, MC, V. **Amenities:** 2 restaurants; bar; babysitting; exercise room; 3 outdoor pools. *In room:* A/C, TV, kitchenette (in most), Wi-Fi ($11 per day).

Hilton Oceanfront Resort ★   This award-winning property isn't the most imposing on the island. Many visitors, however, prefer the Hilton because of its hideaway position—tucked at the end of the main road through Palmetto Dunes—and because its rooms are, on average, a bit larger than those within any other resort on the island. In addition, a $4-million renovation, completed in 2008, adds to its appeal. The low-rise design features hallways that open to sea breezes at either end. The guest rooms offer balconies that angle out toward the beach, allowing sea views from all rooms. **HH Prime**—an upmarket steakhouse that looks a lot more glamorous at night than during the day, when it evokes an upscale coffee shop—is the resort's premier restaurant, although an on-site Pizza Hut serves less expensive fare. In 2007, the resort inaugurated a glossy, urban-looking bar and lounge, which boasts live music.

23 Ocean Lane (PO Box 6165), Hilton Head Island, SC 29938. ✆ **800/845-8001** or 843/842-8000. Fax 843/341-8033. www.hiltonoceanfrontresort.com. 323 units. $139–$349 double; $359–$609 suite. AE, DC, DISC, MC, V. Parking $8–$12. **Amenities:** 4 restaurants; 2 bars; exercise room; 2 outdoor pools; room service; spa. *In room:* A/C, TV, kitchenette, Wi-Fi ($11 per day).

Royal Dunes Resort ★ Comfortable and clean, but blandly standardized and somewhat anonymous, this is a compound of three-bedroom, three-bathroom apartments that have been aggressively marketed to independent investors as a timeshare investment. Whenever the owners aren't in residence, the apartments become available for rentals on the open market. They occupy a quartet of four-story buildings located on the Port Royal Plantation. Each has a washer/dryer; durable wicker, rattan, and Southern colonial furniture; and tub/shower combinations. The compound's location is at the edge of a forested greenbelt, within a 10-minute walk from the beach.

8 Wimbledon Court, Hilton Head, SC 29928. ✆ **843/681-9718.** Fax 843/681-2003. www.spmresorts.com. 56 units. $195–$260 double. AE, MC, V. **Amenities:** Bike rentals; exercise room; Internet (free); 2 outdoor pools. *In room:* A/C, TV, kitchen.

MODERATE

Holiday Inn Oceanfront ★ ⓚ**ids** The island's leading moderately priced hotel, and its oldest, with a history going back to 1970, this sprawling five-story building opens onto a crowded stretch of beach on the southern side of the island, directly across the road from the fast-food joints and souvenir shops of Coligny Plaza. The rooms are spacious and informally but comfortably furnished with rattan furniture and pastel colors. Unfortunately, the balconies are generally too small to actually walk out onto. Only a few of the rooms have actual sea views—most of them have views over parking lots and trees. In summer, planned children's activities are offered. Don't expect glamour, as the place is comfortable, crowded, and family-oriented, with a packed pool and barely enough parking. The staff, despite the many demands on their time, are genuinely concerned and helpful.

1 S. Forest Beach Dr. (PO Box 5728), Hilton Head Island, SC 29938. ✆ **800/423-9897** or 843/785-5126. Fax 843/785-6678. www.hiltonhead.com. 202 units. $129–$234 double. AE, DC, DISC, MC, V. Free parking. **Amenities:** Restaurant; outdoor bar; exercise room; outdoor pool; room service; Wi-Fi (free). *In room:* A/C, TV.

Park Lane Hotel & Suites   Set on the eastern edge of Hilton Head's main traffic artery, midway between the Palmetto Dunes and Shipyard plantations, this is a three-story, all-suite complex in a wooded, park-like setting. The suites are functionally furnished but comfortable. Both cost-conscious families and business travelers on extended stays appreciate the simple cooking facilities in all units.

12 Park Lane (in Central Park), Hilton Head Island, SC 29938. *©* **877/BIRDIE1** (247-3431) or 843/686-5700. Fax 843/686-3952. www.hiltonheadparklanehotel.com. 156 units. $79–$129 suite. Rates include continental breakfast. AE, DC, DISC, MC, V. **Amenities:** Exercise room; Jacuzzi; outdoor pool; 2 tennis courts (lit). *In room:* A/C, TV, kitchenette, Wi-Fi (free).

The South Beach Marina Inn ★ (Finds)   Of the dozens of available accommodations within the Sea Pines Resort, this 1986 clapboard-sided complex of marina-front buildings is the only place offering traditional hotel-style rooms by the night. With lots of nautical, seafaring charm, the inn meanders over a labyrinth of catwalks and stairways above a complex of shops, souvenir kiosks, and restaurants. It is especially known for being located immediately adjacent to the Salty Dog Cafe—one of the island's most popular eateries. Each one- or two-bedroom unit is cozily outfitted with country-style braided rugs, pine-wood floors, and homespun-charm decor celebrating rural 19th-century America.

232 S. Sea Pines Dr. (in the Sea Pines Resort), Hilton Head Island, SC 29920. *©* **800/367-3909** or 843/671-6498. www.sbinn.com. 17 units. $65–$179 1-bedroom; $87–$186 2-bedroom. AE, DISC, MC, V. Free parking. **Amenities:** Outdoor pool. *In room:* A/C, TV, kitchenette, Wi-Fi (free).

INEXPENSIVE

Days Inn   The Days Inn provides easy access to the beach, golf, tennis, marinas, and shopping. The rooms are wheelchair accessible and, although unremarkable, are a good value for expensive Hilton Head. Families save money by using one of the grills outside for a home-style barbecue, to be enjoyed at one of the picnic tables.

9 Marina Side Dr., Hilton Head Island, SC 29928. *©* **800/329-7466** or 843/842-4800. Fax 843/842-5388. www.daysinn.com. 119 units. $89–$139 double; $129–$169 suite. Rates include continental breakfast. Senior discounts available. AE, DISC, MC, V. Free parking. **Amenities:** Breakfast room; outdoor pool. *In room:* A/C, TV, Wi-Fi (free).

Hampton Inn Hilton Head Island   This is one of the two or three most sought-after motels on Hilton Head, especially by families and business travelers who don't mind its lack of resort-style amenities and its straightforward, cost-effective simplicity. It's 5 miles from the Graves bridge and the closest motel to the airport. Rooms in pastel pinks and greens are quite comfortable and well maintained. Some rooms have refrigerators. Local calls are free, and breakfast is included in the rates.

1 Dillon Rd., Hilton Head Island, SC 29926. ✆ **800/HAMPTON** (426-7866) or 843/681-7900. Fax 843/681-4330. www.hamptoninn.com. 125 units. $124–$189 double. Children 17 and under stay free in parent's room. Rates include continental breakfast. AE, DC, DISC, MC, V. **Amenities:** Breakfast room; exercise room; outdoor pool. *In room:* A/C, TV, Internet (free), kitchen (in some).

Hilton Head Metropolitan Hotel (Kids) Favored by families, this is a 1970s-era, five-story, white-concrete hotel set directly across the street from the island's busiest beach. Each room is configured in a bland, generic style duplicated in motels throughout the world. Virtually everything on Hilton Head is within a 15-minute drive. Expect lots of children, especially during the midsummer months.

36 S. Forest Beach Dr., Hilton Head, SC 29928. ✆ **800/535-3248** or 843/842-3100. Fax 843/785-6928. http://hiltonheadmetropolitan.com. 140 units. $49–$139 double. Rates include continental breakfast. AE, DC, DISC, MC, V. **Amenities:** Exercise room; outdoor pool; Wi-Fi (free). *In room:* A/C, TV, kitchenette (in some).

VILLA RENTALS

The **Vacation Company** (✆ **800/845-7018;** www.hiltonheadvacation rentals.com) has been in business for almost a quarter-century and specializes in the rental of homes and villas throughout the region. Its leading competitors include **Beach Properties of Hilton Head** (✆ **800/ 671-5155** or 843/671-5155; www.beach-property.com), **Hilton Head Vacation Rentals** (✆ **800/232-2463;** www.800beachme.com), and **ResortQuest Vacation Home Network** (✆ **800/875-8726** or 843/ 785-7300; www.resortquesthiltonhead.com).

Two developments that we consider especially appealing are reviewed below.

Palmetto Dunes Oceanfront Resort ★ (Kids) This relaxed and informal enclave of privately owned villas is set within the sprawling 1,800-acre complex of Palmetto Dunes Plantation, 7 miles south of the bridge. Accommodations range all the way from one-bedroom condos, booked mostly by groups, to four-bedroom villas, each of the latter furnished in the owner's personal taste. This is the place for longer stays, ideal for families who want a home away from home when they're traveling. In fact, it was ranked the number-one family resort in the continental U.S. and Canada by *Travel + Leisure Family* in 2003 and is still listed among the top 10. Villas are fully equipped and receive housekeeping service; they're located on the ocean, fairways, and lagoons. Each villa comes with a full kitchen, washer and dryer, living room and dining area, and balcony or patio. The resort opens onto a 200-slip marina.

Palmetto Dunes (PO Box 5606), Hilton Head Island, SC 29938. © **800/827-3006.**
www.palmettodunes.com. 500 units. $260–$3,500 per week condo or villa. Golf
and honeymoon packages available. 2-night minimum stay. 50% deposit for reservations. AE, DC, DISC, MC, V. Free parking. **Amenities:** 20 restaurants; 12 bars; 3
18-hole golf courses; 28 outdoor pools; 25 tennis courts (8 lit). *In room:* A/C, TV,
Wi-Fi (in some; free).

The Sea Pines Resort ★★★   Since 1955, this has been one of
the leading condo developments in America, sprawling across 5,500
acres at the southernmost tip of the island. Lodgings vary—everything from one- to four-bedroom villas to opulent private homes that
are available when the owners are away. An additional option is the
separately recommended 60-room Inn at Harbour Town, which
offers the only venue at Sea Pines Resort for rental of conventional
hotel rooms. The clientele here includes hordes of golfers because Sea
Pines is the home of the Verizon Heritage golf tournament, a major
stop on the PGA tour. If you're not a Sea Pines guest, you can eat,
shop, or enjoy aspects of its nightlife.

Sea Pines (PO Box 7000), Hilton Head Island, SC 29938. © **866/561-8802.** Fax
843/842-1475. www.seapines.com. 500 units. $170–$340 1-bedroom villa; $300–
$385 2-bedroom villa; $320–$600 3-bedroom villa. Rates are daily, based on
3-night stay. AE, DC, DISC, MC, V. **Amenities:** 12 restaurants; 12 bars; babysitting;
3 18-hole golf courses; exercise room; 2 outdoor pools; spa; 23 tennis courts (5 lit.);
watersports/rentals. *In room:* A/C, TV, kitchen or kitchenette, Wi-Fi (free).

6 WHERE TO DINE

Hilton Head has the dubious distinction of having the most expensive restaurants in South Carolina. What on the island might be
ranked as moderate would be considered very expensive in other parts
of the state.

EXPENSIVE

Marley's Island Grille ★★ Kids SEAFOOD/STEAK   This
Caribbean-themed restaurant is noted for its fresh, wood-fire-grilled
seafood and steaks, accompanied by the best margaritas and sangria on
the island. Marley's has a fun, albeit kitschy, island vibe, and is popular
with locals, vacationers, and families alike. Try the lobster tacos with
rice and beans or the tortilla-crusted tilapia with jumbo lump crab salsa.
Among our favorite wood-grilled specialties are jerk grilled chicken and
red-chili-rubbed flank steak with chimichurri sauce. After dinner, enjoy
dessert next door at Marley's Ice Cream & Trading Company.

35 Office Park Rd., near Park Plaza. © **843/686-5800.** www.marleyshhi.com.
Reservations recommended. Main courses $13–$37. AE, DISC, MC, V. Sun–Thurs
4:30–10pm; Fri–Sat 5–11pm.

Michael Anthony's ★★★ ITALIAN   Nearly every critic on the island has declared Michael Anthony's the best place to eat in Hilton Head. The place is family owned and operated, with hands-on attention and care paid to every detail. The exquisite menu blends traditional Italian flavors with Low Country ingredients. A local favorite is the homemade gnocchi in a sauce of porcini mushrooms with demiglace and cream. Another delectable specialty is the medallions of veal with spinach, cheese, and Italian sausage, sautéed in white wine. Don't miss the chocolate soufflé cake served with vanilla gelato. *Tip:* Michael Anthony's also has a wine bar where you can enjoy your favorite beverage or dessert or have dinner—no reservations required.

37 New Orleans Rd. (*C*) **843/785-6272.** www.michael-anthonys.com. Reservations required. Main courses $17–$35. AE, DC, DISC, MC, V. Mon–Sat 5:30–10pm.

Ocean Grille ★ AMERICAN/STEAK/SEAFOOD   One of the premier restaurants of Hilton Head is this waterfront eatery overlooking a marina. The skilled chefs specialize in fresh seafood and choice steaks expertly prepared. First-rate appetizers include stone crab claws and coconut-fried calamari. When available, the fresh catch of the day can be ordered grilled, broiled, blackened, or fried. The sublime sauces include lobster butter, tangerine coulis, and garlic saffron aioli. New York strip is grilled and served with buttermilk mashed potatoes.

1 Shelter Cove Lane, Shelter Cove Marina. (*C*) **843/785-3030.** www.oceangrill restaurant.com. Reservations recommended. Main courses $16–$35. AE, DC, MC, V. Daily 4:30-9:30pm; Sun 11am–2pm.

Old Fort Pub ★ INTERNATIONAL   Remote and isolated from the bulk of other Hilton Head eateries, and nestled within the upscale residential community of the Hilton Head Plantation on the island's northwest coast, this is one of the most consistently reliable and upscale restaurants in the Low Country. It is only a few paces from the ruin of what was commissioned by the Union army in 1862 as a fort (Fort Mitchell), and as such, some diners make it a point to traipse around the signposted footpaths. You'll dine in a building that evokes an interconnected series of clapboard-sided houses, amid candlelight and crisp napery, with views over salt marshes and estuaries. Chef Keith Josefiak prepares dishes which include Vidalia onion shoots and goat cheese tarts; spring asparagus en croûte with prosciutto and roasted tomato vinaigrette; a succulent version of local bouillabaisse that just happens to include collards and tasso ham; crab cakes; and pork loin with chanterelles, Vidalia onions, and pistachio nuts.

65 Skull Creek Dr. (*C*) **843/681-2386.** www.oldfortpub.com. Reservations recommended. Main courses $24–$38. AE, DC, DISC, MC, V. Mon–Sat 5–10pm; Sun 11am–2pm (brunch).

Redfish Grill ★ INTERNATIONAL   One of the more talked-about restaurants on Hilton Head Island occupies a rambling villa that contains shopping as well as dining options. A popular pastime involves dropping into the on-site wine shop, selecting a bottle, and for a $10 corkage fee, drinking it with your meal. There are two postmodern, Asian-inspired dining rooms, or the wine shop has a few tables. The menu changes with the seasons, but might include Asian-style marinated tenderloin of beef with Thai cucumbers in a lettuce-leaf wrap; grilled sea bass with a wasabi cream sauce and soy glaze on a bed of udon noodles; seared jumbo scallops served with asparagus and lobster-studded macaroni and cheese; and two upscale and expensive burgers: one made entirely with Kobe beef and accented with foie gras, pepper jack cheese, truffles, and port demi-glace; the other crafted from chunks of Maine lobster mixed with shrimp. This restaurant lies in an isolated residential neighborhood inland from the sea, close to the Cross-Island Bridge.

8 Archer Rd. (✆ **843/686-3388.** www.redfishofhiltonhead.com. Reservations recommended. Main courses $8–$12 lunch, $21–$34 dinner. AE, MC, V. Mon–Sat 11:30am–2pm and 5–10pm; Sun 5–10pm.

MODERATE

All of these so-called moderately priced restaurants have expensive shellfish dishes. However, if you order from the lower end of the price scale, you'll find platters that cost $20 or less. Portions tend to be generous, so you'll rarely need to order appetizers, which will keep your overall costs in the more affordable price range.

Alexander's ★ SEAFOOD/INTERNATIONAL   One of the most visible independent restaurants (in other words, not associated with a hotel) on Hilton Head lies in a gray-stained, wood-sided building just inside the main entrance into Palmetto Dunes. The decor includes Oriental carpets, big-windowed views over the salt marshes, wicker furniture, and an incongruous—some say startling—collection of vintage Harley-Davidson motorcycles, none with more than 1,000 miles on them, dating from 1946, 1948, 1966, and 1993, respectively. Powerful flavors and a forthright approach to food are the rules of the kitchen. The chefs don't allow a lot of innovation on their menu—you've had all these dishes before—but fine ingredients are used, and each dish is prepared with discretion and restraint. Try the oysters Savannah or the bacon-wrapped shrimp, and most definitely have a bowl of Low Country seafood chowder. Guaranteed to set you salivating are the scallops encrusted with sun-dried tomatoes, and the bluefin crab cakes. Steak, duck, rack of lamb, and pork—all in familiar versions—round out the menu.

76 Queen's Folly, Palmetto Dunes. ☎ **843/785-4999.** www.alexandersrestaurant. com. Reservations recommended. Main courses $23–$33. AE, DC, DISC, MC, V. Daily 5–10pm.

Antonio's ★ ITALIAN   This island favorite, with its elegant decor and fine cuisine, continues its bold quest to duplicate the flavors of sunny Italy, and for the most part succeeds admirably. The chef is a whiz at using recipes from all the regions of Italy, although classic seafood preparations are clearly his favorite. Piano music adds to the ambience, as does a visit to the wine cellar, where you can see Hilton Head's most comprehensive assemblage of Italian *vino*. The antipasti selection is one of the island's best, and the succulent pastas include one based on fruit of the sea: sautéed shrimp, scallops, and mussels in a tomato and saffron broth. Veal saltimbocca appears delectably with crispy prosciutto and creamy roasted pancetta sage potatoes.

1000 William Hilton Pkwy., in the Village at Wexford. ☎ **843/842-5505.** www. antonios.net. Reservations recommended. Main courses $9–$32. AE, DC, DISC, MC, V. Daily 5:30–10pm. Closed Dec 24.

Black Marlin Bayside Grill ★ SEAFOOD   Partly because of its location beside a marshy inland channel, a few steps from the most battered-looking boatyard and marina on Hilton Head Island, this is the most raffish of the "grand cuisine" restaurants of Hilton Head. Fun, with lots of salty cosmopolitan charm, and an insouciance that might remind you of Key West, it seems a world removed from the manicured, upscale conservatism of the island's secluded residential zones. Thomas Corey is the chef here, a refugee from the cold Northeast, and an expert at crafting flavor from the fresh seafood that arrives directly from fishermen every morning at dawn. Lunch fare includes meal-size salads and at least a dozen hungryman's sandwiches, pastas, and fried seafood. Dinners are more ambitious, focusing on tuna carpaccio, tempura lobster, fish or shrimp tacos; crab-stuffed flounder, big slabs of steak, and between 7 and 10 dishes that appear only on a blackboard, based on the seafood haul brought in that day.

86 Helmsman Way, at the Palmetto Bay Marina. ☎ **843/785-4950.** www.black marlinhhi.com. Reservations not accepted. Main courses $7.50–$15 lunch; $13–$33 dinner. AE, DC, MC, V. Mon–Fri 11:30am–10pm; Sat–Sun 10am–2pm and 4–10pm.

Charlie's L'Etoile Verte ★★ INTERNATIONAL   Outfitted like a tongue-in-cheek version of a Parisian bistro, our favorite restaurant on Hilton Head Island was also a favorite with former president Clinton during one of his island conferences. The atmosphere is unpretentious but elegant. The service is attentive, polite, and infused with an appealingly hip mixture of Old and New World courtesy.

Begin with roast portobello mushrooms and crab, and move on to tilapia sautéed in a Parmesan crust. End this rare dining experience with biscotti or a "sailor's trifle." The wine list is impressive.

8 New Orleans Rd. (✆ **843/785-9277.** www.charliesgreenstar.com. Reservations required. Main courses $8–$14 lunch, $24–$39 dinner. AE, DISC, MC, V. Tues–Sat 11:30am–2pm; Mon–Sat 5:30–9:30pm.

CQ's ★★ AMERICAN/LOW COUNTRY With a design based on a 19th-century rice barn, this Harbour Town restaurant has been a Hilton Head tradition since 1973. The extensive wine list, some 400 vintages, is one of the best on the island. The well-thought-out menu of American classics reflects the rich bounty of South Carolina—fresh seafood, beef, and game—and also shows a French influence. To start, the Maine lobster and Boursin cheesecake with a sherry butter cream is a delight. Count yourself lucky if you arrive when game is in season, featured in such dishes as seared medallions of venison with roasted onion, shallots, leeks, and asparagus; a Madeira wine reduction adds that extra special flavor.

140-A Lighthouse Rd. (✆ **843/671-2779.** www.cqsrestaurant.com. Reservations recommended. Main courses $26–$40. AE, DC, DISC, MC, V. Apr–Oct daily 5:30–9:30pm; Nov–Mar daily 5–9:30pm.

Crane's Tavern & Steakhouse ★ STEAK/SEAFOOD The original Crane's was launched in Philadelphia at the turn of the 20th century and was one of the most popular taverns there until Prohibition. Always a family business, it was established by Hank Crane, who came over from Ireland, and passed the business down to generations of Crane sons and, now, a daughter. While other Hilton Head restaurants rush to claim the best seafood, Crane's bases its simple menu on prime beef. Each of the choicest cuts is prepared to your taste—can any trencherman cope with the whopper, 20 ounces? A 12-ounce prime rib was the best we could manage, and it was well flavored and quite succulent. The other offerings are good as well, including jumbo lump crab cakes and stuffed chicken. The sweet-potato ravioli in a molasses cream is exquisite.

26 New Orleans Rd. (✆ **843/341-2333.** www.cranestavern.com. Reservations recommended. Main courses $17–$46. AE, DC, DISC, MC, V. Daily 5–10pm. Closed Thanksgiving and Dec 25.

The Crazy Crab North (Kids) SEAFOOD Usually crowded, especially in summer, this is the restaurant that's most likely to be patronized by locals, partly because an entire family can be fed here at relatively modest prices. In a modern, low-slung building near the bridge that connects the island with the South Carolina mainland, it serves baked, broiled, or fried versions of stuffed flounder; seafood kabobs; oysters; the catch of the day; and any combination thereof.

She-crab soup and New England–style clam chowder are prepared fresh daily, children's menus are available, and desserts are a high point for chocoholics. There's a second branch of this restaurant with the same hours and virtually the same prices, at Harbour Town in the Sea Pines Resort (℃ **843/681-5021**).

U.S. 278 at Jarvis Creek. ℃ **843/681-5021**. www.thecrazycrab.com. Reservations not accepted. Main courses $6–$15 lunch, $14–$33 dinner. AE, DISC, MC, V. Daily 11:30am–10pm.

Harbour Town Grill ⟨Finds⟩ AMERICAN   For years, this woodsy-looking refuge of golfers and their guests was open only to members of the nearby golf club. Several years ago, however, it opened to the public at large, a fact that's still not widely publicized in Hilton Head and that sometimes seems to catch some local residents by surprise. Decorated with a simple, aggressively unpretentious style that's vaguely Scottish and punctuated with occasional pieces of golfing memorabilia, this small-scale affair has views over the 9th hole and room for only about 50 diners at a time. Inside, it's sporty-looking and relatively informal during the day, when most of the menu is devoted to thickly stuffed deli-style sandwiches and salads named in honor of golf stars. Dinners are more formal and more elaborate, with good-tasting dishes such as local shrimp sautéed with ginger, Vidalia onions, and collard greens; roasted rack of American lamb with white beans, spinach, and rosemary; and an array of thick-cut slabs of meat that include beef, lamb, veal, and chicken.

In the Harbour Town Golf Links Clubhouse, Sea Pines. ℃ **843/363-8380**. www.seapines.com. Reservations recommended for dinner. Main courses $9–$17 lunch, $16–$38 dinner. AE, DC, DISC, MC, V. Daily 7am–3pm and 5–10pm.

Hudson's Seafood House on the Docks ★ SEAFOOD   Built as a seafood-processing factory in 1912, and an excellent choice if you're looking for an escape from the island's crowded southern tier, this restaurant still processes fish, clams, and oysters for local distribution, so you know that everything is fresh. If you're seated in the north dining room, you'll be eating in the original oyster factory. We strongly recommend the crab cakes, the steamed shrimp, and the especially appealing blackened catch of the day. Local oysters (seasonal) are also a specialty, breaded and deep-fried. Before and after dinner, stroll on the docks past shrimp boats, and enjoy the view of the mainland and nearby Parris Island. Sunsets here are panoramic. Lunch is served in the Oyster Bar.

1 Hudson Rd. (go to Skull Creek just off Square Pope Rd. signposted from U.S. 278). ℃ **843/681-2772**. www.hudsonsonthedocks.com. Reservations not accepted. Main courses $6–$15 lunch, $13–$23 dinner. AE, DC, MC, V. Daily 11am–2:30pm and 5–9pm.

Jump & Phil's Bar & Grill AMERICAN   Cozy and convivial, with dining tables positioned on three sides of a large rectangular bar that does a thriving business with 40- and 50-something owners of nearby homes and condos, this is the brainchild of entrepreneurs Jump and Phil, journalism majors who spent 20 years working in other restaurants before branching out on their own. Outfitted with early-20th-century Americana, some battered antiques, and dark paneling, the place identifies itself as headquarters for Hilton Head's Green Bay Packers fan club. Food is generously portioned, reasonably priced, and utterly unpretentious. Menu items include two-fisted versions of BLTs, Cuban sandwiches, chili dogs, tuna melts, barbecued pork, and burgers. More substantial fare includes grits with shrimp, fried oyster platters, chicken potpie, and grilled rib-eye steaks.

In the Hilton Head Plaza, Greenwood Dr. off Sea Pines Circle. (*) 843/785-9070. www.jumpandphilshhi.com. Sandwiches $7–$12; main courses $11–$24. AE, DISC, MC, V. Daily 11:30am–2am.

Kingfisher ★ SEAFOOD/STEAK   This popular restaurant at Shelter Cove offers live music nightly and a panoramic view of the harbor through large picture windows in all three dining rooms. The catch of the day can be prepared several ways, including the usual grilled or blackened, but also herb-encrusted or Greek style (with tomatoes, onions, mushrooms, spinach, artichokes, and feta). Each day, different varieties of oysters are served on the half shell. Seafood selections range from a very respectable Scottish fish and chips to a Charleston-style shrimp and grits in white gravy. The seared ahi tuna comes with a *ponzu* sauce, wasabi mashed potatoes, and Asian slaw. The filet mignon is tender and full of flavor, and for pasta lovers, the chef makes a creative lasagna every day.

18 Harbourside Lane. (*) 843/785-4442. www.kingfisherseafood.com. Reservations recommended. Main courses $10–$40. AE, DISC, MC, V. Daily 5–10pm. Closed Dec 24–25.

The Old Oyster Factory ★ SEAFOOD/STEAK   Built on the site of one of Hilton Head's original oyster canneries, this always-popular landmark offers waterfront dining overlooking Broad Creek. At sunset, every table enjoys a panoramic view as diners sip their "sundowners." All the dishes here can be found on seafood menus from Maine to Hawaii. But the cuisine is truly palate friendly, beginning with such appetizers as a tangy kettle of clams steamed in a lemon-butter sauce, or else a delectable crab cake sautéed and served in a chili-garlic tartar sauce. Will it be oysters Rockefeller (baked with spinach and a béarnaise sauce) or oysters Savannah (shrimp, crab-meat, and smoked bacon)? Almond-crusted mahimahi is among the more tantalizing main courses, as are seafood pasta and broiled sea

scallops. Those who don't eat seafood can opt for a chargrilled chicken **161**
breast or a steak.

101 Marsh Rd. (© 843/681-6040. www.oldoysterfactory.com. Reservations not accepted. Main courses $17–$33. AE, DC, DISC, MC, V. Daily 5–10pm (closing times can vary).

Reilley's Grill & Bar ★ (Finds) AMERICAN   It rarely advertises, so much of its business is from locals, who come here after dark to hobnob, gossip, eat, and drink within the orbit of patriarch Tom Reil-ley, the island's ultimate F&B insider. If you can manage to pull yourself away from the mahogany and cherry-paneled bar, you'll dis-cover that food items are the most fussed over and most sophisticated of any other eatery within Hilton Head Plaza. Examples include garlic chicken pasta, grilled loin of beef with peppers and onions, pork chops stuffed with spinach and mozzarella with a Gouda cream sauce, upscale salads such as a version with warm Brie and spinach, sandwiches made with such ingredients as tilapia, croissants, meatloaf and cheddar, and Asian-style chicken salad. There's also a roster of grills and a signature version of sirloin topped with an Irish whiskey peppercorn sauce and cheese grits.

In the Hilton Head Plaza, Greenwood Dr. off Sea Pines Circle. (© 843/842-4414. www.reilleyshiltonhead.com. Reservations recommended for dinner. Main courses $7.25–$14 lunch, $10–$25 dinner. AE, MC, V. Daily 11am–2am.

Santa Fe Cafe ★ MEXICAN   The best, most stylish Mexican restaurant on Hilton Head, the Santa Fe Cafe has rustic, Southwest-ern-inspired decor and cuisine that infuses traditional recipes with nouvelle flair. Live music adds to the allure. Menu items are often presented in colors as bright as the Painted Desert. Dishes might include tequila shrimp, herb-roasted chicken with jalapeño cornbread stuffing and mashed potatoes laced with red chilies, grilled tenderloin of pork with smoked habañero sauce and sweet-potato fries, and worthy burritos and chimichangas. The quesadilla is one of the most beautifully presented dishes of any restaurant in town.

700 Plantation Center. (© 843/785-3838. www.santafecafeofhiltonhead.com. Res-ervations recommended. Main courses $7–$14. AE, DISC, MC, V. Mon–Fri noon–2pm and 5–10pm; Sat–Sun 5–10pm.

Skull Creek Boathouse (Kids) SEAFOOD   The nautical decor and the view over salt marshes and Skull Creek form an appropriate venue for the serving of some fine seafood at affordable prices. From some tables, you can see the Pinckney Island National Wildlife Ref-uge and the adjacent marina. Walk under a canopy of giant oaks to enjoy a drink at the Market 13 outdoor bar. Live entertainment is offered, and you can bring the kids, too (there's a children's menu). Plenty of fresh seafood is prepared with that old Charleston flavor, including shrimp and stone-ground grits, excellent crab cakes, Southern catfish with Carolina fixin's, and the chef's own Boathouse bouillabaisse. For meat fanciers, slow-roasted baby back ribs in a sour mash sauce, served with buttermilk "smashed" potatoes and collards, seduce the palate.

397 Squire Pope Rd. ✆ **843/681-3663.** www.skullcreekboathouse.com. Brunch items $6–$11; lunch items $8.75–$15; dinner main courses $16–$28. AE, DC, DISC, MC, V. Daily 11:30am–3pm and 5–9pm. Closed Dec 25.

INEXPENSIVE

The British Open Pub BRITISH/AMERICAN   Except for the fact that the hardworking staff speaks with a Carolina accent, you might believe you've stumbled into a remote, woodsy-looking, and unpretentious corner of Britain. And if you opt for a meal here, you'll be in good company, since the town's mayor and a few of his cohorts have to some degree adopted the place as a regular hangout. Since it rarely advertises, prices remain low. Its name derives from the obsession of its owners with the minutiae of the U.K.'s most famous golf tournament. There's British ale on tap, plus ever-popular versions of fish and chips, lobster potpies, shepherd's pie, and meal-size salads. As for Carolina-inspired food, we recommend Chef Jason's twin crabcake platter, or perhaps the baby back barbecued ribs. If you're looking to escape the crowds of tourists that fill so many Hilton Head bars, this place is a good choice, though the drinks are stiff enough to ensure that locals patronize it in droves.

In the Village at Wexford Shopping Center. ✆ **843/686-6736.** www.britishopen pub.net. Reservations not accepted. Main courses $8–$16. AE, DC, MC, V. Mon–Sat 11am–10pm; Sun 9am–10pm.

One Hot Mama's American Grille ★ (Kids) GRILL/BARBECUE It's fun, it's whimsical, and its reasonably priced platters are served in a setting that evokes a mixture of a rock-'n'-roll cafe and a 1950s-era luncheonette. It's the least expensive of the eateries within "the Triangle" of Hilton Head Plaza, and the most child- and family-friendly. The menu focuses on savory, grease-spattered ribs and barbecue dishes. The baby back barbecued ribs here are scrumptious, the pit-to-plate handpulled pork virtually addictive. Chargrilled steaks and chicken filets will make you call for more, and if you like fried chicken wings, this place serves them in almost 20 different variations, including a version with strawberry-jalapeño sauce. In case you're wondering who the Hot Mama is, she's Orchid, a hardworking entrepreneur whose prototype for this charming place migrated from nearby Bluffton in 2007.

In the Hilton Head Plaza, Greenwood Dr. off Sea Pines Circle. ✆ **843/682-6262.** www.onehotmamas.com. Reservations not accepted. Main courses $7.50–$12 lunch; $7.50–$23 dinner. AE, DC, MC, V. Daily 11:30am–midnight.

San Miguel's (Kids) MEXICAN   Every night since 1977 has been fiesta night here. There's a fun atmosphere, and live music can be enjoyed on the deck. (This eatery opens onto the same marina as Ocean Grille, p. 155.) The food is nothing to rave about, but it's substantial and freshly prepared; there's even a kiddie menu. Most guests start with nachos, quesadillas, or guacamole. After that, proceed to one of the platters, such as chiles rellenos, enchiladas, or sizzling fajitas. If anyone in your party doesn't like Mexican food, the chefs will also serve a shrimp Alfredo or a New York strip steak from the grill.

9 Shelter Cove Lane, Shelter Cove Marina. (℡) **843/842-4555.** www.sanmiguels. com. Main courses $8–$17. MC, V. Mon–Sat 11:30am–3pm; daily 5–11pm.

Sea Shack ★ (Value) SEAFOOD   This unpretentious seafood shack serves the freshest catch of the day in town; you can order it grilled, fried, or blackened. Stand at the counter and make your selection from specialties listed on a board. Find a seat at one of the old tables, and your fresh platter will be brought to you. We always like to begin with the fish soup. At lunch, the fried-oyster sandwich is a local favorite. For dinner, we prefer the grilled grouper. One of the chef's signature dishes is Caribbean jerk grouper, which you don't encounter too often; it's even been featured on the Food Network.

6 Pope Ave. (℡) **843/785-2464.** Main courses $6–$14 lunch, $10–$17 dinner. AE, MC, V. Mon–Sat 11am–3pm and 5–9pm.

Signe's Heaven Bound Bakery & Café SANDWICHES/PASTRIES   Sometime in the early '70s, Signe Gardo, a refugee from the snows of Connecticut, opted to open this bakery. Almost 3,000 wedding cakes and countless danishes later, it's the oldest eatery under a single ownership on Hilton Head, with a roster of loyal clients. It lies in a relatively underpopulated neighborhood of private homes way, way off the island's beaten touristic track. Many come for breakfast, oohing and aahing over Signe's signature deep-dish French toast, her breakfast polenta, and her waffles. (Rachael Ray came here to film a feature story in 2007.) Lunches focus on a half-dozen salads, a spinach-and-feta *spanikopita* pie that might have been inspired by Zorba himself, tomato or crab-cake tarts, and a steaming ration of shrimp and grits. Simple tables on an outdoor deck (no view of the sea, alas) provide a place setting for your meal. Few clients can resist carting off any of the dozen or so homemade breads including Swiss pear, French oat and apricot, and Hilton Head sourdough bread. Equivalent cakes include a Forever Valentine and a version flavored with piña coladas, coconut, and pineapple cream.

93 Arrow Rd. (℡) **866/807-4463** or 843/785-9118. http://signesbakery.com. Reservations not accepted. Main courses $6–$9. AE, MC, V. Mon–Fri 8am–4pm; Sat–Sun 9am–2pm. Closed Sun Nov–Feb.

Smokehouse Bar & House of BBQ (Kids) BARBECUE   This is Hilton Head's only authentic barbecue joint, serving fine hickory-smoked meats in a casual atmosphere. There's a large outdoor deck, and takeout is also available. Locals and visitors (especially families) come here nightly, raving about the man-size portions of pulled pork, sliced or pulled brisket, and barbecued chicken. The specialty is smokehouse ribs, either half or full rack. Other down-home favorites include fried catfish and award-winning chili. Beachgoers are welcome, but must wear shoes.

102 Pope Ave. (C) **843/842-4227.** http://smokehousehhi.com. Reservations recommended. Main courses $12–$22. AE, MC, V. Daily 11:30am–10pm.

Steamer Seafood ★ SEAFOOD/LOW COUNTRY   This casual, convivial tavern is suitable for the whole family. Specialties include she-crab soup and shrimp gumbo. Many old-time Southern coastal classics are also offered, including frogmore stew (shrimp, smoked sausage, onion, and red potatoes). The catch of the day is served grilled or blackened. The "rebel yell" rib-eye is a juicy 14-ounce slab, blackened or chargrilled, as you desire. The biggest seafood platters on the island are dished up here. After all that, dare you try the rich, creamy chocolate-peanut-butter pie or the fruit cobbler of the day?

29 Coligny Plaza (next to the Piggly Wiggly grocery store). (C) **843/785-2070.** www.steamerseafood.com. Lunch items $8–$37; dinner main courses $9–$37. AE, MC, V. Daily 11:30am–10pm.

Truffles Cafe ★ (Finds) INTERNATIONAL   It's no longer on the cutting edge of gastronomic newcomers to Hilton Head, but it's been around so long, and garnered so many fans that it's one of our personal favorites on the island. Within the Sea Pines Center, this cafe has a dark, mostly black decor, with a large copper-topped bar, black banquettes, and a menu that somehow manages to please virtually everybody. Start with a spinach and artichoke dip or coconut fried shrimp, followed by baby back ribs or grouper that's grilled and topped with a basil-Parmesan glaze. You could also try Havana chicken with jack cheese and fresh tomato salsa or meatloaf that's grilled with a honey-flavored barbecue sauce and Vidalia onions. Don't confuse this place with the newer and somehow glossier Truffles Grill on Pope Avenue, between Coligny Circle and Sea Island Circle: The Grill is newer and trendier, but many restaurant insiders swear by the original. If you opt for a meal here, you'll have to pay a $5 charge to enter the Sea Island Resort itself. Most islanders recognize and acknowledge this, and accept that fact simply as the cost of doing business and living on Hilton Head Island.

Sea Pines Center, in the Sea Pines Resort. (C) **843/671-6136.** www.trufflescafe.com. Reservations recommended for dinner. Main courses $8–$29 lunch, $12–$28 dinner. AE, DC, MC, V. Daily 11am–10pm.

Hilton Head doesn't have Myrtle Beach's nightlife, but there's enough here, centered mainly in hotels and resorts. Casual dress (but not swimming attire) is acceptable in most clubs.

Cultural interest focuses on the **Arts Center of Coastal Carolina,** in the Self Family Arts Center, 14 Shelter Cove Lane (© **888/860-2787 or 843/842-ARTS** [2787]; www.artshhi.com), which enjoys one of the best theatrical reputations in the Southeast. The Elizabeth Wallace Theater, a 350-seat, state-of-the-art theater, was added to the multiplex in 1996. The older Dunnagan's Alley Theater is located in a renovated warehouse. A wide range of musicals, contemporary comedies, and classic dramas are presented. Showtimes are 8pm Tuesday to Saturday, with a Sunday matinee at 2pm. Adult ticket prices range from $45 for a musical to $75 for a play. Tickets for children 16 and under are $18 to $35. The box office is open 10am to 5pm Monday to Friday and 10am to curtain time on performance days.

The island abounds in sports bars, far too many to document here. We recommend **Callahan Sports Bar & Grill,** 49 New Orleans Rd. (© **843/686-7665**), and **Casey's Sports Bar & Grill,** 37 New Orleans Rd. (© **843/785-2255;** www.caseyshhi.com).

Jazz Corner   Tucked away into an obscure corner of the shopping center known as the Village at Wexford, this is the closest thing to a shadowy, romantic, and permissive jazz bar on Hilton Head. No other nightclub here attracts such a diverse and noteworthy collection of jazz artists. The best way to find out who's playing here is to visit the website for names and dates of upcoming acts. Doors open nightly at 6pm, performances begin at 8pm, and intermissions are scheduled for 9:30pm. There's an on-site restaurant and a copious drink menu where many of the martinis are ultra-oversize and designed for two drinkers. In the Village at Wexford, Unit C1. © **843/842-8620.** www.thejazzcorner.com.

The Metropolitan Lounge   Consider a martini or two within this very adult, sophisticated nightclub whose decor might be tactfully described as "bordello chic." Here, a sometimes outrageously good-looking female staff in stylish evening décolletage will serve you anything you want from a huge martini list. Laura Moretti is the hardworking director of this glossy and urban-looking cocktail lounge, where live music provides an environment that actually celebrates adulthood. Martinis cost from $7 to $13. There is no cover charge. The lounge is open Tuesday to Saturday 8pm to at least 2am. In the Park Plaza Shopping Center, off Greenwood Dr., near the Sea Pines Traffic Roundabout. © **843/785-8466.** www.metropolitanlounge.com.

The Triangle & How Not to Get Lost In It

Hilton Head's hottest nightlife spot goes by many names. In an area that resembles a shopping center without any shops, the compound is known variously as the Triangle, the Golden Triangle, the Barmuda Triangle, and most officially of all, **Hilton Head Plaza.** Set beside Greenwood Drive, very close to the Sea Pines Traffic Roundabout, it contains five of the busiest nightclub venues and restaurants on Hilton Head.

Ironically, these bars and restaurants spend relatively low amounts on advertising, relying as they do on grass-roots word of mouth for their ongoing success. The names of these bars and restaurants, arranged from the most formal to the least formal, are **Reilley's Grill & Bar, Jump & Phil's Bar & Grill,** and **One Hot Mama's American Grille** (see reviews above). In a close tie for the grungiest, least formal, most youth-oriented, and most raucous are the **Hilton Head Brew Pub** (© 843/785-3900) and the **Lodge** (© 843/842-8966). Of these two, we prefer the Lodge with its pool tables. But they're all so close together that if one place isn't to your liking, you can easily move on to the next one. The Brew Pub is open daily from 11am to 2am, while the Lodge is a nighttime-only affair, open daily from 7pm 'til sometime after midnight every night. None of these bars begin to get busy, however, until after dark.

Quarterdeck   Our favorite waterfront lounge is the best place on the island to watch sunsets, but you can visit any time during the afternoon or evening until 2am. Try to go early and grab one of the outdoor rocking chairs to prepare yourself for nature's light show. There's dancing every night to beach music and Top-40 hits. Quarterdeck is open daily 11am to 2am. Harbour Town, Sea Pines Plantation. © 843/671-2222. http://quarterdeckrestaurant.com.

Side Trips from Charleston

1 MURRELLS INLET ★: THE SEAFOOD CAPITAL OF SOUTH CAROLINA

82 miles N of Charleston

Murrells Inlet is often invaded by Myrtle Beach hordes in quest of a seafood dinner. To join them, just take U.S. 17 north from Charleston and prepare to dig in. This centuries-old fishing village has witnessed a parade of humanity, from Confederate blockade runners to federal gunboats, from bootleggers to today's pleasure craft. The island was also visited by Edward Teach, better known as Blackbeard. Drunken Jack Island lies off Murrells Inlet. During the 1600s, Blackbeard's ship allegedly left a sailor on the island by accident; when the ship returned 2 years later, the crew discovered the abandoned sailor's bones bleaching in the sun, along with 32 empty casks of rum.

In addition to its seafood restaurants (a few are recommended in this chapter), Murrells Inlet is home to Brookgreen Gardens, one of the most-visited attractions along the Grand Strand.

BROOKGREEN GARDENS ★★

Halfway between Georgetown and Myrtle Beach on U.S. 17 (near Litchfield Beach), Brookgreen Gardens, 1931 Brookgreen Dr., in Murrells Inlet (✆ **843/237-4218;** www.brookgreen.org), is a world-class sculpture garden and wildlife park that's a source of enormous civic pride to virtually everyone in the state. It occupies the low-lying flatlands of what functioned 200 years ago as a rice plantation. After the destruction of the original plantation house, the gardens were laid out in 1931 to house the world's largest collection of American garden sculptures, all crafted between 1850 and the present. Archer Milton Huntington and his wife, the sculptor Anna Hyatt Huntington, planned the garden walks in the shape of a butterfly with outspread wings. All walks lead back to the central space, a contemporary building that occupies the site of the original plantation house. On opposite sides of this space are the Small Sculpture Gallery and the original plantation kitchen, now the site of one of the snack bars. An outstanding feature within the wildlife park is the Cypress Bird Sanctuary, a 90-foot-tall aviary housing species of wading birds within half an acre of cypress swamp. The curators of this garden recommend spending at least 2 hours wandering along its byways. Terrain is flat and makes for easy walking. The price of admission grants access to the park and garden for 7 consecutive days.

Admission is $12 for adults, $10 for seniors (65 and older) and students, $6 for children 4 to 12, and free for ages 3 and under. Hours are daily 9:30am to 5pm. Between June and August, the gardens remain open 'til 9pm Wednesday to Friday. The gardens are closed December 4, 11, 18, and 25.

WHERE TO DINE

Bovine's ★ STEAK/SEAFOOD/PIZZA   On the waterfront on the northern fringe of Murrells Inlet, with large windows opening onto views over acres of marshland, this restaurant evokes the Southwest with its use of cowhide and mounted bulls' heads. In the heart of Seafood Row, Bovine's has made a name for itself with its woodfired specialties. You can order honey-crust pizza from the brick oven, along with grilled or blackened rib-eye steak. Barbecued baby back ribs are roasted with bourbon, honey, shrimp and grits, tequila shrimp, and aged balsamic vinegar. Appetizers include crab gazpacho (a refreshing change) and Cajun oyster stew.

3979 Hwy. Business 17. ⓒ **843/651-2888.** www.bovineswoodfired.com. Reservations recommended. Pizza $8–$16; main courses $16–$37. AE, DC, DISC, MC, V. Daily 4pm–midnight.

Capt. Dave's Dockside ★ (Kids) SEAFOOD/SOUTHERN   Family owned and run since 1974, one of the area's best and most famous seafood restaurants offers dining indoors or on the patio outside overlooking the waterfront. Chef Richard ensures that the freshest seafood is featured as the catch of the day. Arrive early if you want to enjoy sundown at the waterfront **Gazebo Bar.** Start a meal with a bowl of Low Country steamed mussels or she-crab soup, either one a delight to the palate. Among the dinner specials are such sublime dishes as a *zuppa di pesce,* a kettle of fish with everything from lobster meat to clams, or grouper prepared in any of at least three different ways. Meat lovers can order a Black Angus New York strip steak. Each day a selection of homemade desserts is featured—count yourself lucky if it's New Orleans bread pudding with a Jack Daniel's sauce. A children's menu is also offered.

On the Waterfront (4037 Hwy. Business 17). $\textcircled{C}$ **843/651-5850.** www.daves 169
dockside.com. Reservations recommended. Main courses $7–$29. AE, DISC, MC, V.
Daily 11:30am–2:30pm and 4pm–midnight.

2 PAWLEYS ISLAND ★ & LITCHFIELD

73 miles N of Charleston

One of the oldest resorts in the South, Pawleys Island has been a popular hideaway for vacationers for more than 3 centuries. Over the years, everyone from George Washington to Franklin Roosevelt to Winston Churchill has visited. During the 18th century, rice planters made the island their summer home so that they could escape the heat and humidity of the Low Country and enjoy ocean breezes. Storms have battered the island, but many of the weather-beaten old properties remain, earning the island the appellation "arrogantly shabby."

This area of South Carolina is sometimes called Waccamaw Neck, a reference to a strip of land 30 miles long and 3 miles wide that extends from the Waccamaw River to the Atlantic Ocean. Both North Litchfield and Litchfield Beach lie between Murrells Inlet and Pawleys Island. (To get here from Charleston, take Hwy. 17 N.)

The beaches here are among the best maintained, least polluted, and widest along coastal South Carolina; however, access to public beach areas is severely limited.

Many visitors from Myrtle Beach come to Pawleys Island to shop for handicrafts, such as the famous Pawleys Island rope hammock. The best place to purchase one is the **Original Hammock Shop** ($\textcircled{C}$ **800/332-3490** or 843/237-9122; www.hammockshop.com), 10880 Ocean Hwy. at Pawleys Island. It's open year-round Monday to Saturday from 9:30am to 6pm and on Sunday from noon to 5pm. At various plantation stores (known as the hammock shops), you'll find pewter, miniature doll furniture, clothing, candles, Christmas items, brass, and china.

ENJOYING THE OUTDOORS

Huntington Beach State Park ★, along Hwy. 17, 3 miles south of Murrells Inlet and across from Brookgreen Gardens ($\textcircled{C}$ **843/237-4440;** www.southcarolinaparks.com), offers one of the best beaches along the Grand Strand. Entrance is $5 for adults, $3.25 for seniors, $3 for children 6 to 15, and free for children 5 and under. The 2,500-acre park has a wide, firm beach, which is slightly orange. Anna Hyatt

Huntington and her husband, Archer, the creators of Brookgreen Gardens, once owned this coastal wilderness. The park is the site of their Iberian-style castle, Atalaya. In the park are 137 campsites, along with picnic shelters, a boardwalk, terrific birding, bike rentals, and toilets. Swimming in specially marked sections is excellent, as is fishing from the jetty at the north side of the beach, or crabbing along the boardwalk. Campsites are rented on a first-come, first-served basis, at a cost of $21 to $28 per day (price depends on whether the particular site has electricity or water). The park is open April to September daily 6am to 10pm, and in the off season Saturday to Thursday 6am to 6pm and Friday 6am to 8pm.

Caledonia Golf & Fish Club, 369 Caledonia Dr., Pawleys Island (© **800/483-6800** or 843/237-3675; www.fishclub.com), opened in 1993. Tees are marked by replicas of native waterfowl that inhabit the old rice fields. The centerpiece of the course is a clubhouse, a replica of a 1700s colonial plantation house. Architect Mike Strantz, a former assistant to Tom Fazio, took care to highlight the natural beauty of the area: huge, centuries-old live oaks; pristine natural lakes; scenic views of the old rice fields; and glimpses of native wildlife. Greens fees are $110 to $175.

WHERE TO STAY

Litchfield Beach and Golf Resort ★   One of the largest developments along coastal South Carolina, this beautifully landscaped complex, known for its oak-lined vistas, sprawls across 4,500 acres, with 7 miles of private beach and some of the best tennis courts in the South. Often catering to groups, it offers a wide range of accommodations, including suites, condos, and cottages. Furnishings are hit-or-miss, described by one returning guest as being "residential beach stuff." The property is well maintained and forms its own private enclave away from the crowds of the Grand Strand. Many of the units have lake, ocean, and marshland views, complete with waterfowl. An on-site restaurant serves standard American food, and there's a grill at the golf club, plus a Starbucks.

14276 Ocean Hwy., Pawleys Island, SC 29585. © **888/766-4633** or 843/237-3000. Fax 843/237-3282. www.litchfieldbeach.com. 300 units. $59–$549 suite or condo; $194–$750 2- to 4-bedroom cottage. 3-night minimum stay July–Aug. AE, DC, DISC, MC, V. Free parking. Amenities: Restaurant; bar; babysitting; 3 18-hole golf courses; health club; Jacuzzi; sauna; 17 tennis courts (lit). In room: A/C, TV, hair dryer, Wi-Fi (in some; free).

Litchfield Plantation   Along the banks of the Waccamaw River, Litchfield Plantation is a stately manor house (ca. 1750) at the end of a quarter-mile avenue of live oaks, making it oft-photographed. A fine country inn, fully restored, it offers four suites. The Ballroom Suite, for example, occupies the north wing of the second floor. This suite includes a bedroom and fireplace, a bathroom with whirlpool, and a large living room (formerly the ballroom) with a Pullman-type kitchen area and a veranda overlooking the grounds. Rates include the use of a cabana and a private beach club at Pawleys Island. There are numerous championship golf courses in the area. There's also a 31-acre equestrian center nearby. Children 5 and under are not permitted.

24 Avenue of the Oak (PO Box 290), Pawleys Island, SC 29585. © **800/869-1410** or 843/237-5300. Fax 843/237-1688. www.litchfieldplantation.com. 38 units. $185–$540 plantation house room; $225–$525 villa. Rates include full breakfast. AE, DC, DISC, MC, V. No children 5 and under. Amenities: Restaurant; bar; outdoor pool; 2 tennis courts (lit). In room: A/C, TV, hair dryer, Wi-Fi (in some; free).

Pawleys Plantation Golf & Country Club ★★★ A group of elegant, regional-style structures border a nature preserve, offering a luxurious country-club aura for those discriminating clients who don't want to pile into a hotel or resort on overcrowded Myrtle Beach. Guests are housed in one-, two-, or three-bedroom luxury villas, each elegantly furnished with a living and dining room, outdoor patio, and full kitchen, plus a tiled bathroom. Many of the villas feature whirl-pools, wet bars, and fireplaces. The villas, with screened-in porches and patios, open onto views of the Jack Nicklaus signature course. Some of the Low Country's best recreational facilities, such as out-door pools and tennis courts, along with beautiful beaches, are found here. The elegantly appointed clubhouse's dining venues all serve first-rate cuisine.

70 Tanglewood Dr., Pawleys Island, SC 29585. © **800/367-9959** or 843/237-6100. Fax 843/237-0418. www.pawleysplantation.com. 80 units. $110–$135 double; $114–$144 1-bedroom suite; $209–$234 2-bedroom suite; $259–$295 3-bedroom suite. AE, DISC, MC, V. Amenities: 3 restaurants; bar; 18-hole golf course; 2 outdoor pools (1 exclusive); room service; 2 tennis courts (lit). In room: A/C, TV, kitchen (in some), Wi-Fi (free).

WHERE TO DINE

Frank's & Frank's Outback ★ Kids LOW COUNTRY/INTER-NATIONAL Frank's has been a Grand Strand tradition since 1988. Its fans think that it's the best restaurant along the beach strip. Chef Pierce Culliton borrows inspiration wherever he finds it, from Arizona to Provence, from China to Thailand. Your seared tuna might arrive over black Thai rice and warm Asian slaw. The rack of lamb with rosemary-and-garlic-laced mushroom sauce is better than many versions of this dish we've sampled in France. With its painted tin ceilings and wood floors, Frank's is an intimate, cozy place. The menu changes every day, based on the chef's inspiration.

In back of the restaurant is **Frank's Outback,** the home of Frank Marlow's mother before its conversion. The candlelit restaurant is slightly less formal than the restaurant up front. In fair weather, tables are set outside in a garden under a canopy of trees.

10434 Ocean Hwy., Pawleys Island. ✆ **843/237-3030.** www.franksandoutback. com. Reservations recommended. Frank's main courses $23–$39, Frank's Outback main courses $23–$42; pizza $14–$16; children's menu $7–$10. AE, DC, DISC, MC, V. Frank's Mon–Sat 5:30–10pm. Frank's Outback Tues–Sat 5:30–10pm.

3 GEORGETOWN ★★

61 miles N of Charleston

The lifestyle of pre–Revolutionary War days comes alive here. Named after George II, this enclave of only 11,000 people boasts more than 50 historic homes and buildings dating back as far as 1737. Masted ships sailed from this riverfront, bound for England with their cargoes of indigo, rice, timber, and "king cotton." You can take a leisurely stroll along the Harbor Walk, tour the antebellum homes, or dine at some of our favorite spots. Georgetown is rarely crowded with visitors. Located 12 miles from the Atlantic, this community is South Carolina's third-oldest city, and it has been rated among the 100 best small towns in America. When Elisha Screven laid out the town in 1729, he couldn't have known that it would become a lively shopping enclave.

ESSENTIALS

GETTING THERE   From Myrtle Beach, take U.S. 17 S. From I-95, take U.S. 521 into Georgetown. From Charleston, take U.S. 17/701.

VISITOR INFORMATION   Providing information about sights, accommodations, and tours, the **Georgetown Chamber of Commerce,** 531 Front St. (PO Box 1776), Georgetown, SC 29440 (✆ **800/777-7705** or 843/546-8436; www.georgetownchamber. com), is most helpful. The staff will also provide you with maps and brochures. It's open Monday to Friday 9am to 5pm.

SEEING THE SIGHTS

Harold Kaminski House Museum   A pre–Revolutionary War home (ca. 1760), this house is visited mainly for its collection of antiques, including a 15th-century Spanish wedding chest, a Chippendale dining table, and some excellent pieces from 1700s Charleston. Many of the interior architectural details, including moldings and the original floors, have been left intact. At one time, the house was occupied by Thomas Daggett, a Confederate sea captain. There's also a museum shop selling items related to the decorative arts and the history of Georgetown.

1003 Front St. ✆ **843/546-7706.** Admission $10 adults, $8 seniors, $6 children 6–12, free for children 5 and under. Mon–Sat 9am–5pm. Closed holidays.

Prince George Winyah Episcopal Church Built around 1750 with brick from English ships' ballast, this church was occupied by British troops during the Revolutionary War and by Union troops during the Civil War. The latter occupation resulted in a great deal of damage. The stained glass behind the rebuilt altar was once part of a slaves' chapel on a nearby plantation. In the churchyard is one of the state's oldest cemeteries, the most ancient marker dating back to 1767.

Broad and Highmarket sts. ✆ **843/546-4358.** Free admission but donations welcome. Sanctuary tours Mar–Oct Mon–Fri 11am–4pm.

Rice Museum This museum is easy to locate. It's in the Old Market Building, which local residents call "the town clock"—Georgetown's answer to Big Ben. The first building in town to be listed on the National Register of Historic Places, it houses a museum devoted to the once-flourishing rice trade. The museum is a repository of maps, artifacts, dioramas, and other exhibits, tracing the development of rice cultivation (which was long Georgetown's primary economic base) from 1700 to 1900. There's also a scale model of a rice mill.

633 Front St. ✆ **843/546-7423.** www.ricemuseum.org. Admission $7 adults, $5 seniors, $3 students and children 6–21, free for children 5 and under with an adult. Mon–Sat 10am–4:30pm.

ORGANIZED TOURS

Nell Morris Cribb, a Georgetown native who conducts tours wearing period dress, complete with a bonnet, provides personalized walking tours of the downtown Historic District. **Miss Nell's Tours** take in about 12 history-rich blocks, last about 1¼ hours, and cost $5 to $9 for adults (free for children 12 and under). Tours begin at HarborWalk Books, 723 Front St. (✆ **843/546-3975**). The tours are given Tuesday, Wednesday, and Thursday at 10:30am and 2:30pm and on Saturday and Sunday by appointment.

OUTDOOR PURSUITS

CANOEING & KAYAKING **Black River expeditions** can be arranged at Kensington Gardens, U.S. 701, 3 miles north of Georgetown (✆ **843/546-4840;** www.blackriveroutdoors.com), open Monday to Saturday 9am to 5:30pm. Half-day canoe rentals cost $35 a day, with kayaks going for $50.

GOLF One of the popular Georgetown championship courses, **Wedgefield Plantation ★**, just north of Georgetown (✆ **843/546-8587** or

448-2124; www.wedgefield.com), is on the site of a former Black River plantation and has wildlife in abundance. It was designed by Porter Gibson, and *Golf Week*'s "America's Best" honored it as one of the top 50 golf courses in South Carolina in 1994. Greens fees are $25 to $60, including cart. The signature hole is the par-4 14th, with both tee and approach shots over water.

RIVER CRUISES The *Carolina Rover* and the *Jolly Rover* (*©* 843/546-8822; www.rovertours.com) set sail from Georgetown Harbor. The *Carolina Rover,* a 40-foot pontoon boat, offers a 3-hour trip including a docked stop on North Island. The 45-minute excursion to this rather remote island includes a nature walk and beach shelling. Trips leave at 9am, 1pm, and 5pm Monday to Saturday. It costs $25 for adults and $15 for children 11 and under. The *Jolly Rover,* an 80-foot topsail schooner, offers a 2-hour tour of Winyah Bay. On board is a storyteller in a pirate's costume, who relates tales about pirates and ghosts who have prowled the Carolina coast. Trips depart Monday to Saturday at 10am, 1pm, and 6pm. The 10am and 1pm tours are pirate adventures. The cost is $30 for adults and $20 for children 11 and under. Reservations are strongly recommended.

WHERE TO STAY

Harbor House Bed & Breakfast ★ This top-rated B&B was created from a 1765 warehouse, opening onto views of the harbor. Immaculately restored, the Harbor House rents out generously sized bedrooms with fireplaces, Oriental carpets, family antiques, heart-pine floors, and deep colonial moldings. Some of the bedrooms contain king-size four-poster beds and all are named for famous ships that once sailed the waters of Winyah Bay. A Low Country breakfast is served, featuring the house specialty of shrimp and grits.

15 Cannon St., Georgetown, SC 29440. *©* 877/511-0101 or 843/546-6532. www.harborhousebb.com. 4 units. $159–$189 double. MC, V. Amenities: Breakfast room; bikes. In room: TV, hair dryer, Wi-Fi (free).

The Shaw House Bed and Breakfast ★★ Nestled among pine trees overlooking miles of marshland, this recently upgraded colonial B&B has spacious rooms with impressive antiques that evoke the grandeur and culture of the Old South. Mary and Joe Shaw are the gracious innkeepers, and their knowledge of the area is encyclopedic. Your day begins with a full Southern breakfast that's probably more than you can eat. Historic walking tours and boat tours can be arranged.

613 Cypress Court, Georgetown, SC 29440. *©* 843/546-9663. www.bbonline.com/sc/shawhouse. 3 units. $100 double. Additional person $10. Rates include full breakfast. AE, MC, V. Amenities: Breakfast room; Internet (free). In room: A/C, TV.

The Rice Paddy SEAFOOD/AMERICAN   The Rice Paddy continues the Georgetown tradition of everything historic. This early-20th-century structure has a minimalist decor that relies on the effectiveness of its exposed-brick walls. The river side of the restaurant offers views of the Sampit River, and if you want to sit even closer to the river, an outdoor dining patio with awnings and ceiling fans seats up to 40 patrons comfortably. Cookery has flair and flavor, with a finesse and consistency that keep the most discriminating palates of Georgetown returning again and again. Main-course choices range from lump crab cakes to rack of lamb. The menu changes seasonally to take advantage of the freshest ingredients.

732 Front St. ✆ **843/546-2021.** www.ricepaddyrestaurant.com. Reservations recommended. Main courses $10–$37. AE, MC, V. Mon–Sat 11:30am–2:30pm and 6–10pm.

River Room SEAFOOD   This is about the best Georgetown gets in terms of seafood dining. Some dishes are a bit overcooked, but locals seem to prefer them that way. Guests are rewarded by waterfront views from cozy precincts; an equally inviting bar is decked out in wood and exposed brick. Diners are smartly dressed in a casual way. Daily specials might include seafood fettuccine or a soft-shell-crab sandwich. Grouper, crab cakes, and other seafood are regularly featured, and you can order such Low Country dishes as yellow grits sautéed with shrimp and sausage.

801 Front St. ✆ **843/527-4110.** www.riverroomgeorgetown.com. Reservations required. Main courses $9–$25. AE, MC, V. Mon–Sat 11am–2:30pm and 5–10pm.

Thomas Cafe LOW COUNTRY   This is the kind of cafe where Charles Kuralt might have come to talk with the locals. With only five tables, a few booths, and a handful of counter stools, it's real Americana. Your waitress might be a spry 80-year-old. Breakfast is a very filling event: grits or hash browns served with eggs, a Cajun omelet, or blueberry pancakes. At lunch, you can have selections like jambalaya, fried chicken, mashed potatoes, and fried green tomatoes. This is the Old South—plenty of hospitality but no nonsense.

703 Front St. ✆ **843/546-7776.** www.thomascafe.net. Reservations not accepted. Breakfast $4–$9; plate lunches $5–$9; sandwiches $5–$8. MC, V. Mon–Sat 7am–2pm.

Appendix:
Fast Facts & Websites

1 FAST FACTS: CHARLESTON

American Express Services in South Carolina are provided through **Abbott & Hill Travel,** 10 Carriage Lane, Charleston (© **843/566-9051;** www.abbottandhilltravel.com).

Area Code It's **843** for Charleston and the South Carolina coast.

Dentists Consult **Atlantic Dental Associates,** in 61 West Building, 1483 Tobias Gadson Blvd., Ste. 105 (© **843/556-3838;** www. atlanticimplantdentistry.com).

Emergencies Dial © **911** for police, ambulance, paramedics, and the fire department. You can also dial 0 and ask the operator to connect you to emergency services.

Hospitals Local hospitals with 24-hour emergency rooms include **Medical University of South Carolina,** 171 Ashley Ave., Charleston (© **843/792-2300;** www.musc.edu), and **East Cooper Regional Medical Center,** 1200 Johnnie Dodds Blvd., Mount Pleasant (© **843/ 881-0100;** www.eastcoopermedctr.com). For medical emergencies, call © **911.**

Liquor Laws The minimum drinking age is 21. Some restaurants are licensed to serve only beer and wine. Beer and wine are sold in grocery stores Monday through Saturday. Liquor is offered through local government-licensed stores, commonly called "ABC" (Alcoholic Beverage Control Commission) stores, which are also closed on Sunday.

Newspapers & Magazines The major local paper is the *Charleston Post and Courier* (www.charleston.net).

Pharmacies Try **CVS Drugs,** 1603 Hwy. 17 N. (© **843/971-0764**), open Monday through Saturday from 8am to 10pm and Sunday from 10am to 8pm.

Post Office The main post office is at 83 Broad St. (© **843/577-0688**), open Monday through Friday from 9am to 5pm.

Safety   Downtown Charleston is well-lit and patrolled throughout the night to ensure public safety. People can generally walk around downtown at night without fear of violence.

Taxes   South Carolina has a 6% sales tax. Charleston County's sales tax adds an additional 5.5%. The total tax on lodgings is 12.5%.

Time   South Carolina is in the Eastern Standard Time (EST) zone. Daylight saving time is in effect from 2am on the second Sunday in March to 2am on the first Sunday in November.

Toilets   These are available throughout the downtown area, including at Broad and Meeting streets, at Queen and Church streets, on Market Street between Meeting and Church streets, and at other clearly marked strategic points in the historic and downtown districts.

Transit Information   Contact the **Charleston Visitor Center,** 375 Meeting St. (© **843/853-8000;** www.charlestoncvb.com).

Visitor Information   Before you leave home, write or call ahead for specific information on sightseeing and outdoor activities. Contact the **South Carolina Department of Parks & Tourism Recreation,** 1205 Pendleton St. (PO Box 71), Columbia, SC 29201 (© **866/224-9339** or 803/734-1700; fax 803/734-0138; www.discover southcarolina.com), or the **Charleston Area Convention & Visitor Bureau (CACVB),** 375 Meeting St., Charleston, SC 29403 (© **800/ 774-0006** or 843/724-7174; www.celebratecharleston.com). The CACVB has four area visitor centers; the main location is the **Charleston Visitor Center,** at 375 Meeting St., open daily from 8:30am to 5pm.

When you enter South Carolina, look for one of the nine **travel information centers** located on virtually every major highway near the border with neighboring states. These will provide general information about South Carolina as well as information about specific destinations.

Weather   Phone © **843/744-3207** for an update.

---

2   AIRLINE WEBSITES

MAJOR U.S. AIRLINES
(*flies internationally as well)

American Airlines*
www.aa.com

Continental Airlines*
www.continental.com

Delta Air Lines*
www.delta.com

United Airlines*
www.united.com

US Airways*
www.usairways.com

INDEX

See also Accommodations and Restaurant indexes, below.